Use Cases

Requirements
in Context

Use
Cases

Requirements
in Context

DARYL KULAK AND EAMONN GUINEY

with illustrations by Erin Lavkulich

ACM Press
New York, New York

ADDISON–WESLEY

Boston • San Francisco • New York • Toronto • Montreal

London • Munich • Paris • Madrid

Capetown • Sydney • Tokyo • Singapore • Mexico City

Many of the designations used by manufacturers and sellers to distinguish their products are claimed as trademarks. Where those designations appear in this book, and we were aware of a trademark claim, the designations have been printed with initial capital letters or in all capitals.

The authors and publisher have taken care in the preparation of this book, but make no expressed or implied warranty of any kind and assume no responsibility for errors or omissions. No liability is assumed for incidental or consequential damages in connection with or arising out of the use of the information or programs contained herein.

The excerpt from "The Single Hound" reprinted by permission of the publishers and the Trustees of Amherst College from *The Poems of Emily Dickinson*, Ralph W. Franklin, ed., Cambridge, Mass.: The Belknap Press of Harvard University Press, Copyright © 1998 by the President and Fellows of Harvard College. Copyright © 1951, 1955, 1979 by the President and Fellows of Harvard College.

This book is published as part of ACM Press Books—a collaboration between the Association for Computing Machinery (ACM) and Addison-Wesley. ACM is the oldest and largest educational and scientific society in the information technology field. Through its high-quality publications and services, ACM is a major force in advancing the skills and knowledge of IT professionals throughout the world. For further information about ACM, contact:

ACM Member Services
1515 Broadway, 17th Floor
New York, NY 10036-5701
Phone: (212) 626-0500
Fax: (212) 944-1318
E-mail: **ACMHELP@ACM.org**

ACM European Service Center
108 Cowley Road
Oxford OX4IJF
United Kingdom
Phone: +44-1865-382338
Fax: +44-1865-381338
E-mail: **acm.europe@acm.org**
URL: **http://www.acm.org**

The publisher offers discounts on this book when ordered in quantity for special sales. For more information, please contact:

Pearson Education Corporate Sales Division
One Lake Street
Upper Saddle River, NJ 07458
(800) 382-3419
corpsales@pearsontechgroup.com

Visit AW on the Web: **www.awl.com/cseng/**

Library of Congress Cataloging-in-Publication Data

Kulak, Daryl, 1963-
  Use cases : requirements in context/Daryl Kulak and Eamonn Guiney.
     p. cm.
  Includes bibliographical references and index.
  ISBN 0-201-65767-8
  1. System design 2. Use cases (Systems engineering) I. Guiney, Eamonn, 1971- II.
Title.

  QA76.9.S88 K85 2000
  658'.05421—dc21

                                                    99-053232

ISBN 0-201-65767-8
Text printed on recycled paper
1 2 3 4 5 6 7 8 9 10—MA—0403020100
First printing, May 2000

To Tamara, my wonderful wife
To my parents, Eunice and Wayne
To my brothers and sisters, Shelley, Todd, Keith, and Zena

D. K.

To my family and the close friends who encouraged me

E. G.

Contents

5 The Filled Iteration

6 The Focused Iteration

9   Working in Teams

10   Classic Mistakes

11 The Case for Use Cases

A Use Cases Beyond Requirements

B Case Study: Sell Property

C   Case Study: Track Costume Sales

Preface

Use Cases: Requirements in Context came about, as most books probably do, as the result of a complaint. We felt that there weren't any good books that addressed use cases for requirements gathering. It seemed that a lot of people agreed that use cases were a perfectly good tool to solve the requirements problem, but no one had put down on paper any detailed process to help people understand how to use them this way. In fact, even as we write today, in late 1999, there is no book of this sort that we know of.

Requirements gathering has been a problem on almost every project we've been involved with. The fuzzy nature of requirements makes working with them slippery and unintuitive for most software analysts. Use cases are the first tool we've seen that addresses the specification and communication concerns usually associated with requirements gathering.

Although use cases in themselves are quite intuitive, the process around them is often done poorly. The questions that people have—How many iterations do I do? How fine-grained should a use case be?—are not answered or even addressed in most texts. This is probably because they are hard questions and the answers can vary greatly from one situation to another. However, they are important questions, and we decided to describe our own best practices as a first volley in what we hope will become a spirited industry dialog on how to generate requirements that will address user needs.

Use Cases: Requirements in Context is a practical book for the everyday practitioner. As consultants in the information technology industry, we employ use cases to specify business systems as part of our daily lives. We think we understand the issues facing people when they deliver software using tools such as the Unified Modeling Language and use cases. Our main intent is not to describe use case notation, although we do address that. Instead, we show a requirements process that addresses requirements gathering in a way that produces quality results.

While writing, we considered the factors that cause problems in requirements gathering, and we developed a use case method for delivering a requirements-oriented set of deliverables. The methodology breaks down the activity of producing requirements into a series of steps, and it answers the questions that usually come up when people employ use cases. This book relates directly to the real work of delivering a specification, managing that effort with a team, and getting the most bang for your buck.

The sample use cases and use case diagrams that appear throughout the book are also presented in Appendixes B and C. These appendixes demonstrate the development of the use cases and other requirements analysis artifacts through each phase of their development. Appendix B documents a business system for real estate, and Appendix C documents a business system for the garment industry.

We hope you enjoy this book. It was a labor of love for us. This is a process that works well for us. If it works for you, too, that's great. If it doesn't, perhaps you can adapt some of the tools, ideas, or suggestions to your own way of addressing the requirements problem.

Acknowledgments

Heartfelt thanks go to the numerous people who helped with this project. Some of them provided material aid and advice; all of them provided enthusiasm and encouragement throughout the project. It is an impossible task to mention everyone, but we would especially like to thank Bill Banze, Tom Barr, David Boyle, Alistair Cockburn, Steve Frison, Helen Goldstein, Peter Gordon, Mat Henshall, Erin Lavkulich, John Lavkulich, Ron Lusk, Bob Morton, Tamara Oakley, George O'Mary, Paul Reed, David Rubin, Mark Thompson, James Tomayko, Sarah Ward, and Ogden Weary.

1

The Trouble with Requirements

> When faced with what they believe is a problem, most engineers rush into offering solutions.
>
> —Alan M. Davis

1.1 First and Least of All . . .

Technical people often pay much more attention to an entity relationship diagram or class diagram than to a requirements list.

Each time a team of systems people sets out to provide a computer system for a group of business people, they proceed through a set of activities that is fairly consistent:

- Requirements gathering
- Analysis
- Design
- Construction
- Testing
- Deployment
- Maintenance

The emphasis that the team gives to each phase determines the direction and quality of the resulting computer system. If one activity is not given its due, there will be predictable problems with the project and the end product. In reality, however, certain activities usually receive more attention than other activities. It is not easy to explain why this occurs, but it does. The activities that are usually ignored or paid lip service are

- Requirements gathering
- Testing
- Deployment
- Maintenance

Traditionally, fewer vendors have brandished flashy tools to accomplish these activities, and maybe that's why they are less interesting and less appealing to practitioners. Certainly, a great deal of creativity and a wide range of skills are required by each activity, but the perception is that anything other than the big three—analysis, design, and construction—does not require much attention or imagination.

This perception is slowly changing, in no small part because vendors are building tools to manage requirements (Rational RequisitePro, TBI Caliber RM), to automate testing (Segue SilkTest, Mercury Interactive WinRunner/LoadRunner, Rational Performance Studio), and to facilitate rollout (Inprise Deployment Server/Java, Marimba Castanet, Forte). Maintenance has also received a boost with the need for Y2K remediation in recent years. We have opinions on ways to improve the visibility, appeal, and effectiveness of these other underappreciated activities, but we'll spare you those points until our next book.

We wrote this book because we care about requirements. In the first place, effective requirements are pivotal to producing a system that meets the needs of the users. It's no exaggeration to say that the requirements *themselves* are the needs of the users.

Moreover, we have grown to care about requirements because we have seen more projects stumble or fail as a result of poor requirements than for any other reason. Because requirements are meant to drive the rest of systems development, any small misstep is amplified into a major flaw by the time deployment is in progress. Correcting those flaws becomes extremely time-consuming (read: expensive!) because so much work has been put into heading in the wrong direction. Unfortunately, requirements do not translate neatly into one discrete module in a coded computer system. Sometimes, they are embodied in principles that cut across many code libraries and components. Because requirements are so abstract and so different from computer programs, it is difficult for people whose skills lie in the concrete aspects of computer programming to get them right.

Traditionally, requirements gathering

- Takes too long
- Documents the wrong thing
- Makes assumptions about activities that haven't happened yet
- Is often completed just in time to do it over again, thanks to swift and dramatic changes in the business

A short time ago, we came across a requirements definition document that contained more than 160 pages of "requirements." The sheer volume of this requirements list was enough to cause us to be filled with panic (or at least dread) at the thought of reading it and attempting to put the pieces together. Table 1.1 contains a sample of the requirements list (which is not so different from other lists we've seen). This list continues for another 159 pages!

Table 1.1   Example of a Requirements List

Requirement	Definition
6.7.1.4.2	The system must provide the capability to capture all of the customer transactions for the fiscal year.
6.7.1.4.3	The system will provide restricted remote inquiry access (via dial-in) to view images and data separately or simultaneously.
6.7.1.4.4	The system will barcode documents automatically prior to distribution. At a minimum, the codes will be used to identify to which work queue the documents should be routed within the organization when they are returned.
6.7.1.4.5	When a workflow is initiated, the system must be able to prefetch the documents that are in electronic image format by document type or grouping of documents by process.
6.7.1.4.6	The system must create an entry in the journal file whenever a letter is created.
6.7.1.4.7	The system must maintain a list of current, open work processes and identify the work process to be executed and the workflow queue for the process. When particular documents are scanned, the system will determine whether there is a process open for that Social Security Number (SSN). If there is an open process, the system will route the document to the appropriate workflow queue, display the work process script, and highlight the current work process.

We dissect these and other requirements statements later, but you can imagine how difficult it would be to read large volumes of information at this level, much less to separate the true requirements from trivialities.

One reason that requirements documents are often so bad is that requirements gathering frequently follows an unproductive route. For example, it may be ignored; in that case, the development team jumps to a solution, resulting in a design based on unwritten assumptions about how the system should work. Or requirements gathering becomes an end in itself, and pages of "requirements" are gathered, documented, cross-referenced, and distributed, resulting in analysis paralysis and cancellation of the project before the first activity can be completed. Or the requirements may be dictated by a single user, system owner, or high-ranking manager, resulting in a system that works only for that person. None of these methods produces satisfactory input to the analysis activity.

Hundreds of application lifecycle activities definitions, taken from various methodologies and processes, litter our bookshelves and the Internet. In Table 1.2 we provide our definitions of these terms because we build on these definitions to explain how to best approach requirements gathering.

Our definitions of lifecycle activities are not taken from any specific methodology. Instead, we've attempted to choose the most commonly used names and definitions for each term. Notice we've chosen the word *activity* instead of the word *phase*. We do this deliberately. In waterfall lifecycles, activities (or workflows) and phases are usually synonymous. However, *activity* relates to something that a person or group does. *Phase* implies a specific time frame and sequence. With iterative and incremental lifecycles, on the other hand, phases and activities are quite different. Activities are done iteratively and incrementally, but phases are simply project management milestones that indicate a number of increments or a natural break in the lifecycle. For example, the Rational Unified Process (RUP) has the following workflows (or activities): business modeling, requirements, analysis, design, implementation, test, deployment, configuration/change management, project management, and environment. It also has the following phases: inception, elaboration, construction, transition, and evolution. We see most methodologies moving in the same direction as the RUP to accommodate developers' as well as project managers' viewpoints.

1.2 What Is a Requirement?

Requirements are the effects that the computer is to exert in the problem domain, by virtue of the computer's programming.

—BENJAMIN L. KOVITZ

A *requirement* is something that a computer application must do for its users. It is a specific function or feature or principle that the system must provide in order for it to merit its existence. Requirements constitute the *scope* of a software development project. Add a few requirements, and the scope increases; take some away, and the scope decreases. The

Table 1.2 Activity Definitions

Activity Name	Description
Requirements gathering[1]	Gather and document the functions that the application should perform for the users in the users' language and from the users' perspective.
Analysis	Build a logical solution that satisfies the requirements but does not necessarily take the physical constraints into account.
Design	Begin with the logical solution and change it to work effectively with the physical constraints (network latency, database performance, caching, availability, and so forth) and produce specifications that can direct the construction effort.
Construction	Use the design to produce working code, which involves making the lowest-level design decisions, writing code, compiling, debugging, and testing by increment.
Testing	Use the constructed application to produce a complete working system by system testing, detecting, and recording issues, fixing problems, and getting user acceptance of the result.
Deployment	Fit the tested application into the production environment by deploying the code libraries to the destined machines, training the users, and fine-tuning the business procedures surrounding the new system.
Maintenance	Administer and make changes to the working system in the production environment to adapt to ongoing business changes (legislative, competitive), technology changes (hardware, software, communications), physical changes (location, configuration), personnel (information technology (IT), user), system issues (code bugs, design problems), and politics.

1. We consider requirements gathering a separate activity from analysis. This is contrary to several other prominent industry luminaries, who lump them together. Neither way is ultimately correct or incorrect; we have simply chosen to separate these activities to emphasize their importance.

requirements also dictate how the system should respond to user interaction. It should do specific things when poked or prodded by the user in a certain way.

Requirements usually seem abstract and intangible, especially to software developers. Requirements and design can tend to blur together in a software person's brain until they become indistinguishable. However, it is crucial to keep design and requirements separate. The following are some of the ways IT people typically get off track with requirements.

- *Embedded design considerations*—Anything that relates to *how* the system should operate, rather than *what* it needs to accomplish, is *design*. Design should not be part of requirements.
- *Vagueness*—If a requirement does not contribute positively to shaping the application design, it is too vague to be useful.
- *The use of computer industry language*—Requirements must always be phrased in the users' language. Jargon is OK as long as it's the users' jargon!

For clarification of this thorny issue, let's look again at the unfortunate requirements shown earlier in Table 1.1. This time let's look at them in detail and try to identify those things that do not constitute requirements.

The system must provide the capability to capture all of the customer transactions for the fiscal year.

This requirement is too vague. How could it translate into a valuable constraint on the design of an application? It implies that the fiscal year has some impact on how customer transactions are organized, but we are not sure *what* impact. We understand that this system has some type of data entry, but that could be stated more specifically. Maybe this is a suggestion about volume, meaning that old transactions can't be archived until they are a year old, but again, that interpretation is a stretch from looking at this requirement.

The system will provide restricted remote inquiry access (via dial-in) to view images and data separately or simultaneously.

Saying "restricted" access is OK, but details about the restriction (who can, who can't) should be stated clearly in this context. Also vague is the reference to remote inquiry. How remote? Saying "remote access" when referring to mobile employees working in the field but still within a couple of miles of the office is one thing—but talking about worldwide access is yet another. Implications on the system design could be huge.

The system will barcode documents automatically prior to distribution. At a minimum, the codes will be used to identify to which work queue the documents should be routed within the organization when they are returned.

This requirement makes several technical assumptions concerning the design. Barcoding is a solution to a problem, not a requirement. This system probably needs a way to identify each document uniquely, but it doesn't have to be barcodes. If all the existing systems use document barcoding (not the case with this system), it would make sense to write a nonfunctional requirement that states, "Unique identification of all documents will be done through barcoding." What's the difference? By embedding the barcoding reference in various functional requirements, you make it difficult for someone to change the identification method from barcoding to glyphs, optical character recognition (OCR), or some other technology, thereby reducing your ability to respond to user needs discovered later in the process.

Another sticky point in this requirement is the reference to work queues. This seems to make an assumption about a workflow-package-oriented system. Workflow tools are solutions, not requirements. A better way to put it might have been, "At a minimum, the unique identification will ensure routing to a specific worker in the organization when the documents are returned."

When a workflow is initiated, the system must be able to prefetch the documents that are in electronic image format by document type or grouping of documents by process.

Look at the reference to a *workflow*. Our suspicions were right! The requirements document has already specified a workflow solution in its requirements. Actually, this whole entry is suspicious. It seems to be saying that we must cache documents by two different criteria: by type or by process. The criteria are good requirements, but the caching (or prefetching) is really a solution to address performance problems and probably is not a requirement.

The system must create an entry in the journal file whenever a letter is created.

This requirement assumes the presence of a journal file, which has entries put into it when a letter is created. This requirement seems focused on the front end ("do this") instead of the back end ("in order to get this"). Why put entries into a journal file? You might do that so that you could create a list of all the letters that were created, when, and by whom. Looking at it from the back end actually makes for a better, clearer requirement. You could create a journal file, but don't think about that until design!

The system must maintain a list of current, open work processes and identify the work process to be executed and the workflow queue for the process. When particular documents are scanned, the system will determine whether there is a process open for that SSN. If there is an open process, the system will route the document to the appropriate workflow queue, display the work process script, and highlight the current work process.

Again, this requirement seems more focused on the *how* than the *what*. Rather than look at the different steps a system must go through, it should clearly document the end in mind. Here is our rewrite for this requirement: "When a new document image is brought into the system, it should be routed to the worker who has the account open for the same SSN as the new document and should be made obvious to that worker. If no worker has an open account, the document should be made available to any worker."

Why not include design in requirements? Why do we keep harping on keeping design out of requirements?

There are several reasons. First, skill sets for a development project are usually matched to the activity being performed. Therefore, the people who are gathering requirements probably have skills that are not suited to design or development, but perhaps they are the same people doing requirements, analysis, and design, and so forth. It is important to keep things separate. Documenting requirements is an effort in understanding the problem at hand. Designing is the activity of solving the problem. The solution for the problem must come after the problem has been identified, documented, and understood.

This can be tricky, especially in an iterative and incremental lifecycle. Perhaps a more accurate way to state our rule is that no system, subsystem, or increment should proceed into design until the requirements for that system, subsystem, or increment have been identified, documented, and understood. Clumsy sentence structure, but good practice. When design precedes requirements, or supplants them, the system tends to take on requirements of its own—requirements that are neither documented nor related to the users' needs. The end result can be a wasted design effort, an unusable system, missed milestones, and unhappy users. Not knowing the problem that your design is solving is dangerous business. It is always advisable (if difficult) to define the problem completely before designing.

Another reason to keep design out of requirements gathering is related to the team environment. If a group is designing a system with no documented requirements, it is likely that group members will be working with different goals in mind. Because they do not have a common document from which to begin, they form the requirements picture in their own minds and use that to formulate their designs. These designs almost certainly will be incompatible and overlapping, causing integration problems, skipped requirements, scope creep, schedule issues, and unhappy users.

1.2.1 Functional Requirements

Without requirements, there is no way to validate a program design—that is, no way to logically connect the program to the customer's desires.

—Benjamin L. Kovitz

Functional requirements are what the users need for the system to work. Functional requirements are functions and features. These are the requirements we typically think of when we describe systems.

Here are some sample functional requirements for an order entry system.

- The system shall accept orders for products and provide notification to the entry clerk as to whether there is sufficient inventory to fulfill the order.
- The system shall use reorder points set by the inventory clerk to order new parts automatically.
- The system shall substitute comparable parts for parts that are out of stock as specified by the inventory manager.
- The system shall produce a nightly report of the orders for the previous day.

1.2.2 Nonfunctional Requirements

Nonfunctional requirements address the hidden areas of the system that are important to the users even though they may not realize it. As you can probably judge by the name, these requirements do not deal with the functionality of a system. Nonfunctional requirements are the global, fuzzy factors that relate to the system's overall success. Many of them end in *-ility*, so we usually call the collection of them the *-ilities*. An example of an *-ility* is scalability: the ability of the system to handle an increased workload without significantly increasing the transaction processing time. (See Section 5.2.3 for details.)

1.3 Requirements Gathering, Definition, and Specification

Requirements gathering is the activity of bringing requirements together. *Requirements definition* is the activity of documenting these requirements and organizing them into something understandable and meaningful. A *requirements specification* is the document that results from the requirements activities.

As the first activity in the lifecycle of application development, requirements gathering sets the stage for the rest of the work. A shoddy or incomplete requirements specification causes the analysis, design, and construction to be based on a shaky foundation—or worse, based on a foundation built in the wrong place entirely. An appropriate and complete requirements specification does nothing to ensure a successful implementation; however, *it makes it possible*.

Software development efforts fail much more often than they should. They fail in very high percentages, and the bigger they are, the harder they seem to fall.

Capers Jones, founder of Software Productivity Research and metrics guru of the software industry, has done much interesting work on projects that fail. Table 1.3 shows that large projects fail in large numbers and small systems fail in small numbers.

The more complex the system, the larger the effort; the larger the effort, the more likely it is to fail. The major difference between developing systems 20 years ago and doing it today is that change is much more pervasive now. Changes to business processes and rules, user personnel, and technology make application development seem like trying to land a Frisbee on top of the head of a wild dog. The moving targets of requirements, tools, and

Homeowner: "Hey, I wanted that foundation laid over there!"

Table 1.3   Probability of Project Failure

Function Points	Probability of Termination Prior to Completion
100	6%
1,000	17%
10,000	45%
100,000	80%

From *Applied Software Measurement: Assuring Productivity and Quality,* Capers Jones, 1997, The McGraw-Hill Companies. Reproduced with permission of The McGraw-Hill Companies.

staff can make life difficult under the bright spotlight of an ongoing software project. The prevalence of change means that systems must be built differently than they were before. They must be flexible enough so that changes can be made on-the-fly to requirements, design, code, testing, staff, and processes. The iterative and incremental lifecycle can address these issues because it accepts that each phase must be repeated multiple times to accommodate change even after the subsequent phases have started.

Software systems are more complex than most other engineering projects human beings undertake, but does that mean we're destined to produce overdue, poor-quality systems that don't last? We believe there are steps the industry can take to reverse this trend. If we focus on the root problems in software development and address them with high-quality processes and tools, we can make a real difference in producing more successful, on-time software that is resilient to changes throughout its lifetime. For example, object orientation, when applied correctly, can address many of the issues of flexibility and extensibility in design and code for computer systems. It can also lessen the problems that occur when maintenance of changes in one area cripples another area. Automated test tools can help address the massive test effort associated with iterative and incremental development. But how do we address requirements?

1.4 The Challenges of Requirements Gathering

If requirements gathering were easy, we wouldn't need to write a book about it. Following are the main challenges that we've observed in the process.

1.4.1 Finding Out What the Users Need

Everyone knows how to do this: "If you want to know what they want, just go ask them." When referring to users of a computer system, though, this advice is not very sound. Users do not know what they want, because the question—what will you want in your new computer system?—is so complex that users can't be expected to answer it. There are too many variables.

Once you are using new business procedures

and

your job has changed

and

the business your company is in changes

and

you are learning a brand new computer application

how would you like it to work?

Users have much more on their minds than your computer application, including their own day-to-day responsibilities. The struggle between users' current responsibilities and their involvement in shaping a new system is legendary. Steve McConnell, in his book *Rapid Development* (1996), gives us a number of ways that users can inhibit the process of requirements gathering.

- Users don't understand what they want.
- Users won't commit to a set of written requirements.
- Users insist on new requirements after the cost and schedule have been fixed.
- Communication with users is slow.
- Users often do not participate in reviews or are incapable of doing so.
- Users are technically unsophisticated.
- Users don't understand the software development process.
- And the list continues.

This list makes users sound like some kind of beasts that rise from the muck to interfere with our quest to develop applications. Of course, they're not. There is simply a tug-of-war between what the users need to concentrate on currently and how you need them to participate in helping you develop the application.

One defense against the struggle for users' time and attention during requirements gathering is simply to concentrate on establishing relationships with your users. The stronger the personal relationships between the analysts and the users, the more likely it is that the users will make the time for questions, meetings, and debates.

Another defense is to work on the visibility of the project. If senior executives in the users' organizations are aware of the system implementation and are touting its importance, it is more likely that the profile of the application among your users will be high enough to encourage them to attend requirements sessions and interviews, and to participate. They need to know that this effort is not just going to be a flash in the pan. Finally, it's important to be respectful of their time. To create the fewest disturbances possible, batch your questions and interviews together.

1.4.2 Documenting Users' Needs

As we said earlier, documenting users' needs is called *requirements definition*. Creating this documentation and then confirming it with them is a difficult process. This book is largely dedicated to making this process easier and clearer for all parties.

The challenge of documenting requirements with traditional tools is that there are often no real checks and balances. It is hard to tell whether a requirement has already been documented, perhaps in a different way or with a conflicting result. It is also hard to see what's missing.

1.4.3 Avoiding Premature Design Assumptions

Premature design assumptions tend to creep into every requirements specification, especially if they're prepared by designers-at-heart. This also tends to happen if the people gathering the requirements don't trust the designers and want to tell them how the system should be designed so that the designers won't mess it up. This tends to happen, in our experience, when the developers are off-site and removed from the requirements gatherers and users. It also happens when the requirements analysts do not trust the designers and developers to make the right decisions later.

1.4.4 Resolving Conflicting Requirements

If requirements, big and small, are listed one after another in a list, as we showed in Section 1.1, there can be requirements in different places of the list that say opposite things. To combat this problem, you need a built-in mechanism to prevent these conflicts. You can use something with more structure than a list, or you can incorporate reviews when conflicts are identified.

1.4.5 Eliminating Redundant Requirements

Redundant requirements are not as bad as conflicts, but they can be confusing if they say *almost* the same thing, but not quite. They also add to the volume of the requirements, which can be its own problem.

1.4.6 Reducing Overwhelming Volume

The greater the volume of the requirements specification, the less likely it is that the development effort can succeed. The volume must be reduced in one or all of the following ways.

- Remove conflicts.
- Remove redundancy.
- Remove design assumptions.
- Find commonality among requirements and abstract them to the level that makes the most sense for the users.
- Separate functional from nonfunctional requirements.

1.4.7 Ensuring Requirements Traceability

When you're gathering requirements, the main thought that should be going through your mind is, Am I documenting things that will be understandable to the users and useful to the designers? Requirements must be traceable throughout the lifecycle of development. You should be able to ask any person in any role the questions contained in Table 1.4.

Unfortunately, these requirements traceability questions can rarely be answered. But if they were, they would provide a solid audit trail for every activity in development and maintenance, and they would describe why they are being done. It would help prevent *developer goldplating*: the addition of system functionality that is not required by the users and therefore does not tie in with any documented requirements.

Table 1.4   Traceability Defined by Role

Role	Traceability
Analyst/designer	What specific requirements does this class on this class diagram relate to?
Developer	What specific requirements does the class you're programming relate to?
Tester	Exactly which requirements are you testing for when you execute this test case?
Maintenance programmer	What requirements have changed that require you to change the code that way?

Automated tools are beginning to address the requirements traceability problem, but they're not there yet. We still need a little old-fashioned people management to maintain a *requirements audit trail*, which runs end-to-end throughout the lifetime of an application.

1.5 Issues with the Standard Approaches

Not only are there issues with the documentation typically produced during requirements gathering (the requirements list), but also there are often issues in the way the documentation is produced. This section looks at several common methods that can be used to bring together requirements for an application.

1.5.1 User Interviews

Obviously, conducting user interviews is necessary when you're building a requirements specification. A user interview normally focuses on users talking about how they do their job now, how they expect it will change after the system goes into production, and the typical problems they encounter with the current process. The requirements analyst is usually writing madly, trying to keep up with the users' remarks and trying to think of the next question to ask.

Often, when one interview with one user is complete and the next user is being interviewed, requirements analysts notice that the two people have conflicting views on the same process or business rule. Then, when people at various levels of management are interviewed, the playing field becomes even more interesting. Conflicting views become a multidimensional puzzle, with pieces that change their shape as the game proceeds. The question might arise in the analyst's mind, How can this company (or department) stay in business and continue to be profitable if no one can agree on how things are run? The answer is that the level of detail required to build a computer application is greater than the level of detail needed to run a business successfully. It is the only possible answer, given our experience with numerous user departments that ran perfectly well even though every employee gives different answers to the same questions.

1.5.2 Joint Requirements Planning Sessions

Joint requirements planning (JRP) sessions are similar to conducting all the user interviews at the same time in the same room. All the people who will influence the direction of the application are brought to one place and give their input into what the system will do. A facilitator leads the group to make sure things don't get out of hand, and a scribe makes sure everything gets documented, usually using a projector and diagramming software.

A JRP is similar in structure to a joint application design (JAD) session except that the focus is different. JAD sessions are focused on *how* the system will work, whereas JRP sessions are focused only on *what* the system will do. But the processes are similar.

*The JRP session provides an opportunity to get input from
a number of stakeholders at the same time.*

The people involved in JRP sessions are key representatives from a variety of interested groups, or *stakeholders*: users, user management, operations, executives, maintenance programming, and so forth. During the JRP session, high-level topics, such as critical success factors and strategic opportunities, are the first agenda items. Then the application's functional and nonfunctional requirements are identified, documented, and prioritized in the presence of everyone.

JRP sessions are valuable and can be significant timesavers for the requirements team. As hard as it is to get all the interested parties into one room (preferably off-site), it can be even harder to schedule time with each individual, given other distractions, interruptions, and priorities.

Our main issue with JRP is the document produced. In most cases, the document is a list of requirements—and you know how we feel about requirements lists.

1.5.3 Requirements Lists

The requirements list has its problems. In most other areas of the software development lifecycle, we have evolved the documentation into effective diagrams along with text that is elegantly structured and useful. Requirements have lagged behind this trend. The requirements list must be replaced by something with more structure and more relevance to users and designers alike. We suggest that use cases, use case diagrams, and business rules replace the traditional requirements list.

Table 1.5 shows another example of a requirements list that needs to be improved. We have a few comments beside each requirement, but please feel free to add your own insights.

Table 1.5   More Requirements

Requirement	Comment
The system will support client inquiries from four access points: in person, paper-based mail, voice communication, and electronic communication (Internet, dial-up, and LAN/WAN).	Four access points are how; we should focus instead on who needs access from where.
The telephone system must be able to support an 800 number system.	An 800 number? Can't use 888 or 877? Again, what's missing is who needs what kind of access from where.
The telephone system must be able to handle 97,000 calls per year and must allow for a growth rate of 15 percent annually. Of these calls it is estimated that 19 percent will be responded to in an automated manner and 81 percent will be routed to call center staff for response. Fifty percent of the calls can be processed without reference to the electronic copy of the paper file, and approximately 50 percent will require access to the system files.	Valuable statistics; this one is actually pretty good.
For the calls that require access to system information, response times for the electronic files must be less than 20 seconds for the first image located on the optical disk, less than 3 seconds for electronic images on a server, and less than 1 second for data files.	Starts out nicely until we mention "optical disk," which is a design assumption. The response times would be good nonfunctional requirements if they weren't linked to design assumptions.
The telephone system must be able to support voice recognition of menu selections, touch-tone menu selections, and default to a human operator. The telephone menu will sequence caller choices in order of most frequently requested information to the least requested.	Pretty good one. Can you find anything wrong?

Requirement	Comment
The telephone system must be able to provide a voice response menu going from a general menu to a secondary menu.	This seems to be trying to provide a dumb designer with some pretty obvious advice.
The system must allow for the caller to provide address information through a digital recording and to indicate whether it is permanent.	"Through a digital recording"? This is a design assumption.
The system must allow for the caller to provide address information through voice recognition and to indicate whether it is permanent.	Sound familiar? (It's redundant.)
The telephone system must be able to store and maintain processor IDs, and personal identification numbers to identify callers and to route calls properly to the appropriate internal response telephone.	Simplify it: "The system must be able to identify callers and route calls to the appropriate internal response telephone."
The telephone system must be able to inform callers of the anticipated wait time based on the number of calls, average duration of calls, and number of calls ahead of them.	Great!
The journal will contain entries for key events that have occurred within the administration of an individual's account. The system will capture date, processor ID, and key event description. The system will store pointers to images that are associated with a journal entry as well as key data system screens that contain more information regarding the entry.	This is a design for the journal. Why have it? What is its purpose?
If an individual double-clicks on an event in a member's journal, the system will display the electronic information and the images associated with the event.	Double-click is a user interface assumption.

continues

Table 1.5 *continued*

Requirement	Comment
The system will restrict options on the information bar by processor function. When an icon is clicked, the screen represented by the icon will be displayed and the system will display appropriate participant information.	This one has lots of user interface assumptions.

1.5.4 Prototypes

The prototype wave hit software development in the mid 1980s as fourth-generation languages become popular and usable. *Prototypes* are mock-ups of the screens or windows of an application that allow users to visualize the application that isn't yet constructed. Prototypes help the users get an idea of what the system will look like, and the users can easily decide which changes are necessary without waiting until after the system is built. When this approach was introduced, the results were astounding. Improvements in communication between user groups and developers were often the result of using prototypes. Early changes to screen designs helped set the stage for fewer changes later and reduced overall costs dramatically.

However, there are issues with prototypes. Users with detail-oriented minds pay more attention to the details of the screens than to the essence of what the prototype is meant to communicate. Executives, once they see the prototype, have a hard time understanding why it will take another year or two to build a system that looks as if it is already built. And some designers feel compelled to use the patched-together prototype code in the real system because they're afraid to throw any code away.

Prototypes will always be a part of systems development. But they cannot be the one and only requirements specification. They contain too much user interface design (which can be distracting to users and designers), and they imply that more of the system is built than is actually completed. They represent only the front end of the system—the presentation. The business rules are not usually represented unless the prototype is fully functional, and this means that a lot of effort must go into the prototype. Prototypes should be used for what they are best at: user interface specification. This means that perhaps prototypes should come along a little later than the bulk of the requirements work.

1.6 Those Troublesome Requirements

The traditional tools and techniques used for gathering requirements have not served us well. We usually get ahead of ourselves and start embedding design into our requirements specifications. We spend either too little or too much effort. We create prototypes that are useful but are also distracting, and we create requirements lists that are difficult to use and don't provide any checks or balances. There must be a better way.

2

In my work, I focus on user goals first, and then I come up with use cases to satisfy them.

—Martin Fowler

Moving to Use Cases

The computer industry has struggled to find a way to represent functionality to users. We have always tended to produce what we're comfortable with: diagrams and specifications that are loaded with terminology and notation that looks a lot more like computer code than anything a user would understand. The traditional modes of expressing functionality to users early in the lifecycle are as follows:

- Requirements specifications
- Data-flow diagrams (DFDs)
- Entity-relationship diagrams (ERDs)
- Prototypes

Typically, requirements are specified in lists and expressed in terms of "the system shall." These lists are often grouped by functionality or subsystem. In such lists, it's easy to inadvertently write duplicate or conflicting requirements, and it happens often. The requirements

The system shall . . .

19

specification does not provide the users with a cohesive view of what the system will accomplish; it is merely an itemization of each of the various functions, as if the functions could be extracted and treated independently.

What requirements lists intend to provide is a comprehensive catalog of every function that the system should perform. Although it seems only natural to list these functions, it turns out that there are better ways to represent this information and provide a better structure than a list.

We recommend that requirements lists be dropped from the analyst's toolbox.

DFDs are useful for technical people but tend to confuse users.

DFDs help show a system as a set of groups of interacting processes. We consider them to represent the dynamic view of the system. The data *flows* from one process to another and then stops in a data store. External entities, such as an outside department or computer system, are referenced whenever they have involvement in the flow of data. Because DFDs focus on what happens inside the system, they are the main input into system design. In our experience, users seem to be confused by these diagrams because the line between system and user responsibility is fuzzy. DFDs also contain a lot more detail than users are prepared to wade through. Some of these details, such as how many data stores are used and what they store, do not concern the users at all.

As with requirements lists, we recommend that DFDs be dropped from the requirements analyst's toolbox. DFDs introduce many technical elements into the requirements picture that are not necessary at this point. DFDs can be replaced by use cases and class, sequence, statechart, and activity diagrams in the Unified Modeling Language (UML).

NOTE: DFDs can still be useful in design, particularly with non-object-oriented systems.

ERDs are critical to database design, but they are not meant for user consumption.

ERDs show how the data is stored in an application. They show details of entities, attributes, and relationships. This diagram can also be used to represent a logical data model and dictate the structure of a relational database. However, ERDs do nothing to show dynamic interaction, and they must always be used along with DFDs to show a complete picture to the users. The difference between a dynamic type of expression (DFDs) and a static or persistent expression (ERDs) is irrelevant and confusing to users.

We recommend that ERDs, too, be dropped from the requirements analyst's toolbox. ERDs are still required if you want to create a logical data model after requirements have been gathered, but ERDs do not provide much meaning to users and seem foreign to them.

Prototypes give users a realistic demonstration of what a system will be able to do when it is completed. These mock-up versions of the system concentrate on the user interface and omit all or most of the background coding. Prototypes are greeted with enthusiasm by users because they help them understand the possibilities much better than do paper diagrams. However, users' enthusiasm is problematic because they immediately get caught up in the details of the user interface and the mock-up data. Soon, they are spending more time requesting button moves and color changes than they spend focusing on the functionality. Prototypes also lead users to the misperception that the prototype *is* the system, and they become impatient when it takes weeks or months to develop the actual system. Prototypes also encourage the team to continue quick-and-dirty coding after actual system development begins, evolving the prototype into the final system.

Prototypes were long held to be the elixir for good requirements capture, but now we realize that they can help much more with proof-of-concept tasks.

We recommend that prototypes no longer be used as the main requirements tool. Instead, they should be used to support use cases and the business rules catalog, which become the central focus of the requirements phase.

Traditional requirements specifications are often never used again after they are produced. DFDs and ERDs are useful for moving into programming and database design, but they do not seem to mean much to users. Prototypes are meaningful to users, but they encourage them to concentrate on the details of user interface implementation and not on the requirements of the system. What's needed is a new medium between users and system designers.

2.1 It's All About Interactions

Clearly, the combination of artifacts produced in our projects contains a lot of information. However, it may be that they contain too much information. What if the diagrams were to concentrate on the requirements of the system from the users' perspectives? The question is then, What do the users see?

Users view computer systems as *black boxes*. This term implies that the perspective of the application is concerned only with what goes in and what comes out. The inner workings are not important to the black-box perspective. Requirements documentation that puts everything in the context of "going in" and "coming out" has more relevance to the users who study it.

When we talk about "going in" and "coming out," we're talking about interactions. Interactions between the users and the computer system are what really matter in requirements gathering. For example, it is important that a user wants to enter numbers in timesheets and have the system print checks. But it is not important to the user that those timesheets go through 18 specific processes before the checks are produced. That's design. The users care only that the checks are produced and that they're right.

Users only care about what goes in and what comes out.

For an IT specialist, grasping this concept is very tough. We have strong tendencies to jump into the *how* before we've defined the *what*. We're typically advised not to get too detailed. But this is not quite accurate. The *what* can become very detailed. For example, the definition of printing the checks "right," in our example, could be very detailed. Information about what the system should do with calculating weekly pay based on a yearly salary, handling hourly employees, dealing with overtime, and incorporating raises at the right time can be excruciatingly detailed. However, the focus must remain on the *what* and not drift into the *how*.

Use cases are a tool that should show the *what* exclusively. DFDs, ERDs, and prototypes include *what* and *how* in their perspectives, and that can confuse users. For this reason, we recommend that use cases be the primary tool for requirements gathering.

2.2 Hello World!

Most of the programming language books we read include a "Hello World" example that shows the new language performing a simple task. Our "Hello World" use case is a *system context use case*, which is abstracted to describe a broad swath of requirements without drilling down into a lot of detail. We present it at this point to consolidate some of the ideas that we have presented about use cases. System context use cases are explained in Chapter 4.

The Origin of Use Cases

Use cases were introduced to the IT world by Ivar Jacobson and his team at Ericsson in Sweden. Their book, *Object-Oriented Software Engineering* (Jacobson et al.1992), took the computing industry by storm, and use cases have been increasing in popularity ever since. Jacobson included use cases as part of an overall system development lifecycle methodology called Objectory, which he marketed as a product and built a company around. Later, Jacobson's Objectory company and methodology were purchased by Rational Software, and Objectory, with its use cases, became part of the Rational Unified Process (Jacobson, Booch, and Rumbaugh 1999). We owe a lot to Jacobson, and this book uses many of his ideas in the definition of use cases. To his ideas we've added the practical application of use cases to solve the requirements problem. As consultants and practitioners, we have worked with use cases on the job for many years, and we understand their good and bad points. In this book, we attempt to improve on use cases, not by changing them fundamentally but by surrounding them with other artifacts and helpful hints to help create a more comprehensive requirements toolset.

A use case has two parts: the use case diagram and the use case itself. The diagram provides an overview of which interactions will be important, and the use case's text details the requirements.

Figure 2.1 is the use case diagram for a real estate system. The use case diagram shows *actors* (entities outside the program) interacting with use cases. In this case, we can see that the buyer, seller, and adviser actors interact to achieve the objective of the use case, which is to sell a property.

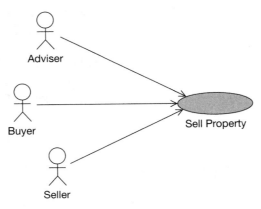

Figure 2.1 *Sell Property Use Case Diagram*

The use case diagram visualizes the system's interactions and captures the scope. The simplicity of these diagrams makes them a great communication tool, and they can be drawn using a software tool or drawn on a napkin during a scope discussion. The use case itself details what the system must do. The following use case (Use Case 2.1) is at the same level of abstraction as the diagram and supplies greater detail than the diagram.

Use Case Name:	**Sell Property**
Iteration:	**Filled**
Summary:	System Context Use Case. The seller lists the property, a buyer purchases the property, and the agent guides them through the process and offers advice, caution, and recommendations.
Basic Course of Events:	1. The seller selects an agent. 2. The system responds by assigning an agent and notifying the seller's agent. 3. The seller lists the property to sell. 4. The system responds by displaying this property in the property listing and linking it for searches. 5. The buyer selects an agent. 6. The buyer reviews the property listings by entering search criteria. 7. The system responds by displaying properties that match the buyer's search criteria. 8. The buyer finds a property and makes an offer on it. 9. The system responds by notifying the seller and the seller's agent. 10. The seller responds to the offer with a counteroffer. 11. The system responds by notifying the buyer and the buyer's agent. 12. The buyer and the seller agree to terms. 13. The system responds by recording the agreement. 14. The buyer indicates that a loan is required. 15. The system responds by locating an appropriate loan provider. 16. The buyer and the loan provider agree to loan terms. 17. The system responds by recording the terms of the loan.

Use Case 2.1   *Use Case Example (continues)*

	18. The buyer and seller close on the property. 19. The system responds by recording the details of the close.
Alternative Paths:	N/A
Extension Points:	N/A
Trigger:	N/A
Assumptions:	N/A
Preconditions:	N/A
Postconditions:	N/A
Related Business Rules:	N/A
Author:	Angela Baltimore
Date:	March 20, 2000—Facade; March 26, 2000—Filled

Use Case 2.1 *continued*

The "Basic Course of Events" section outlines the steps that actors take to achieve the use case's objective. Even highly abstracted, it speaks volumes about the system by showing you how the system will be used.

NOTE: For definitions of the four stages of iteration (Facade, Filled, Focused, and Finished), see Section 3.3.

Before continuing our discussion about use cases, let's put them in the context of the UML, of which use cases are a part.

2.3 The Unified Modeling Language

The Unified Modeling Language.

Use cases aren't a phenomenon unto themselves. They are part of a comprehensive language called the Unified Modeling Language, or UML. This language was brought into existence in January 1997 and has subsequently been adopted as a standard by the Object Management Group (OMG), an industry consortium.

The UML is a *notation*: a way to document system specifications. It is not a methodology. A notation simply tells you how to structure your system documentation. It provides the nomenclature of the diagrams and specifications that you produce. A *methodology*, by contrast, consists of a step-by-step guide to building a system. Methodologies are much more complex and contentious. The UML is not dependent on a particular methodology, nor do methodologies need to be contingent on the UML. The UML requires only that the computer system being built has object-oriented components. In fact, several of the UML diagrams, including use cases, can be used for systems that are not based on object orientation. Methodologies that work with the UML include the Rational Unified Process, the Object Modeling Technique, the Booch method, Objectory, Schlaer-Mellor, FUSION, OPEN, and many others.

Of course, the UML did not appear magically from outer space. It was the result of collaborations between three famous object-oriented methodologists: Grady Booch, James Rumbaugh, and Ivar Jacobson. The "Three Amigos," as they are called, combined their own modeling notations and also got plenty of ideas and unanimous buy-in from every other major methodologist in the industry. Through their efforts, the computer industry has a common language,[1] or notation, with which to specify object-oriented systems—something this industry has never before experienced.

SEE ALSO: http://saturn.csse.swin.edu.au/cotar/OPEN/UML98/UMLCRC.PDF

The UML is composed of nine diagrams:

- Use case diagram
- Sequence diagram
- Collaboration diagram
- Statechart diagram
- Activity diagram
- Class diagram
- Object diagram
- Component diagram
- Deployment diagram

1. There is at least one other notation that we are aware of that competes with the UML. It is called OPEN Modeling Language (OML). The OML is part of a methodology called OPEN, or Object-Oriented Process, Environment, and Notation. OPEN and OML are being championed by Donald Firesmith, Brian Henderson-Sellers, Ian Graham, and Meiler Page-Jones—an impressive roster, to say the least. OML is billed as a "superset of the UML," but it is likely to serve only as a set of recommendations to the OMG for future enhancements to the UML. We do not expect the OML to compete with the UML directly.

These diagrams, used properly within the context of a solid methodology, can convey all the necessary views of a computer system and can provide the basis for constructing, configuring, and deploying the system. There are many interdependencies between these diagrams. Construction on one type of diagram means changes to others. Software tools[2] can help manage these interdependencies. The UML lends itself well to automated analysis and design tools and also provides many possibilities for generating code from design documentation and for *reverse engineering* (creating design from code).

The UML is a well-thought-out notation that serves analysts, designers, and architects. It is comprehensive, especially when compared with earlier object-oriented notations. It is also the new standard for object-oriented systems notation, and that's the best reason of all to use it for all your documentation needs. But remember—to be successful on your project, you must choose and implement a methodology along with the UML. Adopting the UML by itself is not enough.

This book is dedicated to explaining how use cases can solve problems in requirements gathering. It is not meant to provide a tutorial for the UML, but it is important that you understand how use cases fit into the context of the UML. Books on the UML include the following:

- *The Unified Modeling Language Reference Guide* (by James Rumbaugh, Ivar Jacobson, Grady Booch), Addison Wesley, 1999
- *Applying UML and Patterns* (by Craig Larman), Prentice-Hall PTR, 1998
- *The Unified Modeling Language User Guide* (by Grady Booch, James Rumbaugh, Ivar Jacobson), Addison Wesley, 1998

2.3.1 Nine Diagrams

In the following sections we take a look at the nine UML diagrams in some detail.

2.3.1.1 Use Case Diagram

Figure 2.2 shows an example of a *use case diagram*.

Use cases, obviously, are a focus of this book. They are the driver for the rest of the diagrams. Although the UML is not a methodology and therefore does not prescribe steps, it makes the assumption that you diagram use cases before you start the other diagrams. Use cases form the basis of how the system interacts with the outside forces around it: users/ actors, other systems, and other factors (date/time, special environmental conditions, and so on).

Use cases are text descriptions of the interaction between some outside actors and the computer system. Use case diagrams are graphical depictions of the relationships between actors and use cases and between a use case and another use case.

---

2. Our favorite analysis and design tools that support the UML are, in order of preference, Rational Rose, Advanced Software GDPro, and Select Enterprise.

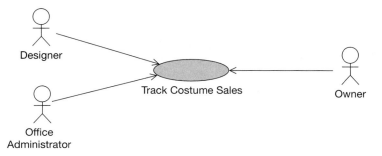

Figure 2.2 *Focused Iteration: Track Costume Sales System Context Use Case Diagram*

Use cases and use case diagrams should be documents that users can interpret easily. They are meant to be written in "user language," devoid of any "objectspeak" or implementation details. Inside each use case is a nice little package of requirements that effectively drives the rest of the system development process.

Use cases drive not only requirements gathering but also the entire software development cycle. Several methodologies, including the popular RUP, are use-case-driven. Use cases have the simplicity to represent a computer system's essence, and yet they have the power to drive the entire methodology, in the process helping to solve problems such as requirements traceability.

2.3.1.2 Sequence and Collaboration Diagrams

Sequence diagrams (Figure 2.3) and *collaboration* diagrams (Figure 2.4) show the internal workings of a use case scenario (see Section 2.4.1.4). They present a dynamic view of a system, showing how messages pass between objects to satisfy a use case.

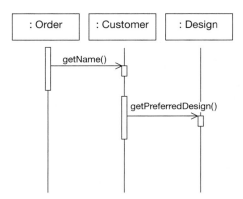

Figure 2.3 *Sequence Diagram Example*

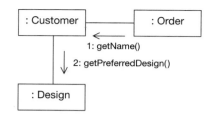

Figure 2.4   *Collaboration Diagram Example*

Collaboration diagrams have the same function as sequence diagrams, but sequence diagrams are geared toward simple, linear interactions, whereas collaboration diagrams are geared toward more complex interactions such as multithreaded or conditional messaging.

2.3.1.3 Statecharts and Activity Diagrams

Statecharts and *activity* diagrams are also part of the dynamic view of a system. In contrast to sequence and collaboration diagrams, statecharts and activity diagrams concentrate on transition from one state to another rather than on the messages that pass between objects. Statecharts (Figure 2.5) are generally used for simpler state transition views, and activity diagrams (Figure 2.6) are used for more complex views.

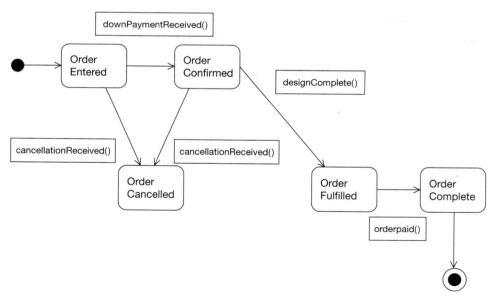

Figure 2.5   *Statechart Diagram Example*

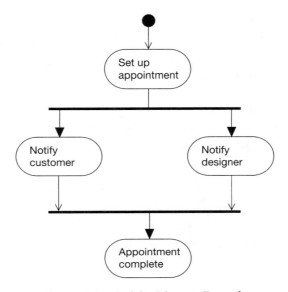

Figure 2.6 *Activity Diagram Example*

2.3.1.4 Class and Object Diagrams

Although the previous diagrams show the dynamic view of a computer system, *class* diagrams are geared toward the static view. Class diagrams (Figure 2.7) show how classes are constructed and list their names, attributes, and operations. They also show how classes are related to one another statically, using associations such as generalization and aggregation (discussed later in this chapter).

Object diagrams show the relationships among *objects*, which are the instances created at runtime from the class templates. The structure of an object diagram is similar to that of a class diagram except that the focus is on the runtime instantiations of the classes.

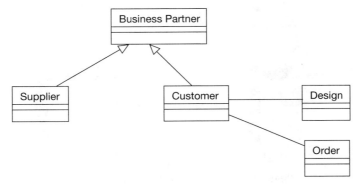

Figure 2.7 *Class Diagram Example*

2.3.1.5 Component Diagram

Component diagrams (Figure 2.8) help move the system from a collection of fine-grained objects to a collection of coarser-grained components, and they help show how these components relate to one another.

2.3.1.6 Deployment Diagram

Deployment diagrams (Figure 2.9) show how components of the system will be deployed to different physical nodes, or machines, in the production environment.

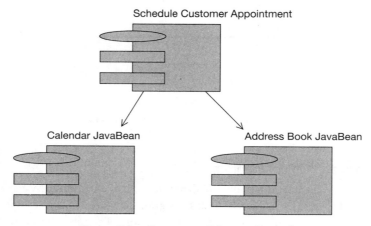

Figure 2.8   *Component Diagram Example*

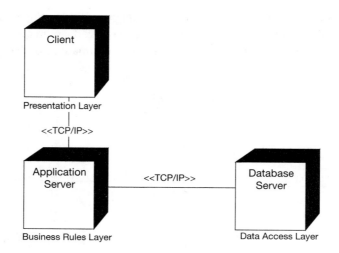

Figure 2.9   *Deployment Diagram Example*

2.3.1.7 Packages

Another convenient UML mechanism is the package metaphor. *Packages* (see Figure 2.10) are a way to hide complexity. They can be used with use cases, classes, components, or deployment nodes.

2.3.2 Extending the UML with Stereotyping

We hope that the UML will last for years and years. But how can a modeling language last in the computer field, where the only constant is change? And how can this general-purpose language be useful for each specific situation, when circumstances may require new types of elements or diagrams?

The UML addresses these issues with a feature called *stereotypes*. Stereotyping lets you *extend* the UML to represent new types of abstractions or concepts. Stereotyping is extremely powerful and enables you to customize the UML for your project. It also means that the UML will not go out of date as quickly as most modeling languages because it can be adapted to handle the changes it faces.

What are stereotypes? Stereotypes are a way to classify UML building blocks (or elements) in a more specific way to add meaning to a diagram. Stereotypes let you group characteristics that are common among several use cases, for example, and thereby change the specification of a use case to a more specialized form, perhaps a mission-critical use case. The *mission-critical* stereotype might specify that a requirement of all use cases of this stereotype is that they respond to the actor within three seconds on each interaction.

In addition to use cases, all other UML elements—components, nodes, associations, and objects—can be stereotyped. The most common UML element to be stereotyped is classes.

The UML has several built-in stereotypes. For example, on the use case diagram, associations between use cases are stereotyped as *includes* or *extends* to show special kinds of associations that are unique to the use case diagram.

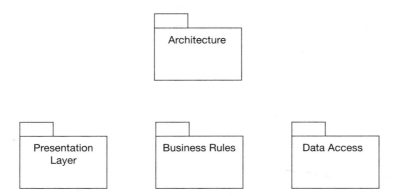

Figure 2.10 *Package Diagram Example*

This book uses several kinds of stereotypes to increase the relevance of use cases to requirements gathering. We discuss these stereotypes in later chapters.

Stereotypes can be introduced by anyone who uses the UML, including individual practitioners. For the purposes of this book, we use stereotyping to help clarify the concepts we are introducing. (You can read more about our new stereotypes in Chapter 3.)

In the sample use case diagram in Figure 2.11, the *Process Loan* use case is classified with the stereotype *mission-critical*. This means that all use cases marked with this stereotype must meet certain criteria; in this case, the transaction must be secure and must have less than a ten-second response time. The definition for *mission-critical* might be specified in a separate document that addresses all stereotypes.

2.4 Introducing Use Cases, Use Case Diagrams, and Scenarios

Part of our solution to the requirements-gathering problem is to deploy use cases, a deceptively simple tool that examines a computer system by expressing the interactions between the system and its environment: what goes in and what comes out. This sounds simple, but in practice it becomes very difficult. In our experience, systems professionals have an extremely hard time producing use cases that mean anything to the users. Systems people are used to dealing with systems as white boxes, not black boxes, and are focused on the *how*. Users see only the black box: the *what*.

In the book *Zen and the Art of Motorcycle Maintenance*, Robert Pirsig (1974) uses historical terms to describe differing views of a motorcycle: the *classic* view and the *romantic* view. The classic view sees a motorcycle in terms of its subsystems: power train, braking, steering, safety, and so on. The romantic view sees the motorcycle as what it can do for the rider: speed up, slow down, weave through traffic, avoid accidents, and so forth. Each view sees exactly the same motorcycle, but they see it from much different perspectives.

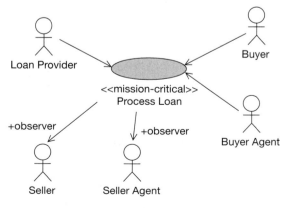

Figure 2.11 *Use Case Stereotypes*

*Two people see a motorcycle in two ways: as the subsystems that make
up the bike and as the things a person can do with the bike.*

Use cases in the requirements activity see the system from the romantic view. They are concerned only with what the system can do for the users. This makes them extremely effective for conveying information to users because they cut out all classic viewpoints and boil down the requirements to the barest essentials.

To apply use cases effectively to the requirements-gathering process, you need to understand the goals of use cases, which are discussed in the next section. Use cases are simple in structure, but preparing them correctly is difficult. This is often the case with simple representations of complex things. In the following subsections, we explore the notation of the use case and how it fits in with the rest of the UML.

2.4.1 The Goals of Use Cases

Following are the goals of creating use cases for requirements.

2.4.1.1 Interactions That Provide Value to Actors

Use cases are meant to show the interactions between the system and the entities external *to* the system. External entities, or actors, include users, other computer systems, or external events, such as reaching a specific date or time. Each interaction should provide something of value to the external entity. If it does not, it should contribute directly to a value provided to an external entity that does not participate in the interaction. For example, a management information system may not provide value to the clerk who keys in volumes of data, but the data contributes directly to the manager, who uses the data to make business decisions. Similarly, a production accounting system may gather information from a metering system but actually provide the value to another actor, perhaps a general ledger system. When the interaction occurs between the system and an external event such as date/

time, the external event does not gain a value from the interaction; nevertheless, some other external entity should benefit from the interaction.

2.4.1.2 No Implementation-Specific Language

As mentioned previously, use cases are black-box representations, and this means that use cases do not include any *implementation-specific language.* As the use case author, you avoid using implementation-specific language by not making any assumptions about how this use case is realized in program code or the user interface. Table 2.1 provides examples of implementation-specific language and our suggestions for improving it.

Be careful about using implementation-specific terms in these areas:

- Specific people (instead of roles)
- Specific departments in the organization
- User interface widgets (buttons, menu navigation, hardware references)
- Assumptions about where the work is being done physically
- IF-THEN-ELSE statements in use case text
- Pseudocode in use case text
- The use of any kind of constraint language in use case text (such as Object Constraint Language [OCL])

Table 2.1   Removing Implementation-Specific Language

Don't	Do	Assumptions Removed
The clerk pushes the OK button.	The clerk signifies completion of the transaction.	User interface button
The account holder folds the envelope with the cash or check and deposit slip and places it inside the slot on the automated teller machine (ATM).	The account holder provides the deposit, including cash, check, and deposit summary data.	Envelope, deposit slip, slot, ATM
The customers use the mouse to click on their part selection for the zip code they specified in the pull-down box and then click on the hyper-link to the Order Finalization Web page.	The customer chooses a part from a list of available parts in the specified zip code.	Mouse clicks, pull-down box, hyperlink, Web page, navigation from one page to another

Hand in hand with the rejection of implementation-specific language, use cases should be written in the users' vocabulary. All data items and interactions should be termed and phrased using the same language that the users adopt to describe their jobs.

We call use cases that have no implementation references *context-free* use cases. It means that we can apply these use cases to any context—technical, implementation, user interface, workflow, and so forth—and they will still be perfectly applicable.

Sometimes, implementation-specific language is OK. Having stated firmly that you should never put implementation-specific details in use cases, now let's discuss when you should do it: when they are being produced or refined outside the boundaries of requirements gathering. Because use cases drive the whole lifecycle, it is reasonable to assume that they are modified throughout the lifecycle. In fact, use cases become increasingly implementation-specific as time goes on, reflecting the work being done at the time. Another term for implementation-specific, in this context, is *real*. The term *real use cases* comes from Constantine and Lockwood 1999 and is documented in Craig Larman's book (1997). Any use cases that reflect the requirements view should be saved separately, but they can also become input to use cases that help manage the work of design, construction, testing, and architecture. There is much more on this topic in Appendix A, Use Cases Beyond Requirements.

2.4.1.3 User-Appropriate Level of Detail

As you proceed through requirements gathering, use cases go from being general to being detailed. As IT professionals, we tend to migrate to the details quickly. It is important to at least start at a general level before jumping to the details. Keep in mind that use cases should always be in the users' vocabulary. This may help you keep to a suitable level of detail.

2.4.1.4 User-Appropriate Volume

At the Object-Oriented Programming System, Languages, and Applications (OOPSLA) conference in 1996, Ivar Jacobson said that a very large system should have no more than 70 to 80 use cases. Sound impossible? This means that most systems would have perhaps 20 to 50 use cases, and some small systems even fewer.

We have found that if we use good judgment, it is not only possible but also extremely wise to keep the number of use cases very small. In producing such a small number of use cases for functionality so grand, the analysts and users are forced to abstract the activities of the system until they truly represent what the system must accomplish. After the distractions and assumptions are pulled out, two processes that may seem to be unique begin to merge, and a better abstraction results.

Please note that we refer to the number of use cases and not the number of scenarios. *Scenarios* are individual instances of use cases that traverse a specific path using specific data. There can be a large number of scenarios, depending on how detailed the testing effort becomes or how much confusion exists between users and requirements analysts.

Remember that each use case represents a fairly abstract interaction between actor and system. The individual paths through the use case, shown in the Alternative Path and Exception

Path sections in the use case template (discussed in Section 2.4.3), form the basis for the detailed processing that usually requires volumes of documentation to represent.

2.4.2 How Use Case Diagrams Show Relationships

Use cases are text documents. To show two kinds of relationships—those between use cases and those between use cases and actors—we employ use case diagrams. As with all UML diagrams, use case diagrams have specific rules about notation. The following subsections explain these rules.

2.4.2.1 Actors and Roles

Use cases never initiate actions on their own. The initiator of all interactions is the actor: something outside the computer application. Actors can be people, other computer systems, or something more abstract, such as a specific date and time. Actors shown on the use case diagram should be those that interact directly with the system or are influenced directly by the system.

The use case actor.

It is often hard to decide which actors to show on a use case diagram. For example, when a supplier provides an invoice to a company clerk and the clerk enters the invoice into the system, should the supplier be included in the diagram? If the supplier is shown, it is called a *secondary* actor. Our rule is that the supplier should be shown in the diagram if the supplier's behavior impacts the system in any way. For example, if a supplier sends a shipment late and that changes how the system reacts, then the supplier should be in the diagram.

Computer systems can also be actors. For example, when your system feeds postings to a general ledger system, that general ledger system becomes an actor in your use case diagram. Similarly, if other systems feed your system, they should also appear in your diagrams. A trigger of some sort can also be an actor. For example, if a system goes into action when a certain date or time is reached, such as 7:00 PM on the last workday of the month, then the date/time becomes the actor. Similarly, if a system is initiated by a condition of its environment, such as the pressure in a natural gas pipeline increasing above a certain level, then the pressure in the pipeline becomes the actor.

Actors are external to the system and outside its responsibility. It might be helpful to treat each actor as an *assumption*. You assume that the actor is out of scope and that the system will interact with it but not automate it.

Actors can be treated as use cases when analysts begin looking at the use cases to start building an object model. Actors may influence how the classes are constructed; in fact, they themselves may become classes. Therefore, it makes sense to take care in creating the right actor to interact with the use cases. (We talk about how actors in use cases influence security in Appendix A, Use Cases Beyond Requirements.)

Interactions between actors and use cases are shown with a straight, unbroken line with arrows. It is not customary to label these lines. The description of what is behind these lines is what constitutes the Basic Course of Events section in the use case text.

Good actor names are quite specific but are not linked to organizational positions or certain users.

When to Show Secondary Actors

You should show secondary actors on use case diagrams when the specific actions of the secondary actor have an effect on the responses the application provides. Another rule of thumb is to make early judgment about whether the data regarding this secondary actor will be stored in the system in any way.

Role Names

You may notice that there are names at the actor ends of the arrows in the use case diagram examples. These are *role names*. Role names are useful when the association between an actor and a use case needs information beyond the fact that they interact. In this example, these associations are special because the actors are only *observers*. This role must be defined according to its implications. Perhaps they have read-only access to some data. This information is captured now, at requirements time, and is useful later in design.

2.4.2.2 Associations

Associations can exist between an actor and a use case, between use cases, and between actors. Let's examine each type of association.

Generalization

Generalization is a concept that is borrowed from the object-oriented world. When several use cases, for example, have something in common that can be abstracted into another, higher-level use case, they are said to be generalized.

Figure 2.12 shows two *subactors* being generalized into a *superactor*. Two types of representatives—customer and field—have behavior or attributes in common that are described under the service representative superactor. This type of generalization of actors should be done for one of two reasons.

- The superactors and subactors all have interactions with the use cases.
- There is considerable description that is common between the two subactors that would otherwise be duplicated.

The superactor should interact with use cases when all its subactors interact the same way with use cases. The subactors should interact with use cases when their individual interactions differ from that of the superactor.

Use cases can also be generalized using the same notation, but it is not used very often. We usually create one use case diagram that contains nothing but the actor generalizations.

Extend and *Include* Adornments

Use case associations stereotyped as <<*extend*>> indicate a relationship in which a special use case (the blunt side of the association) extends an original use case (the sharp side of the association). The <<*include*>> association stereotype allows use case designers to avoid duplicating steps across multiple use cases. You deploy it as a reuse strategy for use case text

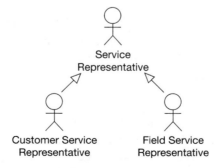

Figure 2.12   *Customer and Field Representative Generalized as Service Representative*

instead of cutting and pasting steps into multiple use case documents. These types of association, also called *adornments*, are useful when certain special cases would clutter the original use case.

In Figure 2.13, *Enter Costume Order* and *Schedule Customer Appointment* have some similar steps that can be drawn out into a separate use case called *Schedule Designer*. There may be other pieces of these use cases that are common, and they, too, could become separate use cases with *include* associations back to the owning use cases.

The *extending* use case (the blunt side of the arrow) is a special case of the *extended* use case (the sharp side of the arrow), and therefore the *extending* use case would not exist without the *extended* use case.

Be sparing in your use of the *extend* and *include* associations. It can be tempting to overengineer use cases and to go into design mode when you should really be continuing to gather requirements. Use these associations to simplify your use cases and to exploit similarity between groups of requirements. Do not use them to design a solution.

NOTE: You can think of *included* use cases the way you might think of function calls in programming. They are common pieces of logic that are reused from several calling modules.

2.4.3 The Use Case Template

Most of the UML elements are diagrams. A use case is actually a page or two of text representing each oval in the use case diagram.

You need a common template for use cases in a project. Figure 2.14 presents a sample template. Standardization on a template is more important than what the template itself looks like. You can use our template or the template supplied with the RUP. Or, best of all, you can create your own template that uniquely addresses the requirements of your organization. It is helpful, however, if the same template is used for all projects within an organization. We have these rules for creating good-quality templates.

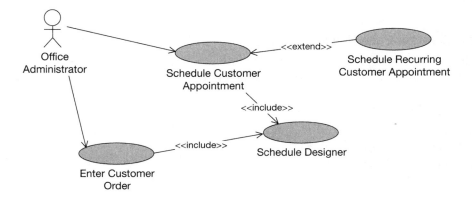

Figure 2.13 *Include and Extend Notation Example*

Use Case Name:	
Iteration:	
Summary:	
Basic Course of Events:	
Alternative Paths:	
Exception Paths:	
Extension Points:	
Triggers:	
Assumptions:	
Preconditions:	
Postconditions	
Related Business Rules:	
Author:	
Date:	

Figure 2.14   *A Sample Use Case Template*

- Make each section meaningful. For example, don't have a section for Goals and another one for Objectives. For use cases, these are probably variations of the same thing.
- Use as few sections as possible to accomplish the job. We found ourselves creating more and more boxes on our form, but if users are to use this template easily, the fewer boxes the better. Users like use case templates that allow them to speed-read when they are reviewing the documents, so organize the template with that in mind.
- Each use case will probably be a page or more of text. Give yourself plenty of space to work with and don't constrain your line length by having more than one column in a page.

2.4.3.1 Use Case Name

The use case name provides a unique identification. We prefer a unique identifier that is written in English. Long ID numbers tend to turn off users.

2.4.3.2 Iteration

Iteration relates to each of the four stages through which we see use cases progressing: facade, filled, focused, and finished (see Section 3.3). Each use case progresses through these iterations at its own pace.

2.4.3.3 Summary

In one or two sentences, describe the interaction that occurs in this use case. Try not to regurgitate the basic course of events. Remember that each section should add its own unique value. The summary section may provide some context that other sections don't contain.

2.4.3.4 Basic Course of Events

This is the meat of the use case. Describe the steps that the actors and the system go through to accomplish the goal of this use case. The actor always takes the first step, and then the system responds. This goes back and forth until the goal has been accomplished, with some value being provided to the actor.

The basic course of events represents the "simple, correct path" through the use case. This means that no errors or missteps occur, either by the actor or the system. It also means that it shows the most common path taken. For example, a retailer may find that 80 percent of all orders use purchase orders (POs), with only occasional cash, check, or credit card use. This means that the basic course of events should show the details of a PO without concern for the other types of payment.

Sometimes, courses of events are shown with separate columns for the actor's actions and the system's actions. This arrangement helps to show the interaction that occurs. However, it also makes the use case confusing if more than one actor is involved, something that may happen in some specialized cases (for details, see Section 2.4.2.1).

Although we state that use cases are text and not diagrams, we'd like to hedge that definition slightly. The structure, or template, of the use case is text. However, if some kind of picture helps the understanding of a use case, it should be included or attached to the use case. For example, it's quite acceptable to include a price schedule in table format. Furthermore, pictures of decision trees, calculations, flowcharts, or Petri nets are also quite acceptable either inside the use case or as attachments. Again, let the users' perspectives be your guide. If the users will understand the use case better with the pictures, include them.

2.4.3.5 Alternative Paths

The Alternative Paths section shows the less-common paths that need to be addressed. They include situations in which unusual types of processing occur. An alternative path would be taken when an uncommon condition occurs, such as the cash, check, or credit card payment mentioned previously.

A single use case often includes several types of alternatives. For example, the *Enter Sale* use case, which has different types of payment, may also contain alternatives relating to the type of customer, whether industrial or consumer. An industrial customer might have a standing account to which orders are collected and billed monthly, whereas walk-in consumer business is conducted with cash or credit card. Each alternative should indicate which step, in the basic course of events, is its starting point.

Alternative paths listed separately from a basic course of events allow you to avoid IF-THEN-ELSE structures. Users usually do not understand programming structures of any kind: IF-THEN-ELSE, DO-WHILE, TRY-CATCH, and so on.

Sometimes it is difficult to determine the most common alternative. It is a good rule of thumb to try to determine the statistics of use. If they are not available, choose the simplest interaction. If cash is the easiest, involving the least number of steps and verifications, then choose it as your basic course of events. The main objective is to avoid confusing the users by creating a use case that does not reflect their daily work because they seldom see that type of transaction. The Alternative Paths section is where the less common interactions are documented.

2.4.3.6 Exception Paths

Exception paths, like alternative paths, show uncommon processing. Exception paths, however, show the interactions that occur when an error happens.

For example, an exception path is taken when an actor enters an invalid date. The system provides an error message, and the actor reenters the date.

2.4.3.7 Extension Points

In Section 2.4.2.2 we talk about the *extend* relationship, an association between use cases. The *extend* relationship exists between two use cases when one use case provides an optional sequence of events that is included in the other use case. The extension points show the steps in a use case from which the extending use cases extend.

2.4.3.8 Triggers

Triggers describe the entry criteria for the use case. They are a list of the conditions that you expect to be true when an actor begins a use case. Triggers may describe a business need or be time-related, or a trigger could be the completion of another use case. Triggers answer the question "When or why will the actors enter this use case?"

2.4.3.9 Assumptions

From the project manager's point of view, this is a critical section. It is here that you document the things that you assume to be true but that might not be true. For example, if you assume that the actor has access to a current pricing list (which is not in the scope of this system) and if this use case's interactions depend on that, mention it here.

2.4.3.10 Preconditions

List the preconditions of this interaction. Preconditions are things that must be in place before the interaction can occur. They are part of the contract between this use case and the outside world.

Preconditions relate to conditions outside the scope of this use case and the computer system being developed. An example of a precondition is that a ledger exists for the incoming transaction.

2.4.3.11 Postconditions

Postconditions, like preconditions, are part of the contract between this use case and the outside world. After this use case has been completed successfully, the postconditions are satisfied.

Postconditions should be independent of the alternative path taken inside the use case. However, they do not need to be so generic that they deal with what happens when there is an error, especially an error in the input from the actor. An example of a postcondition is that a transaction is posted successfully to a ledger.

2.4.3.12 Related Business Rules

Business rules are the written and unwritten rules that dictate how a company conducts its business. This section in the use case template allows you to document or to refer to business rules that relate to the requirements presented in the use case. We find it more convenient to reference business rules than to include their entire text. In Section 3.9 we describe a business rules catalog for this purpose.

2.4.3.13 Author

You were probably expecting to see Author and Date at the top of the template, but we put them at the bottom. The most critical information should be at the top, where it can be spotted and read quickly and easily. We have heard users remark that if they can't speed-read a use case, they want it rewritten. This makes good sense, and it should be a guiding principle for designing use case templates.

2.4.3.14 Date

The Date section contains the date the use case was originally written, with references to when it was completed at each iteration. Here's an example.

Facade complete	Jan 29, 2000
Filled complete	Feb 4, 2000
Focused complete	Feb 12, 2000
Finished complete	Feb 14, 2000

These descriptions relate to how the use case template works best for us in our projects. Feel free to make the use case template your own by adding, deleting, or changing sections or changing the way it's used. We ask only that you stick to the guiding principles mentioned at the beginning of this section.

2.4.4 Paths and Scenarios

Use cases cannot tell the whole story. They are not highly detailed, and there are not many of them. To focus on the detailed interactions, we require a different tool: scenarios. Use Case 2.2 is a sample scenario that details each of the use case's interactions.

This example also demonstrates how we use the word *scenario*. In the world of requirements gathering, perhaps no term is as maligned as this one. As far as we know, there are at least three definitions of the term. For clarification, we provide each of the definitions in this section. We start with an extract of steps and alternatives from a simplified use case for a welfare application system. Then we put forth several contradicting definitions of what the scenarios would be given this use case.

Use Case Name:	**Schedule Customer Appointment**
Iteration:	**Filled**

Scenario:	1. Jenny Carmela, a fitness instructor, calls for an appointment on July 5, 2000. She needs a posing bikini and fitness outfit for the Nationals on August 22.
	2. Terri, the office administrator, logs on to the system with her user ID and password and requests a list of open times when Karen, the designer, can meet with Jenny for a consultation.
	3. The system responds with the following openings:
	  • July 7 1 PM–8 PM
	  • July 15 1 PM–9 PM
	  • July 16 1 PM–9 PM
	  • Etc.
	4. Jenny requests July 7 at 3:30 PM, which Terri chooses in the system.
	5. The system responds by recording this appointment with Karen and Jenny.
	6. When Karen logs on to the system July 6 at 4 PM, the system notifies her of her upcoming appointment.

Author:	Tammie Thurber with Karen Lavton
Date:	June 6, 2000

Use Case 2.2   *Scenario of Schedule Customer Appointment*

Use Case Name: Determine Benefits Eligibility for Enrollee

Use Case Steps

1. This use case starts when the social worker enters the enrollee's name and employment situation.
2. This use case ends when the system responds with a determination of whether the enrollee is eligible for benefits and the financial extent of the benefits.

Alternative Path:

- In step 1, if the enrollee has applied for benefits previously, based on the enrollee's own disclosure, the social worker enters the enrollee's name to search for his or her previous records.[3]

Scenario Definition 1, The Alternative Path: Example of a Scenario

1. This scenario starts when the social worker determines that the enrollee has applied for benefits previously, based on the enrollee's own disclosure, and therefore enters the enrollee's name to search for his or her previous records.
2. The system responds with the enrollee's previous records, including the number of previous applications and the benefit eligibility results.
3. The social worker asks the enrollee whether he or she has applied previously for and/or received benefits through this agency. If the enrollee has applied previously for benefits, the social worker enters the enrollee's welfare recipient number or searches by name if the enrollee cannot supply the welfare recipient number.

Scenario Definition 2, The Instance

A scenario is a realization of a use case, meaning that it is one possible path (similar to scenario definition 1), but it also includes the specific data.

Example of Scenario

1. The social worker asks Edward Trueman if he has applied previously for and/or received benefits, and Mr. Trueman replies that he has applied previously.
2. The social worker provides Mr. Trueman's name as the search criterion.
3. The system provides Mr. Trueman's previous records, which state that he applied for benefits on December 9, 1997, and was determined to be ineligible on December 9, 1997, because of his current part-time employment status at Boeing Aerospace in the capacity of assembly line worker.

Scenario Definition 3, The Synonym

Scenario is a synonym for *use case* (which is a synonym for *script*). This is the way some methodologists who provided input into the UML, such as Peter Coad, identified their version of the use case.

---

3. Let's say that there is a government regulation that the social worker is not allowed to look for previous applications unless the enrollee discloses them.

If you choose definition 1 (the alternative path), there is no need for scenarios as separate artifacts because they merely restate what was listed more succinctly in the Alternative Paths section of the use case. If you choose definition 3 (the synonym), you do not require scenarios as separate artifacts because they *are* use cases.

Our view is that definition 2 (the instance) is the only definition that provides additional value. By including sample data, preferably taken from production files, you can prove effectively that a use case can handle that set of circumstances. Scenarios can be used in two places in the development lifecycle to prove that a use case reflects accurately what the users need it to do. First, they can be used during the requirements activity to provide immediate feedback to the users and analysts as to whether the use cases are accurate reflections of the users' needs. Second, they can be used during the testing activity to test whether the computer system reflects the requirements. This is only one way that use cases drive the rest of the lifecycle. We talk more about this in Appendix A, Use Cases Beyond Requirements.

To summarize, scenarios are *instances* of use cases (complete with production data) that effectively test one path through a use case. They are meant to demonstrate whether a use case reflects accurately the needs of the users, using terms and examples that the users understand. Scenarios are a useful vehicle for testing the validity of use cases early in the lifecycle.

The Difference between Exception Path and Alternative Path

Exception path and *alternative path* sound as if they're describing the same thing. However, they are worth differentiating. An exception path contains steps that execute if something goes wrong, such as an input from the actor that the system cannot handle or a condition or series of conditions that occurs that are not part of the functionality. An example of an exception path is an actor keying in a record for a search and the record not being found.

An alternative path is actually much closer to the basic course of events because everything happens correctly (in other words, there are no errors); an alternative path simply is less likely to happen than the basic course of events. An example of an alternative path is the use of an unusual form of payment, such as the use of a credit card when a PO is more common.

When designing the use case template for your project, you may decide to lump exception and alternative paths together under one heading or to keep them separate. In our template, we separate them because we think it helps when producing scenarios. It is more important to generate scenarios, including a wide variety of alternative paths, than to worry about exceptions.

2.5 Use Cases Apply Here

Use cases apply to a wide range of activities and not only to requirements gathering. In this section we look at the application of use cases in a couple of areas that you might not have thought of. Also, in Appendix A we show how use cases apply to other activities in the lifecycle.

2.5.1 Use Cases for Inquiry-Only Systems

Use cases make sense for any system that has interactions with the outside world. It is not outrageous to say that any computer system should interact with the outside world. The most common application of use cases occurs in transaction-processing systems. However, inquiry-only systems, such as data warehouses, are also good candidates for use case requirements gathering. For example, Use Case 2.3 is primarily an inquiry-only use case and demonstrates how a use case can capture and communicate requirements even if there are few transaction-processing requirements present.

There are a few caveats. Inquiry-only use cases are usually more abstract than transaction-processing use cases. Data warehouses are built to offer users flexible interfaces that can provide multiple views of volumes of data. This flexibility means that the users' actual interactions may not be well known at the time of requirements gathering. However, at an abstract level, the interactions are quite clear. As with transaction processing, documenting the actors for a use case for inquiry-only systems is very useful. You always need to know your audience!

Use Case Name:	**Review Listings**
Iteration:	**Finished**
Summary:	The buyer browses through the listings of properties with the help of the buyer's agent.
Basic Course of Events:	1. This use case begins when the buyer requests to view properties. 2. The system responds by providing the buyer with methods for searching keyword or specific criteria, for example: price, location, photo, size, floor plan, age, and so on. 3. The buyer's agent enters advice for the buyer into the system and also points out certain properties that the buyer may have overlooked.
Alternative Paths:	In step 3, if no agent was chosen by the buyer, this step does not exist.
Exception Paths:	None
Extension Points:	None
Trigger:	The buyer wishes to purchase a property but does not know of a suitable property yet.

Use Case 2.3 *Review Listings (continues)*

Assumptions:	None
Preconditions:	At least one property has been listed.
Postconditions:	None
Related Business Rules:	None
Author:	Ed Towson
Date:	March 23, 2000—Facade; March 26, 2000—Filled; April 1, 2000—Focused; April 7, 2000—Finished

Use Case 2.3   *continued*

2.5.2 Use Cases for Requests for Proposals

Requests for proposals (RFPs) are often used between a customer and a contractor. The customer issues an RFP to multiple contractors, the contractors bid to win the business by submitting proposals, and the customer picks a winner based on the compliance of the responses to the RFP.

RFPs can be tricky business for the customer and for the contractors. Especially with government work, the RFP for a computer system must be complete and unambiguous because the requirements that are itemized in it become the foundation for the creation of the system. Requirements lists are often used in RFPs, and because everyone is worried about legality and wants to avoid missing anything, these requirements lists can sometimes run hundreds of pages.

We suggest that you employ use cases for RFPs. If the customer were to create a set of use cases and scenarios in the RFP, the contractors could respond more easily and the solution would more likely reflect the business needs. Use cases can simplify RFPs and proposal responses in the same way that use cases simplify requirements for other types of systems requirements specifications.

2.5.3 Use Cases for Software Package Evaluation

Use cases have special applicability to software package evaluation efforts. Use cases can help clarify the "gap analysis" by comparing package functionality to business requirements. We have used this approach and have seen it used elsewhere with great success.

2.5.4 Use Cases for Non-Object-Oriented Systems

There is a predisposition in our industry to associate use cases with object-oriented systems. We believe that use cases can be used easily for non-object-oriented systems, and our experiences bear this out. Our use cases have been used to document requirements for a number of non-object-oriented systems.

The fact that use cases are part of the UML encourages the viewpoint that use cases are exclusively for object-oriented systems. However, we view use cases as a great way to document requirements for any system. In fact, we use them not only for system development efforts but also for evaluations and package implementation. Use cases are a good way to boil down the essential requirements of the required interactions, whether they are used for a new system being built or to help someone make a choice between packages that already exist.

2.6 Applying Use Cases to the Requirements Problem

We hope that you find this chapter a good primer to use cases. We love use cases, and we hope you've developed an appreciation for them as you've read through this chapter. We think they make a lot of sense as a tool for requirements, and, to this end, we've developed our own process for incorporating them into the requirements-gathering activity. Chapter 3 provides a view of our overall approach. Chapters 4 through 7, the methodology chapters, describe how to iterate through levels of fidelity with your use cases until you have everything you need to build a great system.

SEE ALSO: http://www.stsc.hill.af.mil/CrossTalk/1998/dec/ham.html

3

A Use Case–Driven Approach to Requirements Gathering

3.1 Requirements Specification Tools

In this chapter we propose a specific group of tools that help drive requirements gathering to a successful end product. In this context, *tools* does not refer to software applications; instead, tools are the techniques and methods that assist in requirements gathering and refining.

3.2 Principles for Requirements Success

We propose an approach to gathering and documenting requirements that differs substantially from what we have called the traditional approach. Our approach is *use case–driven* and employs a number of tools that are either borrowed from the traditional approach, perhaps with slight changes, or are completely new. Chapters 1 and 2 discuss the current state of requirements gathering and the simple elegance of use cases. Now let's look at a solution to the requirements problem. Table 3.1 outlines several guiding principles and ways to succeed in fulfilling those principles.

Table 3.1   Guiding Principles

Guiding Principle	Comments
Reduce risk.	The obvious result of a high-risk project is a high failure rate caused by unhappy users and management. Culprits in increasing risk are big-bang requirements and micro-management. Possible ways to reduce risk are an iterative or incremental approach, increased user involvement (users writing use cases), and requirements reviews.
Focus on business interactions.	Very often, technologists focus on technology and not on the business interactions required for a system. To focus the effort on the business, you must separate analysis and design activities and keep use cases devoid of technical language and considerations.
Reduce volume.	By turning requirements *specification* into requirements *engineering* (a term we've avoided), teams often produce huge amounts of requirements documentation. When they are asked to review it, users rebel, either by rubber-stamping everything (and complaining later) or by refusing to deal with it, causing schedule delays. Strategies for reducing volume are to leave the rote requirements (table maintenance and the like) until the end and to abstract use cases and business rules as much as possible.
Reduce duplicates and inconsistencies.	When a requirements specification exceeds 30 to 40 pages of text, confusion and sloppiness begin to creep in. The requirements become a poor basis from which the designers must work, and they give users a poor view of the system-to-be. The strategies for reducing duplicates and inconsistencies are the same as those used to reduce volume.
Create requirements that users can understand easily.	The main culprits of user-inappropriate requirements are premature design, overspecification, and insufficient user involvement or authoring. The main strategy for avoiding this issue is to employ use cases as specified in this book, avoiding implementation-specific language.
Create requirements that are useful to designers, developers, and project managers.	When requirements are useless, the main culprit is the requirements list. Failure to group, classify, cross-reference, or automate listed requirements hurts their usefulness. Also, if the requirements are not easily

	traceable to design artifacts, code, and test cases, they get no attention from designers, developers, and testers. By using use cases and a use case–driven lifecycle, you can minimize or avoid these issues.
Leave a requirements trail.	Even with use cases and business rules, it is important to cross-reference the artifacts properly so that later traceability is possible. By taking a use case–driven approach and creating real use cases from abstract use cases, the team can help leave a requirements trail that ensures a system built as it was specified (and promised!).
Leave design until later.	If requirements analysts are really designers-in-disguise, then design considerations can easily creep into requirements specifications.
Keep the plan in mind.	It is easy to get caught up in today's set of requirements tasks and forget what is to be done with these documents. It is the responsibility of the project manager to help the team keep a far-sighted perspective. Thinking about the use case paths as increments of development helps the team in making decisions on granularity of use cases.

3.3 Four Steps for Gathering Requirements

We suggest that requirements be created iteratively. Iterative and incremental approaches help reduce risk by treating risky items earlier in the lifecycle. Requirements specifications, as much or more than other lifecycle artifacts, change constantly and require frequent modifications and overhauls. This is because requirements are based on several people's fuzzy ideas about a computer application to be created. Other artifacts have the luxury of tying back to the requirements, but the requirements tie back only to fuzzy ideas.

Iterative creation of artifacts is highly dependent on individual situations. It would be silly to suggest that exactly the same number of iterations is needed to complete requirements in all situations. However, it is possible to say that iterative requirements specification always proceeds through the same logical steps in every situation. In this book we make a case for four logical steps: outlining, widening, focusing, and touching up the artifacts. We have created names for each of these steps and have assigned those names to iterations. We do not want to specify that there always must be four iterations, only that there are four mind-sets to adopt throughout requirements. The iteration names are

- *Facade*—Outline and high-level descriptions
- *Filled*—Broadening and deepening

- *Focused*—Narrowing and pruning
- *Finished*—Touching up and fine-tuning

Chapters 4 through 7 provide the details of these iterations.

The iterative and incremental lifecycle is not a set of lifecycle phases for requirements, something that would be cumbersome; rather, it is a way to categorize the activities needed to develop use cases. It is likely that most of the use cases will be in the same iteration at the same time, but we emphasize that it is not necessary to force use cases into iterations if it's not needed.

We created these named iterations because we've often been asked, "How many iterations are right?" "What should I do in each iteration?" It made sense to us to categorize requirements-gathering activities into a set of iterations, but please do not assume that we are asking you to approach these iterations rigidly as a set of lifecycle phases.

Throughout the iterations we create and refine several tools that define the requirements deliverable set. These tools include use cases (which require the most effort), and they provide comprehensive coverage of this part of the software development lifecycle.

- Problem statement
- Statement of work
- Risk analysis
- Prototype
- Use cases and use case diagrams
- Business rule catalog

Let's take a look at each of these tools and its role in the requirements activity.

3.4 The Role of the Problem Statement

The *problem statement* of an application, probably the first document to be created, outlines the business problem to be solved. The authors of the problem statement must be the high-level executives who are approving the need to solve the problem. Here is an example of a problem statement from a system one of us worked on a few years ago:

> The department must find a way to pay our contractors promptly to avoid incurring interest on late payments. Currently, the department allocates 10 percent of its yearly budget allocation toward contractor interest payments. This line item needs to be reduced or eliminated.

NOTE: As simple as this real-life problem statement sounded, it kicked off an effort with this governmental department to create a computer application that cost approximately $10,000,000, including hardware, software, and services. At the end of the project, contractor payments were being paid promptly. In fact, there were some complaints that the accelerated payment process was causing a cash-flow problem within the department, something that was subsequently addressed. A problem solved too well!

3.5 The Role of the Statement of Work

The *statement of work* defines the scope of the work and a general view of how the work is to be accomplished, including a general workplan and staffing assignments. The following is a sample outline of a statement of work, again from one of our previous engagements (with a little help from the RUP).

1. Scope
2. Objectives
3. Application overview
4. User demography
5. Constraints
6. Assumptions
7. Staffing and cost
8. Deliverable outlines
9. Expected duration

The statement of work becomes a contract between the IT group and the user department. It is also the tool that is used to define a contract between a consulting company and a customer.

3.6 The Role of the Risk Analysis

A *risk analysis* is a list of the risks that may influence the development of the application; the risks are prioritized by the impact of each risk if realized and the likelihood of the risk. The risk analysis helps establish clearly whether this development effort should even be attempted. Table 3.2 is an example of a risk analysis.

The *risk rating* is calculated by multiplying the days lost if it occurs and the likelihood it will happen. It represents the total days that should be reserved as a contingency to handle the possibility of this risk.

NOTE: This idea is from *Rapid Development* (McConnell 1996).

3.7 The Role of the Prototype

A prototype is a software mock-up of a system's user interface, but no more. It helps round out the requirements picture, showing the user interface requirements clearly and, often, interactively.

In our approach, we propose moving the prototype to a later stage in the lifecycle: after the requirements have had a chance to gel. Introducing user interfaces onscreen at this later stage is less of a distraction for the users and helps you to avoid the temptation to solve problems before they are understood. This problem is discussed further in Chapter 7.

Table 3.2 Sample Risk Analysis

Number	Category	Risk	Resolution Needed By	Status	Days Lost If It Occurs	Likelihood It Will Happen	Risk Rating
001	Interfaces	The new application needs to interface with SAP, which has not been put into production yet. There could be schedule delays if this project has to wait two months for the SAP project.	Jul 1, 2000	Unresolved	50	50%	25
002	User time	The majority of the user group is heavily involved in a reengineering effort. If the project team members cannot get their time, the project will be delayed.	May 15, 2000	Being investigated	70	80%	56

Technical prototyping is a design activity that reduces technological risk by letting the team try out the technically tough pieces of the solution before the design and build activities are properly under way. This is a great way test your technical assumptions, especially when the problems or toolkit involved is new. Prototyping performed simultaneously with requirements activities is not a part of the requirements process and is outside this book's scope.

3.8 The Roles of Use Cases

The major artifacts of this approach are use cases. The following few paragraphs describe the different roles played by use cases as tools of requirements specification.

3.8.1 Use Cases Are Effective Communication Vehicles

Use cases are the centerpiece of our approach to requirements gathering. The interactions they illustrate form the basis of most of the requirements that must be documented.

In our experience, use cases have the additional tremendous benefit of aiding effective communication between IT staff and users. Users seem to catch on to use cases better than almost any other document that IT people produce. Because use cases are boiled down to the essence of the desired interactions, users are not distracted by computer-specific jargon or nomenclature (DFDs, ERDs, class diagrams, and so forth) or by user interface details (graphical user interface [GUI] mock-ups, user interface storyboards, prototypes, and so on). All that remains is the most basic information about the interactions between actor and application.

3.8.2 Use Cases Can Be Used for Functional and Nonfunctional Requirements

Use cases can portray functional and nonfunctional requirements effectively. Generally, functional requirements can be put into terms of interactions between an actor and the application. The exceptions can be specified as business rules (see Section 3.9). Nonfunctional requirements—such as performance, extensibility, and maintainability—can often be stated in terms of use case stereotypes. These stereotypes are added to the use case model after most of the functional requirements are incorporated.

The definitions of the stereotypes that handle nonfunctional requirements should be quite detailed and should be reviewed by users in the same way that use cases are reviewed.

3.8.3 Use Cases Help Ensure Requirements Traceability

Use cases can provide requirements traceability effectively through the lifecycle because they are a building block for system design, units of work, construction iterations, test cases, and delivery stages. The status of each use case, including how it has changed over time, becomes completely obvious to the users and the IT staff. If a new use case is added, it becomes evident that the scope has increased and therefore something about the project plan must change.

When use cases drive the lifecycle, it also helps to assure the stakeholders that all the requirements are being addressed as development progresses. For example, at any point in the lifecycle, anyone who is creating artifacts—whether they are design deliverables or code—should be able to answer this question: Which use case (or scenario) are you elaborating?

3.8.4 Use Cases Discourage Premature Design

Use cases discourage (although nothing can prevent) premature design. When design creeps into a use case, it becomes quite obvious. When the system is performing several steps before responding to a user, it sounds an alarm that perhaps internal system design is being created and exposed.

3.9 The Role of the Business Rules Catalog

Use cases are an important part of the requirements picture, but by themselves they are not enough. Use cases capture the interactions between users and the system, but they cannot portray all the subtleties of how a business is run. For this, we need *business rules*.

A list of business rules is not the same thing as a list of requirements. Business rules are the written and unwritten rules that dictate how a company or agency conducts its business. Requirements relate to a specific application being considered or developed.

In our methodology, we use a combination of use cases and business rules. Use cases cover a great many of the requirements by specifying interactions between actors and an application. However, these interactions are governed by the business rules that set the tone and environment in which the application operates. Some businesses create lists of business rules for their businesses even though they may not be building any new computer applications. It is simply important to them to document how their business runs.

According to Ron Ross, the business rules guru, there are five categories of business rules.

- *Structural facts*—Facts or conditions that must be true. Example: The first customer contact is always with a salesperson.
- *Action restricting*—Prohibiting one or more actions based on a condition. Example: Do not accept a check from a customer who does not have an acceptable credit history.
- *Action triggering*—Instigating an action when one or more conditions become true. Example: Send the shipment as soon as the pick items (items selected from inventory) have been collected.
- *Inferences*—Drawing a conclusion when one or more conditions become true. Example: Members who fly more than 100,000 miles in one calendar year become Elite members.
- *Calculations*—Calculating one value given a set of other values. Example: The sales amount is the total retail value of the line items but does not include state or federal tax.

Business rules must be *atomic*: Each business rule should be stated at the finest level of granularity possible. Methods of atomizing tend to be more art than science.

The best way to get a feel for business rules is to see lots of examples (see Table 3.3). We've provided some examples from our experiences and our imagination and have categorized them in several ways:

- Type of rule
- Likelihood of change (whether the rule is static or dynamic)
- Source

Your business rules catalog may look significantly different, depending on the type of data you record and cross-reference.

NOTE: It is easy to slip into the trap of creating a list of business rules that is actually a list of requirements. Remember that business rules always relate to how a company operates; they do not relate to the requirements of a specific application. A requirement is usually phrased, "The system shall," whereas a business rule states, "The business works like this."

Table 3.3 We-Rent-All Equipment Rentals Co. Business Rules Catalog Sample

No.	Rule Definition	Type of Rule	Static/ Dynamic	Source
001	Cash, personal check, and credit card are accepted for rental payment.	Action restricting	Dynamic	Management policy
002	Customers who rent driving equipment must possess a U.S. driver's license.	Action restricting	Static	Management policy
003	Customers who rent driving equipment must provide proof of insurance for the rental.	Action restricting	Static	Management policy
004	Rentals must be returned by the next day at the same time as the conclusion of the rental transaction, unless otherwise specified at the time of rental or in a requested extension.	Action restricting	Static	Management policy

continues

Table 3.3   *continued*

No.	Rule Definition	Type of Rule	Static/ Dynamic	Source
005	If a rental item is not available, substitute using the substitution part chart.	Action triggering	Static	Management policy
006	Customers can make reservations up to six months in advance.	Action restricting	Dynamic; advance limit may change	Management policy
007	Rental items will be serviced according to the part service chart.	Action triggering	Static	Management policy
008	If a rental item that was reserved is not available to the customer on the day of the rental for any reason, the customer service representative will arrange for the customer to rent it from a competitor at our cost.	Action triggering	Dynamic; customer service level may change	Management policy
009	If customers are renting firearms, a background check must be initiated and a 30-day waiting period is required.	Action triggering	Dynamic; law may change	Federal law
010	A customer may return an item only if it has not yet been taken out of the store.	Structural facts	Static	Management policy

3.10 Managing Success

Adopting a use case–driven approach can help you organize and systematize your software development efforts. This chapter describes a series of steps you can take to produce a set of documents that will help you carefully define your system's requirements. The next four chapters discuss the four iterations that we recommend, explaining how the use cases we've introduced are used to drive and guide the process overall.

4

The Facade Iteration

4.1 Objectives

The first iteration in the requirements lifecycle is the Facade iteration. Its purpose is to create placeholders for each major interaction you expect the users to have with the proposed application.

A Facade use case contains only the minimum information that is needed as a placeholder, including names and short descriptions of each interaction. It also identifies the major actors. Writing this iteration is difficult because you don't yet have a concept of an

application. For this reason, the team will do its best work if the environment encourages openness and creativity.

As you develop a definition of the proposed system, you can call on the following sources for ideas and opinions:

- Users
- Project team
- Industry Experts
- IT management
- User management
- Owners of the data

The users have the major influence on the definition of proposed system interactions. They are the focus of the new system, and their input and buy-in are critical.

However, as anyone knows who has been through requirements definition even once, the users cannot tell you the whole story. They are not equipped to define fully what the new system should do. Why? First, the new system is probably not being created merely to automate an existing system. Many new business processes, perhaps not yet built, will dictate the system interactions. In addition, the users often know their domain so well that they assume that most of what they do is terribly obvious. Alternatively, they've been put into their current role recently as a result of organizational restructuring, and they haven't had time to become familiar with their environment. One department in an oil and gas company for which we worked had a 110 percent annual staff attrition rate, so relying solely on the users was not possible for that development effort. In any case, the requirements-gathering team has its work cut out for it.

There's another issue. If you don't have a *subject matter expert* (SME) on your project team who knows this domain as well as a user, your team will not have the opportunity to "read between the lines" of what the users tell you. You need to make these kinds of inferences to identify better, faster, cheaper processes and to recognize the vital pieces of the puzzle that the users have left out—omissions that will come back to bite you in three months' time. SMEs are often ex-users themselves, or they may be IT people who have specialized in an industry and have a number of system implementations under their belts.

The project team, too, has input into how the user-system interactions should occur. After all, the team is responsible for the work! The project team should have a laser focus on setting standards for interaction, maintaining scope, making inferences from user input, and documenting, storing, and indexing the requirements. The major guiding force behind these interactions should be the users and the SMEs on your project team. The task of the rest of the team is to transmute these models into use cases. The users provide the information on how they do things now and what they would like to see changed, and the SMEs help to shape the system into more refined, elegant, and profitable processes.

The challenge of the project team members is to take *user-centric* information offered by computer industry experts and luminaries and to determine whether it applies to this situation. Industry experts can provide only rules of thumb, and rules are meant to be broken.

Determine your position on the industry "advice-of-the-day," and if you decide to deviate from it be prepared to defend your position. Whatever you do, don't simply follow the experts blindly. Unless you believe in your direction, your project won't work.

The IT management group always has opinions on how the interactions of the system should be described. If you are a member of the in-house IT group, you must balance these opinions with the user needs and wants. If you are an outside consultant the same balancing act is required, but sometimes it is easier being a third party. The IT group can provide valuable input regarding systems that have been developed previously, interfaces between user departments, previous incarnations of this functionality, and other contextual information.

As with user input, you should be cautious in weighing IT viewpoints. IT staff (yes, this means us!) have a strong tendency to push requirements gathering into something that is technology-centered. Technology-centric solutions have no place in this early activity of system development. It is dangerous to commit an application to a specific technology or to focus more on the technical implementation than the needs of the users. This practice leads to systems that fit neatly into technology niches but are lacking in functionality or may even deliver functions that are not required. It's easy to fall into the technology trap, especially for someone who is steeped in technical know-how. At this stage, there should be no discussion of technical solutions, only a focus on business solutions. Technical solutions enter into the picture during systems analysis and design, which are the next activities of the lifecycle.

User management personnel are involved in the major decisions for the application's life or death, so it is important to try to involve them early and often. They need to know of major changes in the project's scope and should be kept up-to-date on major decisions that are made throughout the life of the project—for example, whether to use distributed updates or centralized updates.

*It can be hard for a requirements analyst not
to stray from the path of business requirements
into the land of the latest technologies.*

User-Centric Versus Technology-Centric Solutions

User-centric solutions focus on what the user needs. All requirements that drive the development of use cases come from actual business needs of the users. This principle applies to the entire development cycle and not just requirements gathering.

Technology-centric solutions focus on using the "technology of the hour" for whatever business problem might pop up. Applying a technical solution—whether a new programming language, operating system, architecture, partitioning scheme, or methodology—becomes an end in itself rather than a tool. It is sometimes a fine distinction, but it is possible to tell the difference.

We're not saying you shouldn't try out new technology to solve business problems, but when you find yourself adding features the user didn't request simply because your new tool supports them, you've crossed the line into a technology-centric approach. By the same token, when you are trying to convince the users that they should not want a feature because your favorite tool doesn't support it, you are being technology-centric. When you start making up business problems so that you can use your new techno-toy, you are also being technology-centric.

Our best advice: Start user-centric and never lose that focus. The time to start deciding how to "make it happen" is during design. If there are critical requirements that can't be fulfilled, decide then to take them out.

The users of the proposed application may not be the owners of the data—that is, the people who are responsible for the integrity of the data in the database. From a technical standpoint, of course, the database administrators are responsible for data integrity. But from a user perspective, there may be an administrative group, such as an audit or finance group, that is responsible for seeing that the data is accurate and current. Whoever they are, they will also want input into the requirements and should be involved as much as possible.

4.2 Steps in the Facade Iteration

Following are the steps to completing the Facade iteration.

1. Create a problem statement.
2. Identify and review existing documentation and intellectual capital.
3. Get the executive sponsor's unique viewpoint.
4. Identify the users, the user group management, the stakeholders, the customers being served by the user group, and the owners of the data.
5. Interview the stakeholders.
6. Find the actors.

7. Create the Facade use cases.
8. Start the business rules catalog.
9. Create a risk analysis.
10. Create a statement of work.
11. Get informal approval from the executive sponsor.

4.2.1 Create a Problem Statement

The executive sponsor leads the effort to create a problem statement for the application and distributes it widely to generate support and awareness. This document essentially becomes the mission statement for the application development team, including the requirements analysts. For an example of a problem statement, refer to Chapter 3.

4.2.2 Identify and Review Existing Documentation and Intellectual Capital

To familiarize yourself with the history of this effort, read every memo, deliverable, proposal, and e-mail message you can get your hands on. If there is too much for one person to read, use a team approach. Each person takes a stack of paper or electronic documents and wades through it, reporting the interesting findings to the group. Here are the questions you're trying to answer.

- What elements of the proposed system were ruled out previously and by whom? Who introduced those items in the first place?
- Who are the people who want this system built? Who doesn't want it built?
- Have any commercial off-the-shelf (COTS) packages been considered? Which ones?
- Is this project visible to upper management? Who?
- How long has this idea been kicked around? What were its previous incarnations?

The benefit of completing this step is that you create a *reuse strategy* at the first level: requirements. If someone has already done part of this work, it is worthwhile to try reusing it. Of course, reuse always comes with some overhead, so you must judge whether it is worth it. Often, it is. Major stumbling blocks are revealed, and fortuitous shortcuts will become clear.

Let's take a closer look at each of these questions.

4.2.2.1 What Elements of the Proposed System Were Ruled Out Previously and by Whom?

You're not searching for great detail here, only the subsystem name and general functionality that was killed before this effort started. Usually there is a long "fuzzy front end" (McConnell 1996) during which not much gets done but people mull the possibility of developing such a system. What was ruled out during this time?

4.2.2.2 Who Are the People Who Want This System Built? Who Doesn't Want It Built?

This question may be more important than the first one. Find out the enemies of this system and their motivations. If possible, arrange to meet with them, or at least people in the organization who know something about them. At this point, don't try to convince them that they're wrong. Just gather data. They may have valid suggestions, and implementing them might result in only a small change to the requirements that would be easy to include at this early point. The motives of these naysayers may be political, and it will require your tact, charm, and negotiation skills to work with them. If you're a consultant or a low-ranking IT team member, this is a difficult step because the upper-level IT managers may not understand why this kind of discussion is important. However, you should still see how far you can go. Consider it practice in office politics for when you're in management. Remember that numerous systems have died for political and not technical reasons.

4.2.2.3 Have Any Packages Been Considered? Which Ones?

It is important to ferret out this information. There may have been some investigation into whether any COTS packages could fulfill the requirements for this system. It is also likely that those COTS packages have evolved since the investigation. Check into it. During design, you can evaluate the suitability of these products.

4.2.2.4 Is This Project Visible to Upper Management? Who?

High project visibility is both a curse and a gift. The curse is often that everyone wants his or her trademark on the visible project and wants to be associated with it—until it begins to look as if there are problems. However, project visibility is a greater gift than a curse. When resources are required, it helps tremendously because no one wants to stand in the way of an initiative that has support and visibility at high levels of management. Quite simply, the higher the visibility in the organization, the better.

4.2.2.5 How Long Has This Idea Been Kicked Around? What Were Its Previous Incarnations?

Find out what you can in this area, but don't go into great detail. Because elements of these previous incarnations will show up in your requirements, it pays to at least speak the language: "Oh, that sounds like it comes from the ORMS idea a few years ago." It's likely that this system has been attempted once or twice before and then stopped.

4.2.3 Get the Executive Sponsor's Unique Viewpoint

It can be hard to get time from your executive sponsor. She is rushing from one high-flying meeting to another, and she has already started organizing her next big launch. As far as she's concerned, you should be self-sufficient. Yet your success rides on getting the exact definition of the problem from her. Get at least a sliver of her time, whatever it takes. Try this as your opening line: "Our team has our own answers to these questions, but we want to make absolutely sure that we're right." Then ask her these questions.

- What is the problem being solved?
- Why is a system required?
- Why is a computer system required?
- Who will be affected by the system implementation? How?

This must be done in a face-to-face meeting at best or a telephone meeting at worst. E-mail does not work. This must be interactive. Certain things the sponsor says will spur other questions, and you should ask them. It is important to try to catch every nuance, every uncomfortable moment, every glance at her shoes. Body language and silences will warn you of the dangers to come. Remember, if she's not happy with the result, you've failed. Period.

4.2.3.1 What Is the Problem Being Solved?

This should be a problem statement, perhaps four or five sentences at the most. It should describe the business reason for the system. Usually, business systems are developed to help the organization stay competitive in the marketplace, to provide better customer service, to automate certain functions, to comply with government legislation, or to meet any other of a variety of environmental demands. State the factor that is pushing the need for this system, and state what is likely to occur if it is not developed. If there is a drop-dead date that has relevance to the problem statement, include it.

4.2.3.2 Why Is a System Required?

What is the worst thing that would happen if this problem were not resolved? How much money would the new process save (or make) the company? What is a reasonable payback time? This question addresses only the business process and not necessarily a computer system. That's next.

4.2.3.3 Why Is a Computer System Required?

Why can't this task be done manually? If the business process has been proven, why can't it be a manual process? This is a difficult question. If the executive sponsor starts to think about it, she may decide that an electronic system isn't needed at all, and that means you will have to find another project to work on! As project managers, we tend to jump too quickly into a self-fulfilling prophecy: We want to make a project happen whether or not it is *meant* to happen. If you take a hard, objective look at whether this system really should be built now, you might save countless heartaches later.

If you and the executive sponsor end up talking each other out of a computer system to attack this problem, the executive sponsor may see you as someone who has just saved her budget millions of dollars, and she may be more likely to come to you again with requests, knowing that you'll take an objective view. Play the devil's advocate with the sponsor. Pretend that you need to be convinced of the need for this process to be automated. It's what's best for the business.

4.2.3.4 Who Will Be Affected by the System Implementation? How?

Identify all the groups that will be affected by this implementation. Determine the relative benefits or obstacles they will experience from this system. Judge this over a period of time. For example, the data entry clerks might be disadvantaged by the system at first but then realize its benefits after two months. This technique is called *other people's views*, or OPV (de Bono 1982). Don't limit the list to those directly affected; include the indirect effects as well. This step will give you valuable information later as you calculate costs versus benefits.

4.2.4 Identify the Users, Customers, and Related Groups

Get an up-to-date organization chart for the user group that includes management and all participants. Try to find out where the informal power lies. If you can also get last year's organization chart, so much the better. Seeing the way things have been reorganized will help you understand where the organization is trying to go and how a system could help it get there.

If possible, talk to a sampling of the users. Take some of them out for lunch. Include not only the managers but also a decent sampling across the board. These are get-to-know-you sessions and not requirements gathering—yet. That comes later.

By *customers*, we mean the real, honest-to-goodness customers outside the organization, not internal customers. Building a system for a grocery chain? Identify the people who would benefit: the clerks, the shoppers, the pharmacists. How about a manufacturing firm?

Other People's Views: The Selling Property Application

At the beginning of a project to design a real estate application, the following people and groups were identified as those who would be affected by the application.

All customers want a system that is easy to use, doesn't cost much, handles transactions quickly, and stays out of the way, allowing productivity.

Buyers want to buy a property that fits their exact needs and want some advice on shaping their own needs.

Sellers want to sell property quickly and as close to their target price as possible.

Agents want to earn maximum fees in minimal time and want to feel a sense of accomplishment from helping people exchange money and property.

The owner of the agency wants the application to increase the agency's profits, wants the application to be delivered quickly, and wants control of and information about the status of the development.

Designers and developers want requirements that show the needs of the users accurately, want no design assumptions embedded in requirements, and want to build an application that is state-of-the-art.

Identify the wholesalers and the final customers, assuming that your system will change how they view the firm.

4.2.5 Interview the Stakeholders

You can do this task in several ways. You can conduct individual interviews with the users, user management, and a sampling of their customers. You can hold a concentrated joint requirements planning session, during which all interested parties get together in a hotel conference room and work through all the issues until a semblance of requirements emerges. The differences in these approaches change the speed, but not the content, of your iterations. You will most likely emerge from the JRP with a set of Filled use cases, which will need to be consolidated with the Focused and Finished iterations before they are completely usable. This means that to avoid wasting the participants' time you may need to walk into the JRP with a set of Facade use cases. With individual interviews, on the other hand, the interview notes will come together as input to your Facade use cases.

SEE ALSO: http://www.valiantsys.com/jrpjad.htm

The "Internal Customer" Problem

A recent movement promotes the idea of treating everyone in the organization as your customer. The IT shop treats the accountants as its customers, the accountants treat manufacturing as their customer, and so forth. Here's the issue with internal customers. Let's say you work for an internal IT shop that's building a sales tracking system, and you consider your internal customer to be the sales department. Your internal customers will tell you exactly what they want so that they can sell more stuff, properly credit their commissions, and widen their markets. That's part of why you're building this system. But there's more. The *actual* customers will want a sales tracking system that increases their level of customer service, allows them to cancel orders late in the order process, and is flexible enough to handle their specialized requests. They may also offer some insights into what the future may hold for this company in terms of the changing marketplace. Christopher Alexander, an insightful building architect who has greatly influenced the computer industry, said at the 1996 OOPSLA conference in San Jose that computer analysts and programmers treat themselves as "guns for hire" in their organizations (Alexander 1996). They say, "Just tell us what to build, and we'll build it"—without asking about the larger circumstances. By including the external customers in the process of requirements gathering, we broaden our purview to include the health and wealth of the entire business, and perhaps society, in the development of a system. We believe that it is the obligation of computer analysts and programmers everywhere to delve deeply to determine the true requirements of the systems they build.

4.2.6 Find the Actors

Actors are the people and applications that interact with this application. Ask the executive sponsor who she thinks the actors are, and ask each stakeholder.

Your definition of the actors may be fuzzy at this point, and that is OK. Define them as they arise and push concerns about duplication and definition into later iterations.

4.2.7 Create the Facade Use Cases

The output of this step is a set of sketchy use cases that outlines the scope of the proposed system. The level of detail is crucial because too much detail here will hurt the iterative nature of this process. It is important to identify the need for the use case, describe in two or three sentences what is involved, and move on.

Use cases focus on the ingredients that go in and the result that comes out.

We're creating use cases that treat the system as if it were a bread-making machine. You put the ingredients into the machine, and after a while you take out a loaf of bread. The focus is on the ingredients going in and the product coming out. What goes on inside the bread-making machine is not our concern, and certainly not part of requirements.

The top-level use case in a system is the *system context use case*. There is only one. Below that are the Facade use cases, which show the basic, essential, high-level interactions that this system must support (Constantine and Lockwood 1999).

When you're creating use cases, do

- Name the use case in user terminology
- Write a two- or three-sentence description of what the use case accomplishes
- Use role names and not user titles
- Group input or output information without specifying field-by-field details, which can come in later iterations

Don't

- Skip use cases, because the goal is to create "shell" use cases for each of the main user interactions expected for this system (placeholders, remember?)

Use Case 4.1 is an example of a Facade use case. Notice that the Basic Course of Events and Alternative Paths sections are usually blank in this iteration because they require more detail than you have at this point. If you happen to already have the information, however, it would be silly not to document it now.

Actor names and use case names can be quite informal and may not be completely consistent in Facade. They can be cleaned up later.

Use Case Name:	**Track Costume Sales**
Iteration:	**Facade**
Summary:	System Context Use Case. This system needs to track the information related to customers, appointments, designs, orders, and sales. The purpose of the system is to provide historical sales data that allows the owner to visualize trends.
Basic Course of Events:	
Alternative Paths:	
Exception Paths:	
Extension Points:	
Trigger:	
Assumptions:	
Preconditions:	
Postconditions:	
Related Business Rules:	
Author:	Tammie Thurber
Date:	June 2, 2000—Facade

Use Case 4.1   *Track Costume Sales*

4.2.8 Start the Business Rules Catalog

Business rules (see Chapter 3) govern how the organization conducts its business, so they likely apply to several or all use cases.

Look for business rules that constrain the construction of use cases for this application. Try to produce at least a few rules in this early iteration, but there is no need to create a comprehensive catalog yet. See Table 4.1 for an example.

4.2.9 Create a Risk Analysis

Create a risk analysis document in this iteration as a repository for the risks that surface as you proceed through discussions with the users. Chapter 3 describes the format and role of the risk analysis.

4.2.10 Create a Statement of Work

Create a statement of work as a contract to fulfill during this development effort. This document outlines a set of scope boundaries that you and the user groups agree to. Chapter 3 describes the format and role of the statement of work.

4.2.11 Get Informal Approval from the Executive Sponsor

It is doubtful that you'll get your executive sponsor's attention long enough to leaf through a set of partially finished (Facade) use cases at this point. Instead, summarize what you believe are the sticking points: areas that are unclear, fraught with danger, or contentious. Bring these up with your sponsor and create an action item for each one as necessary. This is really all you need to do for this step.

4.3 Tools

There are several tools that you'll need to use in this iteration. This section describes each of them in detail.

4.3.1 System Context Use Case

This highest-level use case explains the overall function of the entire system. It is rather like a mission statement for the application. Going through the exercise of writing the system context use case can be enlightening, especially as a way of confirming the users' overall expected functionality. What you actually come up with may be less valuable than the process you go through to get there.

You do not need to show every actor or every step. Instead, show what is significant at this general level.

Table 4.1 Business Rules Example

Rule ID	Name	Description	Static/Category	Dynamic	Source
001	Provide discounts for referrals	If a current customer provides a referral to the company and the referral makes a purchase, the person referring the business receives a $20 discount off future costume purchases.	Inference	Dynamic	Interview with owner 5/7/2000
002	Referral discounts must be used quickly	If a referral discount has been granted to a customer, that discount must be used on a costume within 1 year unless the customer contacts the company to request an extension.	Structural fact	Dynamic	Interview with owner 5/7/2000

The use case diagram visualizes the system interactions and captures the scope. The simplicity of the diagrams makes them a great communication tool. They can be drawn using a software tool or on a napkin during a scope discussion. The use case itself details what the system must do. Use Case 4.2 is at the same level of abstraction as Figure 4.1 and supplies greater detail than the diagram.

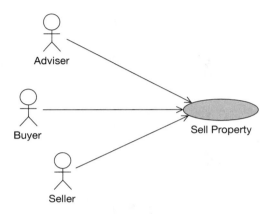

Figure 4.1 *Sell Property Use Case Diagram*

Use Case Name:	**Sell Property**
Iteration:	**Filled**
Summary:	System Context Use Case. The seller lists the property, a buyer purchases the property, and the agent guides them through the process and offers advice, caution, and recommendations.
Basic Course of Events:	1. The seller selects an agent.
	2. The system responds by assigning an agent and notifying the seller agent.
	3. The seller lists the property to sell.
	4. The system responds by displaying this property in the property listing and linking it for searches.
	5. The buyer selects an agent.
	6. The buyer reviews the property listings by entering search criteria.
	7. The system responds by displaying properties that match the buyer's search criteria.
	8. The buyer finds a property and makes an offer on it.

Use Case 4.2 *Sell Property (continues)*

	9. The system responds by notifying the seller and the seller's agent. 10. The seller responds to the offer with a counteroffer. 11. The system responds by notifying the buyer and the buyer's agent. 12. The buyer and the seller agree to terms. 13. The system responds by recording the agreement. 14. The buyer indicates that a loan is required. 15. The system responds by locating an appropriate loan provider. 16. The buyer and the loan provider agree to loan terms. 17. The system responds by recording the terms of the loan. 18. The buyer and the seller close on the property. 19. The system responds by recording the details of the close.
Alternative Paths:	N/A
Extension Points:	N/A
Trigger:	N/A
Assumptions:	N/A
Preconditions:	N/A
Postconditions:	N/A
Related Business Rules:	N/A
Author:	Angela Baltimore
Date:	March 20, 2000—Facade; March 26, 2000—Filled

Use Case 4.2   *continued*

4.3.2 Use Case Name Filters

When you're considering use case names, it's a good idea to run them through the following filters. Use case names

- Should conform to verb-noun construction: mail checks, determine eligibility, trace shipment, print letter
- Can contain adjectives or adverbs
- Should not be instances of classes and should not contain any situation-specific data
- Should not be tied to an organization structure, paper forms, or computer implementation: enter form 104-B, complete approval window, get approval from immediate supervisor in Accounting Department

- Should not use "weak verbs" (discussed later) that do not describe the action: *process, complete, do, track*

4.3.3 Candidate Use Case List

The candidate use case list (Table 4.2) is a useful tool at this point. Next to each use case name, IN or OUT designates whether a given use case is in or out of scope at this time. This list is a general adaptation of the traditional requirements list.

4.3.4 Actor Filter

A single person can play multiple roles, and actors can include external systems or devices. Therefore, the names of actors that involve human actions should reflect the roles that people play and not the names of actual people. Actors get value, provide value to the system, or both. Generalizing several layers of actors is best left until the Filled iteration (discussed in Chapter 5).

Be careful not to link a use case actor to your current organization chart. Although the actor's name must be recognizable to the users, there may be a more generic or abstract name that would still make sense to the users and would not tie your use cases into the current org chart (see Table 4.3).

Table 4.2 Candidate Use Case List Example

Use Case Name	Summary	In/Out Scope
Enter payment	Enter the basic payment information and notify the agency that the account is no longer outstanding.	IN
Activate agency	Set the agency to active.	IN
Merge agencies	Merge two or more agencies into one in case of mergers or acquisitions.	OUT
Remove audit records for agency	Archive audit records to reduce online storage required.	OUT

Table 4.3 Evaluating Actor Names

Good Actor Names	Poor Actor Names
Pension clerk	Clerk
Sales supervisor	Third-Level Supervisor
Production accountant	Data Entry Clerk #165
Customer service representative	Eddie "The Dawg" Taylor

4.3.5 Verb Filter

Concrete ("strong") verbs are more meaningful in use case names than are generalized ("weak") verbs (see Table 4.4 for examples). If you find yourself using weak verbs in use case names, it may be that you are unsure of exactly what this use case is accomplishing. You may be recording a use case that provides no value to the actor, or you may be bowing to time pressure, reducing the quality of your work.

NOTE: In some situations, verbs we've designated as "weak" are quite acceptable, such as an industry-specific verb. For example, in our *Sell Property* use case examples, we show *List Property* as a use case. Here, *list* is a real estate term that means to place a property for sale. Similarly, *Process Loan* refers to the bank processing of a loan and not an application process. There are always exceptions to the rules.

Table 4.4 Strong and Weak Verbs

Concrete (Strong) Verbs in Use Case Names	General (Weak) Verbs in Use Case Names
Create	Make
Remove	Report
Merge	Use
Defer	Copy
Switch	Organize
Calculate	Record
Pay	Repeat
Credit	Find
Register	Process
Deactivate	Maintain
Review	Display
View	List
Enter	Retrieve
Change	Integrate
Combine	Input
Release	
Search	
Migrate	
Receive	
Debit	
Activate	
Archive	
Browse	

4.3.6 Noun Filter

Strong (concrete) nouns, like strong verbs, show that use case authors know what they are talking about and aren't hedging. Table 4.5 shows examples.

4.3.7 Packages As Placeholders for Functionality

Packages can be a convenient tool for creating placeholders for large areas of functionality that are not addressed during the Facade iteration. Interactions between the unknown functional area (indicated by the package) and the rest of the system (defined in the Facade use cases) can ensure that the only thing that remains undocumented is the functionality inside the package itself.

NOTE: The principle of the Facade iteration is to write use cases to create placeholders for each functional area. The focus should be on the functionality that is the hardest to define or the most nebulous. Therefore, it's a good idea to take a close look at those functional areas that you wish to put inside packages during this iteration. It may be important to break those packages down into Facade use cases instead of leaving them as amorphous packages. Packages are more useful when they hold a place for functionality that cannot be defined at this time or that is known to be simple and is not worth documenting now.

4.3.8 Facade Filter

At what level should Facade use cases exist? Facade use cases represent the most important interactions between the actors and the system. There should be only a few use cases that represent the major interactions. Activities such as security, audit, backup, and recovery merely support the major business interactions. Leave them until later.

Table 4.5   Weak and Strong Nouns

Strong	Weak
Property	Data
Loan	Paper
Agent	Report
Supplies	System
Price	Form
Costs	Template
Offer	
Account	
Trend	
Date	
Sales	

Facade use cases should be relatively abstract. Abstract use cases can cover a variety of actual proposed interactions with just one abstract interaction. Constantine and Lockwood (1999) talk about "essential use cases," which are abstract enough to define truly how the system interacts with the user without any regard for implementation details.

Omit from this iteration all use case diagram adornments, such as *extends* or *includes*. These are stereotypes that you'll add later. Also, there is no need to spend time on the Basic Course of Events section in the use case template. Just fill in a brief summary for each use case as a placeholder. Use Cases 4.3 and 4.4 illustrate two Facade use cases from the real estate example we've cited before.

Use Case Name:	**Agree to Terms**
Iteration:	**Facade**
Summary:	The buyer and seller agree to the terms of the sale, including any required changes to the existing property, the items included with the property, the date of possession, the financing, and any other conditions of sale. The agents help their respective customers by offering advice, caution, or recommendations. The financial analyst helps the buyer understand the extent to which the buyer's finances stretch. The legal analyst provides advice on legal issues and approves the contract.
Basic Course of Events:	
Alternative Paths:	
Exception Paths:	
Extension Points:	
Trigger:	
Assumptions:	
Preconditions:	
Postconditions:	
Related Business Rules:	
Author:	Angela Baltimore
Date:	March 20, 2000—Facade

Use Case 4.3 *Agree to Terms*

Use Case Name:	**List Property**
Iteration:	**Facade**
Summary:	The seller lists the property, providing information on location, price, floor layout, and so forth. The seller's agent checks the listing and solicits the seller for any additional items required before it can be listed publicly.
Basic Course of Events:	
Alternative Paths:	
Exception Paths:	
Extension Points:	
Trigger:	
Assumptions:	
Preconditions:	
Postconditions:	
Related Business Rules:	
Author:	Ed Towson
Date:	March 20, 2000—Facade

Use Case 4.4   *List Property Facade*

4.3.9 Peer Review

Think of use case *peer reviews* as code walk-throughs except that peer reviews are much more brief. It is simple to review five use cases in one sitting. Have a technical architect present who can begin to estimate how much architecture is required by these interactions. Also, include an SME who understands the business domain. That person watches for major "gotchas" that you want to catch before you make a fool of yourself in front of the user.

Have peer reviews often and informally. Don't hesitate to pass your Facade use cases by your coworkers during this phase, or perhaps use an outside quality assurance authority. The more involvement there is by these various parties at this time, the easier the later iterations will be, and certainly the easier design and development will become.

The input is the Facade use cases, perhaps partially completed. The process is a review of the use cases for problems in nomenclature, standards, and so on. The output is improved use cases and a list of changes for the author to make. If this is the final review before user review, the output includes a deadline for making the changes.

4.3.10 User Review

User review of your Facade use cases is critical. Plan one or several face-to-face meetings (if possible) with your users to walk through the use cases. You are already iterating through your use case development (Facade, Filled, Focused, Finished), so you do not need to have multiple sessions with the same users, but you may need to schedule multiple sessions to include each user who requires involvement. Every hour you spend in user review is an investment in problem avoidance that repays you tenfold later.

4.4 Deliverables

The Facade iteration is complete when

- A system context use case is documented
- The project manager has an 80 percent confidence that all Facade-level use cases have been identified
- Every use case identified has been documented

Some planning is required before you move on to your next use case iteration. It is during the Filled iteration that you widen your scope, deepen your analyses, and broaden your context. You will take many of the ideas that surfaced in Facade and bring them to life.

The outputs from the Facade iteration are as follows.

Problem statement	Complete
Statement of work	Complete
Risk analysis	Partially complete
Prototype	Not started
Use case diagrams	Facade level
Use cases	Facade level
Business rules	Facade level

4.5 Roles

Table 4.6 shows the roles that are involved in this iteration.

4.6 Context

The Facade iteration creates placeholders for each use case. This iteration provides a structure for the use cases to come.

Table 4.6   Roles in the Facade Iteration

Role	Duties
Requirements analyst	Create Facade use cases, use case diagrams, and business rules
Stakeholder	Participate in interviews
Executive sponsor	Review problem statement, informal review, occasional status
Technical architect	Attend peer reviews
Project manager	Assist in developing the statement of work, provide updates to problem statement

4.7 Summary

Start your requirements effort with the Facade iteration. This process gives you a high-level view of the system that you are going to build, and it organizes your efforts by giving you placeholders for the tasks that remain.

To create the Facade iteration, dig into the system and talk to the stakeholders. As you build a mental image of the system, describe its components in simple use cases. When you have Facade use cases written for the major parts of the system, the work remaining for other iterations is to increase the value of each one until you have documented sufficient detail to build the system.

Several tools are at your disposal to help keep this iteration on track. The verb, use case name, and actor filters will help you avoid classic use case traps. The supporting requirements documentation (see Chapter 3), together with the Facade use cases, immediately reduces the ambiguity of what the system must do for its users, and this is the central point of requirements gathering.

5

For every problem, there is one solution which is simple, neat and wrong.

—H. L. Mencken

The Filled Iteration

5.1 Objectives

Putting together comprehensive requirements for a nontrivial application is a complex task. During the Filled iteration, you face the magnitude of this task.

The objective of the Filled iteration is to create a comprehensive set of use cases and business rules that describe the application. Although these requirements are rough and unpolished, they contain a lot of detail and include functional and nonfunctional requirements and business rules.

During this iteration, you spend most of your time working to understand the requirements and exploring possible solutions to the business problems. You write use cases by finding interactions and analyzing processes, asking, Is this the right way? Can we simplify this?

85

Use cases are the mechanism with which you can explore the possibilities and opportunities offered by the application. The exploratory nature of this process produces well-documented system requirements that benefit developers, designers, users, and testers.

5.2 Steps

To create the Filled iteration artifacts, you follow these steps.

1. Break out detailed use cases.
2. Create Filled use cases.
3. Collect and document the nonfunctional requirements.
4. Add business rules.
5. Test the Filled use cases.
6. Put some things off.

Even within the Filled iteration, the process is iterative. Expect to revisit the majority of the use cases at least twice, and the complicated use cases as many as four times. Getting use case granularity right, for example, is difficult the first time through, so plan to go through the process several times until you are satisfied.

5.2.1 Break Out Detailed Use Cases

During the Facade iteration, you created use cases for each major interaction. As you delve into more detail during the Filled iteration, you will find that some of these Facade use cases are too general and need to be broken down into several Filled use cases. This challenging task poses questions such as What size should a use case be? Where is the natural breakdown between functionality?

Before we answer these questions, let's expand step 1, breaking out detailed use cases, into more-detailed steps.

1. Identify and summarize each use case.
2. Add detail to the use case diagrams.
3. Review use case granularity.
4. Repeat steps 1, 2, and 3 as necessary.

Creating a consistent breakdown that has a suitable granularity is a challenging task. But you'll find that a successful decomposition of any overgeneralized Facade use cases gives you a solid basis for supporting future design and development. In addition, you gain experience in the difficult task of choosing the granularity of use cases. The more often you do this, the easier it becomes.

5.2.1.1 Identify and Summarize Each Use Case

Identify and describe all the use cases that make up the system. Tackle the overall system using the input from the Facade iteration. First, review the documentation identified during the Facade iteration so that you understand the background; then interview the stakeholders again. Have the stakeholders walk through the functionality, giving them the opportunity to tell you what their needs are. Next, pick each *macro* piece of functionality (discussed next) and assign it to a use case. Include the details provided by the stakeholder in the summary of the use case (and eventually in its body). Supplement these details with questions such as Who does this? What results are you looking for? What are the inputs to the process? What steps do you take? Go into as much detail as you can, and follow each process through to its conclusion. The additional detail will increase your understanding and may reveal additional use cases. If something looks like a possible use case, document it. Chapter 4 contains more information on getting as much value from this meeting as possible.

A macro piece of functionality is a subjective explanation of how something works from the stakeholder's perspective. Remember that use cases are not a primary input to the programmers; the design team is responsible for providing the level of detail that they require, and that is not your job during this activity. Instead, you are looking for coherent sets of functionality that you can group in a way that makes sense from a business perspective. Of the users being interviewed, those who are actually going to work with the system are a good source for this breakdown. Pay attention to their sense that a piece of work is finished. In the costume design examples in Appendix C, the users naturally break down a garment lifecycle into consultation, design, sewing, and fitting, followed by alterations. Take this kind of breakdown as your starting point, and think of the use case as you start to add detail. Big changes in the users' view of what is important can indicate a reasonable place to start a new use case. For example, while describing the consultation process, the user may start to go into less detail about understanding the needs of the customer and begin to provide more detail on estimating the cost of the finished garment. Even though providing a price for the garment is part of the consultation, it is a different set of tasks and is an ideal activity for a separate use case.

Pay most attention to the use cases that contain the bulk of the application's business functionality. These use cases provide the most valuable user-application interactions, and they require more effort than use cases containing mainly CRUD (create-read-update-delete) table maintenance operations.

Next, write the summaries for the detailed use cases. By itself, the use case name is too short to communicate its purpose to everyone. If you write an appropriate summary you will have a lot more success in remembering your intentions for the use case. Write as much as you need to convey the purpose of the use case, including some of the important steps. The summary information becomes the use case description when you write the full use case. What are the important elements in the summary? It should identify all the major results of the use case.

Repeat this process until you have identified and summarized detailed use cases for the entire system. Section 5.3.3 describes a tool that helps you check whether you have covered the entire system.

Although you may be tempted to combine use cases to take advantage of their similarity, hold back at this point. Your objective is to understand the system, so you should avoid combining use cases until you have a sufficient understanding of why they are similar.

The combination of use case name and summary comprises the candidate list. You cannot expect to finalize this entity early in the requirements-gathering process. Expect it to evolve as you investigate various areas and as you develop the appropriate granularity for the requirements.

5.2.1.2 Add Detail to the Use Case Diagrams

You created an initial set of use case diagrams for the Facade iteration. During the Filled iteration, you break down the overgeneralized Facade use cases into several Filled use cases, adding any other details that are uncovered as you get into greater detail in the text use cases.

Figure 5.1, taken from Appendix B, is an example of a Filled use case with an appropriate amount of detail for this iteration.

5.2.1.3 Review Use Case Granularity

Earlier we posed the question, What size should a use case be? "Size" does not refer to the amount of documentation that supports a use case, nor does it indicate how detailed a use case should be. Rather, it refers to how you define the boundaries between system functionality. Another way to look at the issue is to ask, How do we split system functionality into use cases? How many use cases should we employ to describe the system? The answer lies in *use case granularity*.

NOTE: Use case granularity is the relative scope of individual use cases compared to the application's scope.

You can describe a system in a few or a great many use cases. The fewer the use cases, the coarser the granularity of each use case.

Granularity is a relative measure, and there are no metrics established to determine correct granularity for all projects. Instead, you choose granularity that is appropriate for a specific development effort. Your goal in gathering requirements is to understand and communicate scope, complexity, and detail. The granularity you choose for documenting

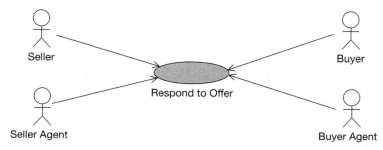

Figure 5.1 *Sell Property—Respond to Offer Filled Use Case Diagram*

requirements must facilitate division of work among analysts and must allow ease of change. In addition, the granularity must be acceptable to your stakeholders.

The best way to finalize the granularity decision is to provide the team with guidelines and discuss the factors that guided the choices. Consistency and consensus are important criteria for successful granularity across use cases. One guideline that we've used successfully is to think of the iterations of design and development. Iterations are often set as one to three weeks. Making this assumption, think about what can be accomplished in one week (or two or three). Choose a single example of functionality and revalidate the requirements, doing analysis, design, construction, testing, and deployment. Given one of the paths (scenarios) of the use cases you've created, could your team implement it in a week? Two? Three? The answer to that question becomes a good acid test for use case granularity.

What differences will granularity make to the use cases? A too-fine granularity may not be able to provide the "big picture" in a single use case, and that may make it difficult to grasp a business concept. A too-coarse granularity increases complexity and decreases readability.

After you have completed the initial identification of the detailed use cases, it is time to review their granularity and change it if necessary. Ask the following questions of the detailed use cases.

- Does each use case provide a sufficient "big picture" view of its functionality?
- If you broke down the use cases, would they be easier to understand?
- Can you make them easier to work on?
- If you needed to change some details in a use case, would it be difficult?
- Can one analyst work on one use case, or is it so big that two or more analysts would have to work on it?
- Could a reasonably sized team take one path (scenario) from the use case from requirements to deployment in one, two, or three weeks?

When you have found a granularity that works well, apply it also to the use case diagram. Group related use cases into packages, and draw a use case diagram for each package. The system context use case diagram shows the big picture, and each package's diagram will contain the detail for each set of use cases.

NOTE: Chapter 9 identifies the implementation of a configuration management system as being crucial to the success of use case development. Such a system facilitates rapid changes to granularity by allowing you to revert to a previous iteration if the change was not beneficial. Chapter 9 also discusses granularity from a team perspective.

After you implement any changes due to granularity, review the use cases and their summaries to ensure that you have not omitted considerations of scope. Name and summarize any additional use cases, and then update the use case diagram. You will complete these use cases, so it is important to identify all the necessary use cases as placeholders at this time.

5.2.2 Create Filled Use Cases

Now that you have summarized all the use cases in the application (we hope!), you are ready to build each one. Because you have chosen an appropriate granularity, you can safely take the time to build the detailed use cases.

Stakeholder meetings have formed the input into most of these steps. If more information is needed, head back to the stakeholders to confirm, probe, and query.

The following sections show the steps for completing the Filled use cases.

5.2.2.1 Identify Triggers

A use case *trigger* is the impulse or event that initiates the use case.

Triggers answer the questions, When does this use case start? What impulse or event signaled the start of this use case? A use case may have more than one trigger. To help discover all the triggers, ask the stakeholder to describe the process flow.

Describe the trigger in the active voice ("The build manager asks the developer to build a product release") rather than the passive voice ("The developer is asked to build a product release"), and state the condition simply. Do not describe the trigger in terms of the software system; instead, relate it to the business being modeled. For example, a use case should not start when a user opens a window; instead, it should start when a sales agent receives a telephone order.

Clarify whether a trigger is also an automation requirement. For example, suppose that a trigger for a use case that captures a telephone purchase order is "Sales agent receives a telephone call." The problem with this description is that it does not specify whether the telephone or the sales agent triggered the use case. Talk to the stakeholders about the level of automation they require, and document it clearly to avoid this kind of ambiguous requirement. In such a discussion, it is useful to distinguish between "possible but expensive" versus "realistic" requirements.

Here are two examples of triggers.

- The build manager asks the developer to build a product release.
- The system detects a work file in the inbound processing queue.

5.2.2.2 Identify Preconditions

Preconditions describe a mandatory state of the system at the inception of the use case.

A precondition is anything that the use case assumes has occurred before its starting point that is relevant to the use case. Describe the business conditions that must precede use case initiation. Ask the stakeholder questions such as What must happen before we can do this? What do you need to have before you can perform this functionality?

Examine the inputs to the use case—whether the input is a piece of information (such as a form) or an event (such as someone retiring)—and ask how this use case will be aware of it. For example, suppose that in your use case, the actor keys data. Ask where the data came from. If it is mailed and if this is the first time the system comes into contact with it, then a precondition is that the data entry sheets are available. A related trigger could be that at least ten data entry forms have accumulated.

Preconditions and use case triggers are related. Together, they describe the state of the system when the use case starts. The difference between a precondition and a trigger is that satisfying the preconditions is not, by itself, a sufficient condition to initiate the use case. The trigger provides the impetus to start the use case, and that initialization is successful only if the preconditions have also been satisfied. All preconditions must be satisfied for the trigger to be able to initiate the use case.

Also note that a condition should not be included in both the precondition and the exception area of a use case. If the condition is included in both, you have introduced redundancy. The exception cannot occur because the use case would not begin until the condition was satisfied.

Another use case, an actor, or a system actor must be capable of satisfying all preconditions of any use case.

5.2.2.3 Refine the Use Case Name

The *name* of a use case describes the primary actor's objective. This is a verb-noun combination.

Ask the stakeholder to define the most important objective of the use case. Answering this question is difficult, so encourage the user to explore the possibilities and to examine the use case's completion criteria. One area that confuses users when discussing objectives is this: From whose perspective should the objective be considered?

For example, in a book-ordering system, the customer's criterion for use case completion is that she receive the book that she ordered. From the perspective of the sales clerk, the objective is to collect the order, address, and payment information and to send the order to the dispatching warehouse.

The use case name should reflect the objective of the primary actor. In our example, the sales clerk is the primary actor, and the customer is a secondary actor, so the use case name should be *Create Sales Order*. To avoid confusion when you name use cases, discuss with the stakeholder which of the actors is the primary one. In addition to helping you identify a good use case name, gaining a clear understanding of the objectives will improve all areas of the use case.

Section 4.3 describes several tools that help in this process, including a use case name filter that helps you avoid using weak use case names.

5.2.2.4 Refine the Actors

The use case *actor* is an abstraction of any role that interacts with the use case.

The use case diagram indicates the roles that interact with a use case as actors. These are the stick-figure people attached to the use cases. Each actor is a role and can represent a person or a system.

It is important that you understand "who does what" in each use case. Ask the stakeholder questions such as What roles are involved in this task? How do they interact? To prevent confusion regarding similar roles, collect any relevant information about each actor in an actor profile. For example, if an actor is someone who sometimes works remotely, record this in the profile.

5.2.2.5 Specify the Basic Course of Events

The Basic Course of Events section of a use case specifies the actor's interactions with the system and with other actors to achieve the actor's goals. The events tell a story that describes how a triggered use case progresses toward its objective and the steps in between.

Write the basic course of events as numbered instructions that tell the actor what to do and that show how the system responds.

For example, let's say that during the Facade iteration, a use case called *Process Loan* (see Appendix B) has the following summary and little other information:

> The loan provider and the buyer work out the terms of the loan, if the buyer requires one. Terms include the interest rate, points, term, escrow, insurance, and so forth.

In Use Case 5.1, we add the Basic Course of Events.

Each statement in the Basic Course of Events section is part of the dialog between the actor and the system. This section describes the straight line through the process; variations and exceptions have their own section. The information in the basic course of events comes from your interview with the stakeholders. Have the stakeholders describe how they envision the actor achieving the objectives of the use case. Ask them to list all the steps that they can think of. This information will give you the first cut at the course of events. Go into detail for these steps. If they say, "We enter the customer's demographics," ask them to elaborate on these details. Ask, What happens if . . .? If there are multiple actors in a use case, ask, Who does what? Don't be afraid to ask persistent questions. Repeat the interviews to clarify any details that remain obscure.

If there is an existing system or manual process, it makes it easier for the stakeholders to give you the detail needed for these steps. If there is no existing system, encourage them to imagine it and to think of all the detail they need for the process. Walk the stakeholders through the steps to encourage them to remember additional details.

The Basic Course of Events section must expose complex processes and reveal simple, easily read steps. To "open the black box" and make the process clear is your goal for writing this section. Aim to elaborate a process sufficiently to reveal all its intricacies.

Avoid naming user interface controls in the steps. Always translate the requirement into a format that excludes GUI specifics, and ask the stakeholder for the underlying requirement. For example, don't write, "Click the OK button." Instead, write, "Save the demographic details."

TIP: Maintain a glossary of all the business terms included in the use cases. The glossary should explain the terms used and has the dual function of clarifying and confirming your use of the specific terms. This action reduces jargon confusion between stakeholders and analysts during the requirements-gathering activity, and it clarifies your use cases to the designers.

Use Case Name:	**Process Loan**
Iteration:	**Filled**
Summary:	The loan provider and the buyer work out the terms of the loan, if the buyer requires one. Terms include the interest rate, points, term, escrow, insurance, and so forth.
Basic Course of Events:	1. This use case begins when the buyer and the seller have agreed to terms. 2. The buyer indicates that a loan is required. 3. The system responds by contacting the loan provider with the details of the buyer's loan requirement. 4. The loan provider uses the buyer's loan requirement as input to create a loan proposal. 5. The system responds by sending the loan proposal to the buyer and the buyer's agent. 6. The buyer makes a counteroffer to the loan provider. 7. The system responds by sending the counteroffer to the loan provider. 8. The loan provider accepts the counteroffer. 9. The system responds by sending notification of the loan provider's acceptance to the buyer and the buyer's agent. 10. The buyer indicates acceptance of the loan. 11. The system responds by recording the buyer's acceptance of the loan and files the approved loan application with the loan provider.

Use Case 5.1   *Process Loan*

5.2.2.6 Indicate Repetition

Repetition is the reiteration of a process by an actor until a condition changes.

The basic course of events must often show repeating steps as well as alternative paths and exception paths. Use a tiered numbering scheme to indicate repetition. For example:

1. Indicate customer's color choice from the set displayed.
   • (Optional) Indicate as many as five alternative choices.
2. Next step

Ask, What is the condition for ending the repetition? Will there be the same number of repetitions each time? Then translate the answers into the requirements that the user interface designers and data designers must know. Additionally, this information is valuable for defining scope.

5.2.2.7 Document Exceptions

Exceptions specify the actor's interactions with the system, and with other actors, when the basic course of events is not followed.

The exceptions and alternatives listed in Use Case 5.2 apply to the Basic Course of Events section of Use Case 5.1.

The exceptions have their own section in the use case template, immediately below the Basic Course of Events section. If there is ambiguity regarding which step the exception relates to, clarify by referring to the step's number. If the description of the exception requires multiple statements, use tiered numbering like that used in the Basic Course of Events section. The default is to return to the next event statement; if that is not the default, show the event number to return to. If an exception ends a use case, state it.

Write your use cases so that all levels of users are comfortable reading them. When you are writing exceptions, avoid the use of IF-THEN-ELSE construction. Such pseudocode breaks the flow of the use case story, and executive-level users may not be comfortable with it. Write exceptions so that they can be read naturally, and do not capitalize words such as *otherwise*.

The Basic Course of Events section specifies the straight line through from trigger to use case completion. This is the basic process. Most use cases have exceptions in response to specific circumstances. We document these because the system must be able to handle them. Exceptions document the answers to the range of questions that begin with, What will the actor do if . . .?

Identify the business process exceptions to respond to real-world inputs; do not document possible software exceptions. To identify the relevant exception, discover how the actor should interact with the system when the process deviates from typical processing. In this

Alternative Paths:	In step 6, if the buyer approves the initial loan proposal, jump to step 8.
Exception Paths:	In step 6, if the buyer decides that this loan provider cannot provide an appropriate loan for this purchase, the buyer will indicate to the system that another loan provider is needed. The system will respond by returning to step 3. In step 4, if the loan provider decides that the buyer is not eligible for any loan, the loan provider makes note of this in the system and the system responds by notifying the buyer that no loan is possible from this loan provider. The buyer may then choose another loan provider or may cancel the offer.

Use Case 5.2   *Exceptions and Alternatives Sections of Use Case 5.1*

> **When Should You Make an Exception into a New Use Case?**
>
> While writing use cases, guard against creating a use case that is too large to be managed. When the size of an exception is comparable to that of the use case, it can be a warning signal that the exception, even if it appears to be related to the use case, should be a separate use case.
>
> If your exception is too large or if it has exceptions of its own, create a separate use case for it. At this point do not relate it to other use cases with *include* and *extend* relationships. Do this in the next iteration.

way, the use case can describe the interaction between actors and the system that accomplishes real business. Ask the stakeholder what-happens-if questions to discover the exceptions. But be sure to distinguish between exceptions and improbable occurrences. The focus of most business development is to create a system that functions correctly for the majority of the business cases that it handles. Typically, the system designers decide not to explicitly handle every possible business exception. Embedded systems and mission-critical systems may need to handle a larger set of improbable conditions. As with the majority of the rules surrounding use cases, you are free to make and break them as you choose.

5.2.2.8 Refine the Use of Language

It sounds basic, but grammar and spelling in your use cases are important. Use cases are written in natural language, so the only syntax that guides you when writing them is the use of language. You can be sure that your work will be judged on the quality of the writing in the use cases as much as anything else.

In general, use the active voice ("The actor did it") rather than the passive voice ("It was done by the actor"). Writing in the passive voice may be a clue that information is missing. If you're saying, "It was done," without specifying who did it, perhaps it is time to find out who did it.

Also, try to keep technical jargon out of your use cases.

5.2.3 Collect and Document Nonfunctional Requirements

There are three steps to identifying and documenting nonfunctional requirements in this iteration.

1. Identify the requirement in the notes from previous interviews.
2. Validate the requirement with additional interviews with the associated stakeholders.
3. Document the requirement: Capture an understanding of the requirement, its effects, and the system and business degradation that would result if the requirement were not satisfied.

In the Filled and Finished iterations, you refine your nonfunctional requirements and create a stereotype to relate nonfunctional requirements to the use cases. Stereotypes are first explored in Chapter 2, in which we describe how this feature of the UML can be employed to associate related information to a number of use cases. For this iteration, we only capture and document these requirements.

5.2.3.1 Identify Nonfunctional Requirements

The best time to identify nonfunctional requirements (see Table 5.1) is while you are exploring the functional requirements. Whenever you identify a candidate nonfunctional requirement, document it. Do not wait to attempt to do this as a single task later. Your group of users is an excellent source for identifying nonfunctional requirements. When you interview stakeholders while building the use cases, use this opportunity to gather the nonfunctional requirements, too.

Ask the users about response time needs, and ask them what annoys them about the way the system works now. The answers will give you valuable leads for nonfunctional requirements. If there is a legacy system, it can be another good source for nonfunctional requirements. Ask users what they liked and disliked about it. Be careful not to confuse business-related gripes with those that provide nonfunctional requirements. For example, "The existing system only allows us to capture three lines of miscellaneous information about a customer." Increasing this length constraint can be documented as a normal requirement. The flow of events would contain the statement "Enter the miscellaneous information provided by the customer (no length constraint)."

These nonfunctional requirements, and many others like them, contribute to the usefulness of a system. For a number of reasons, however, it is common for these topics never to come up during requirements discussions. They are important nevertheless.

TIP: One way to deal with nonfunctional requirements is to rate their relative importance, numbering them 1 through n.

Nonfunctional requirements are principles that run through parts or most of the system and dictate how the system is structured. The way an application is structured is part of its architecture, so you can see how nonfunctional requirements contribute to the architecture of an application.

5.2.3.2 Validate the Requirements

At this point, it helps to recap the functional and nonfunctional requirements and walk through them to test whether they make sense as a group.

5.2.3.3 Documenting Nonfunctional Requirements

Figure 5.2 presents a template for documenting the nonfunctional requirements.

Describe the requirement, include the exceptions that are special cases of the requirement, and name the use cases that it applies to. Some nonfunctional requirements, such as

Table 5.1   Definitions of Nonfunctional Requirements

Nonfunctional Requirement	Definition
Availability	Rate of hardware and software component failure (mean time between failures)
Cost of ownership	Overall operating costs to the organization after the system is in production
Maintainability	Ability of the support programming staff to keep the system in a steady running state, including enhancements
Data integrity	Tolerance for loss, corruption, or duplication of data
Development cost	Overall cost of development
Extensibility	Ability to accommodate increased functionality
Flexibility	Ability to handle requirement changes
Functionality	Number, variety, and breadth of user-oriented features
Installability	Ease of system installation on all necessary platforms
Leverageability/Reuse	Ability to leverage common components across multiple products
Operability	Ease of everyday operation; level of support requirements
Performance	Ability to meet real-time constraints in batch and online
Portability	Ability to move the application to different platforms or operating systems
Quality	Reduced number of severe defects
Robustness	Ability to handle error and boundary conditions while running
Scalability	Ability to handle a wide variety of system configuration sizes

Requirement	Exceptions	Applies to Use Cases

Figure 5.2   *Technical Requirements Template*

system constraints, apply to many use cases. It is not necessary to list all of them; instead, write, "Most data entry use cases." This approach spares you from having to write the same requirement for many use cases and makes it easier to alter.

Be careful to avoid including assumptions in the nonfunctional requirements. For example, a technical requirement might be "Back up nightly to tape storage." The requirement is to prevent data loss, and it describes the frequency of this task. The mention of a tape solution, however, is either a platitude or a technical constraint. Ask the user which it is. If it is a technical constraint, you have identified an additional nonfunctional requirement. If it is not, you risk adding an invalid assumption to your requirements. In this case, the specification of a tape backup is invalid because, for example, a number of highly reliable backup vendors have popped up on the Internet. They back up your data across an Internet link and provide you with instant restoration when required. For a small business, the mention of tape in the requirement may lock it into an assumption that the tape solution is the only possible one, perhaps precluding a better solution.

SEE ALSO: http://www.@backup.com

@backup is an Internet backup company oriented toward consumers and small businesses. Daryl uses it and loves it!

Avoid documenting platitudes such as "Each window must have a method of closing it as part of the interface." Such statements do not add value to your use cases, but they may be appropriate rules in the user interface standards document (see Chapter 7).

Table 5.2 lists nonfunctional requirements for one use case example.

TIP: When you're looking for nonfunctional requirements, refer to standards documents, where some technical constraints and requirements have probably been documented. Many organizations create and maintain standards documents to describe solutions to recurring problems. They can include everything from GUI standards to the software and

Table 5.2   *Sell Property* Nonfunctional Requirements

Requirement	Exceptions	Applies to Use Cases
When an offer is changed, this information must be available to all users simultaneously.	None	Making and responding to offers.
Other users, and anyone outside the system, must not be able to see details of any transactions being posted.	Authorized system administrators may view the details of any transaction.	All

Nonfunctional Versus System Maintenance Requirements

Are system maintenance requirements different from nonfunctional requirements?

Yes. If you can model a requirement by writing a narrative description of the interaction between actor and system, then it is a functional requirement. Use cases can document any functional requirement, whether it involves maintaining a system or supporting a business process. Therefore, you should not document administrative functions as part of the nonfunctional requirements. A system administrator is another actor, and use cases are an appropriate vehicle to document the administrator's interactions. Write these use cases just as you would any other.

For example, many data-intensive applications use lookup tables to constrain the data. The requirement that the system administrator needs access and can change these tables is a functional requirement. This requirement could be documented in a use case titled *Edit List of States* with the actor *system administrator*.

Remember to investigate and document maintenance requirements. Because they are not core to the business, they are sometimes neglected.

hardware that is normally used. You should review these documents and become familiar with their contents. When you discover an already defined nonfunctional requirement, simply determine that it relates to your use case and state that it follows the established standard. This fits our principle of documenting only in one place whenever possible.

5.2.4 Add Business Rules

Collect the business rules in parallel with developing the use cases and identifying the non-functional requirements. During the Filled iteration, you are simply adding business rules as they appear during use case creation. At this point there is no need to comply with strict formats or categorizations for business rules. You can apply these in later iterations.

5.2.5 Test the Filled Use Cases

After you have built the use cases, check their completeness and quality. Because the use cases are not ready to be examined by the stakeholders, this should be an internal review. It is for your benefit only. It allows you to identify vague points in your use cases and to return to the stakeholders for clarification.

Employ scenarios for testing use cases. Chapter 2 defines a scenario as a possible path through a use case. Create a scenario by choosing data that will drive a use case through a specific set of main flow and exception statements.

Helping Users Help You Test a Use Case

How do you guide users through testing a use case, given the differences between use cases and scenarios?

When a user is explaining to you the rules from which a business process executes, both of you can experience a great deal of ambiguity because of the differences in how each of you views the events. The interviewer tends to ask the questions in use case language, and the interviewee tends to provide answers in "scenario land." Business users typically describe the set of circumstances in which they find themselves. If they have a specialty within the business process being described, their descriptions of the straight line path and the exceptions will reflect it. Under these circumstances, the dialog is likely to be misleading.

Be especially aware of the potential for this problem when the user is describing scenarios without first describing the main path and listing the exceptions. For example, if the business user says, "The customer calls to verify the order that was received via the Web," this is a danger sign. It is possible that the conditions described actually reflect an exception and not the main flow. Ask questions to determine whether this is so and to determine the additional paths that the business process could follow.

Apply a scenario by reading each step, supplying data to it, and obeying the use case's rules. Applying a scenario allows you to walk through a use case by following the flow and exceptions dictated by the data. This process helps you identify missing steps and discover additional exceptions, and that makes it a useful tool for quality-checking your work.

Each use case may have many possible scenarios. You may want to create scenario data for the normal processing scenario and for the more important exceptions. Scenarios do not have to be formalized, or recorded, to be an effective testing tool.

While you walk through a scenario, ask whether the use case documents the modeled system sufficiently. Test a use case comprehensively by executing a scenario for each path in the use case. Check that the exceptions are called and that the use case handles each exception.

Scenarios can be used to test both system requirements and the finished product. If you do formalize a scenario, it will be useful to the testing team. See Appendix A for additional detail on how to leverage your use case efforts throughout the software development lifecycle.

5.2.6 Put Some Things Off

Certain tasks should be put off until later iterations. The Filled iteration is the time to expand the detail of the documented requirements but not to increase or decrease the scope dramatically. It is good to wait on the following tasks:

- Identifying common behavior and merging use cases
- Handling software exceptions

Above all, keep working on gathering *what* and not *how*. Keeping this focus can be difficult because describing the *how* alleviates people's fear that they are being misunderstood or the fear that the system will not match their expectations. When you are given a description that includes a *how* component, look for the reason it was expressed during requirements gathering. Perhaps an additional nonfunctional requirement lurks behind the veil of design assumptions. For example, suppose that a requirement is expressed as follows.

When the user has entered the salary, interest rate, and credit rating, the system stores the profile and calculates a band of possible loan amounts. The calculation must be performed on the server and never on the client.

Note that the last line of this requirement contains *how* information. A design decision has been expressed. If you inquire further into this statement, you may discover that the user community is worried that the calculation will not be made quickly because a previous legacy system performed the calculation on a client machine, which took several minutes. The unstated nonfunctional requirement is actually that the calculation result be returned to the user within, say, three seconds.

Here's another example.

The data system passes the Social Security number to the imaging system via API calls that will bring up the folder of personal information about the account holder through which the user can browse.

The specific *how* elements in this requirement are the mention of application programming interface (API) calls and the use of Social Security numbers as a unique identity in an imaging system. Further conversation with this user may indicate that he wants it documented that the imaging system is integrated with his business system and that he will not have to invoke the imaging system manually to search for an account. It is a simple step to remove the unique key and API references from this requirement and still describe the interaction successfully.

Also, do not worry about the user interface requirements at this point. The way the application presents or accepts information to and from the users (the *how*) is a detail that should wait until a later iteration.

5.3 Tools

There are a number of tools (techniques and approaches) that you can employ to ease the tasks involved in the Filled iteration. Let's look at each of them in turn.

5.3.1 The Stakeholder Interview

The stakeholder interview is your primary tool for gathering requirements and for getting additional information about confusing requirements. Refer to Chapter 4 for details on interviewing stakeholders and holding joint requirements planning sessions.

5.3.2 IPA Filter

IPA stands for includes, preconditions, and assumptions (and not India Pale Ale).

There are three parts of a use case that can be easily confused:

- An *include* association between use cases
- A *precondition* on a given use case
- An *assumption* for a use case

When should you use each of these elements? Table 5.3 lists our rules of thumb for the types of information that should populate each of these fields.

5.3.3 White Space Analysis Filter

Think of *white space analysis filter* as a way to examine a "day in the life" (although it may refer to any period—say, a month or a year—in the life). When you walk through the existing or newly modeled business processes, you can discover that there are missing interactions, perhaps significant areas that have not been addressed in the use cases so far. We call these unaddressed areas the *white space* in your requirements picture. If this system is part of a business process engineering effort, the business process definitions can help structure the

Table 5.3   Includes, Preconditions, and Assumptions Compared

Use This	Under These Conditions
Include association	When the reused use case does not provide value to an actor and it is only an intermediate step that is used by use cases within this development effort that really provide the value, it signifies an include relationship.
Precondition	When something inside the system being built, but outside this use case, must be in place before this use case can run, it is an example of a precondition.
Assumption	When something outside the control of this development effort (especially things that have been ruled beyond the scope of this project) must be in place before this use case can run, you've found an assumption.

discussions. Or, if this system is automating existing procedures, those process definitions can be used. Or, more likely, the information stored in people's heads can guide the process.

Go through a day in the life of each actor, and then move on to end-of-week, end-of-month, end-of-quarter, and end-of-year processes. These walk-throughs should help you identify interactions that may not have been obvious earlier.

5.3.4 Abstraction Filter

When you're gathering requirements and making them understandable to all the stakeholders, an important function is *abstraction*. Abstraction is a process of generalization that allows you to consider the similarity between requirements and to make decisions consistently across the business domain. Take a reality check on how abstract the use cases are. The primary reason for modeling requirements with use cases is to communicate the requirements to the users, application designers, and testers. If the use cases are too abstract, they will not provide sufficient, meaningful detail. If they are not abstract enough, you will repeat similar information in many different places, resulting in problems with consistency and documentation volume.

Read your use cases and think about the various people who must rely on them. Have you provided sufficient detail, or are the use cases too abstract? Have a sample use case reviewed by a user and by an application designer. Then discuss the use case with them to ensure that they are comfortable with the level of abstraction.

5.3.5 Testing Use Cases with Scenarios

The way to attack use case testing is to use scenarios. Scenarios, discussed earlier in Section 5.2.5, are effective testing tools for use cases because they help users and IT staff walk through what would happen in an everyday interaction with the application. Use Case 5.3 is actually a scenario related to our real estate example. It provides an example of a real-life situation with real data embedded that help a user decide whether this use case represents interactions with an application that would be useful.

Use Case Name:	**Agree to Terms**
Iteration:	**Filled**
Scenario:	1. The buyer (John Forrest) and seller (Tina Hart) indicate that an agreement is possible.
	2. The system responds by notifying John Forrest, Tina Hart, the buyer's agent (Harold Beanton), and the seller's agent (Claretta Watersmith) that the agreement process is ready to begin.

Use Case 5.3   *Testing Scenario (continues)*

	3. Tina Hart submits a proposal of terms. 4. The system responds by allowing all actors to view the proposal of terms and make their changes. 5. John Forrest changes the possession date from February 15 to February 10, and Tina Hart includes a set of shelves in the garage with the property. The others do not make any changes. 6. The system makes John Forrest's changes public to all other actors. 7. The actors discuss John Forrest's possession date change and Tina Hart asks that it be moved to February 11. Everyone agrees to the new possession date. The set of shelves is also added. 8. The system responds by consolidating the agreed-to changes and making the proposal of terms public again to all actors. 9. The actors indicate their agreement. 10. The system responds by indicating that the proposal of terms is final.
Author:	Angela Baltimore with Claretta Watersmith
Date:	March 27, 2000

Use Case 5.3   *continued*

5.3.6 Review

Peer reviews and user reviews should conclude this iteration to identify existing issues with the documentation.

5.3.7 Additional Use Cases

There are peripheral use cases that are often forgotten in requirements gathering.

- *Security*—authentication and authorization of users
- *Audit*—logs of online or batch activity
- *Backup and Recovery*—creating and maintaining copies of the system data
- *Remote users*—interactions of customers or supply chain partners
- *Reporting requirements*—queries and reports

The Filled iteration is the time to create these use cases.

5.4 Deliverables

The deliverables from the Filled iteration are as follows.

Candidate use case list	Partially complete
Use cases	Filled level
Use case diagrams	Filled level
Business rules catalog	Partially complete
Scenarios	Several for each use case tested

5.5 Roles

Table 5.4 shows the roles that participate in the Filled iteration.

5.6 Context

During the Filled iteration, you emphasize broadening and deepening the requirements specification. During the next iteration, which we call Focused, you will concentrate on narrowing the scope and level of detail that will be most helpful to the designers and developers.

5.7 Summary

In the Filled iteration you deal with the meat of requirements gathering, when you ask questions, write use cases, and have the majority of your contact with the system stakeholders. When this iteration is complete, you will have collected sufficient information to describe the system. For many projects, design can start from use cases like the ones you create in this iteration.

Table 5.4 Roles in the Filled Iteration

Role	Duties
Requirements analyst	Adds detail to use cases and business rules, reinterviews stakeholders to validate earlier assumptions, documents Filled use cases
Stakeholder	Participates in interviews
Executive sponsor	Reviews occasional status update
Technical architect	Helps determine nonfunctional requirements
Project manager	Provides statement of work updates and problem statement updates

6

The Focused Iteration

A man is rich in proportion to
the things he can afford to let
alone.

—Henry David Thoreau

6.1 Objectives

Arranged in your computer is a collection of use case documents, and each one describes a possible system component. This set of requirements is discouragingly large. You must now select the best options identified during the Filled iteration and include only these in the project scope.

The Focused iteration clears a path through the paperwork and leaves you with clear project requirements. At the end of this iteration, you will have defined the system and will have gathered sufficient information to build a successful application.

The Focused iteration separates the essential from the nice-to-have. It is now that you decide what is important, what will be built, and why. You examine the business problem from the context of your proposed solution, and you make sure that the solution doesn't solve unnecessary problems. For this reason, the Focused iteration is a difficult one.

When this iteration is complete, the use case model will describe the users' interactions with the system. These interactions allow the users to solve the business problems that initiated this development effort. The deliverables you create during the Focused iteration give you a detailed understanding of the scope of the system as well as its complexity and the risks involved.

To build systems that fulfill users' needs, you must understand the essential core functionality and help them understand which functionality is necessary. You can eliminate waste by carefully examining the scope and thus reduce the system to its essentials. Removing functionality at this stage is a real moneysaver. You avoid the effort of prototyping, designing, reviewing, building, and testing the additional functionality.

The following sections describe the steps in the Focused iteration.

6.2 What Are Focused Use Cases?

Focused use cases build on the work you have performed thus far. You make difficult choices about the current project, decide on the feature set, determine the scope, and eliminate duplication.

Focused use cases describe the users' interaction with a system. You hone each interaction to provide a solution to a limited set of business problems. At this point, you have analyzed the business sufficiently to remove contradictory requirements and to describe from a business perspective how the use cases share functionality and assist one another in reaching an understood goal. This varies considerably from the output of the Filled iteration. Focused use cases are clear and crisp. There is no additional detail, and the focus of the system is apparent. Use Case 6.1 is an example of a Focused use case.

Use Case Name:	**Agree to Terms**
Iteration:	**Focused**
Summary:	The buyer and seller agree to the terms of the sale, including the changes to the existing property that are required, the items included with the property, the date of possession, the financing, and any other conditions of sale. The agents help their respective customers by offering advice, caution, or recommendations.
Basic Course of Events:	1. This use case begins when the buyer and seller both indicate that an agreement is possible. 2. The system responds by notifying the buyer, the buyer's agent, the seller, the seller's agent, the legal analyst, and the financial analyst that the agreement process is ready to begin.

Use Case 6.1   *Sell Property—Agree to Terms: A Focused Use Case (continues)*

	3. The buyer or the seller submits a proposal of terms. 4. The system responds by allowing all actors to view the proposal of terms and make their changes. 5. The actors make their changes. 6. The system responds by making the actors' changes public to all. 7. The actors discuss the changes and come to an agreement on each proposed change, item by item. 8. The system responds by consolidating the agreed-to changes and again making the proposal of terms public. 9. The actors indicate their agreement. 10. This use case ends when the system indicates that the proposal of terms is final.
Alternative Paths:	In step 3, the buyer's agent may submit a proposal of terms to the buyer, who may then submit it as his own. In step 3, the seller may also be the one to submit a proposal of terms. In step 3, the seller's agent may submit a proposal of terms to the seller, who may then submit it as his own.
Exception Paths:	In step 9, if the buyer or the seller does not agree to the proposal of terms as it stands, the objecting party enters his issue; then the objecting party modifies the proposal, and processing returns to step 4.
Extension Points:	None
Trigger:	One of the actors indicates that the agreement to terms can begin.
Assumptions:	None
Preconditions:	An offer has been made and accepted
Postconditions:	Terms are agreed to by the buyer and the seller
Related Business Rules:	None
Author:	Angela Baltimore
Date:	March 20, 2000—Facade; March 28, 2000—Filled; April 2, 2000—Focused

Use Case 6.1 *continued*

6.3 Steps

To create the Focused iteration artifacts, follow these steps.

1. Create the context matrix.
2. Remove duplicate processes.

6.3.1 Create the Context Matrix

The context matrix puts each of the use cases in context with the others. Its purpose is to show dependencies between use cases. When a use case is ruled out of scope, it is important to be able to name the other use cases that may become unusable if that use case is eliminated.

Use the context matrix tool in Section 6.10.1 of this chapter to complete this step.

6.3.2 Remove Duplicate Processes

Examine the contents of each use case in relation to the remaining use cases. If you can share a process with other use cases, you reduce the scope of the project. To reduce the number of use cases, you remove duplicates, generalizing similar use cases. To reduce the size of individual use cases, you remove duplicate processes and generalize processes.

Many processes in a business are essentially the same. Early discovery of these similar processes in the development lifecycle will prevent you from designing, building, and testing duplicate code.

To find and remove duplicates, follow these steps.

1. Identify duplicates.
2. Split the duplicated piece into its own use case.

The Payback of Removing Duplicate Processes

The detection and removal of duplicate processes enhances your ability to perform a number of tasks, including the following.

- Choosing better candidate use cases.
- Simplifying the application documentation.
- Prioritizing use cases.
- Creating accurate estimates. If a use case can be used elsewhere, you can let the estimators know that.
- Improving your development process. For example, if a core set of use cases is employed diversely throughout the system, it might be economical to develop an automated system to test and regression-test these use cases.
- Planning project iterations.

3. Use *extend* or *include* relationships to employ this functionality in additional use cases.
4. Update the context matrix.
5. Update the use case diagram.

Removal of duplicates is crucial in this iteration. Duplicate functionality in use cases is a serious problem when you begin to implement the requirements in code. It also complicates maintenance because a single change means that you must update several processes.

6.4 Bring Focus to Each Use Case

Analysts, designers, architects, project managers, and programmers rely on use cases. In addition to extracting scope information from them, these individuals need sufficient data to be able to build and test the system. Each use case must be complete, accurate, and concise. In the Focused iteration, you edit each use case to make sure that your descriptions are complete and provide sufficient information without being wasteful or vague. You must ensure that you define the terms used for the business domain and that you have accurately defined the actors.

For this task, look into the following.

- *Interfaces to other systems (ports, APIs, telephony, Internet, and so on)*—Have you neglected any of these?
- *The relationships between the interfaces and the use cases*—For example, can the telephony interface provide the correct services to each of the use cases that depend on it?
- *Improving the processes*—Walk through each of the processes from the point of view of the user. What does this tell you about the process? Have you inadvertently retained the manual process? If you have, is it efficient enough for the future system?
- *Prioritizing the use cases*—Have you numbered them in order of importance and urgency to the users? This helps you to identify which use cases should be in the early design and development increments and stages of delivery.
- *Defining the inputs and outputs*—Examine these with the processes to ensure that you have not missed something.

6.5 Scope Changes During This Iteration

Requirements change. This moving target, often called *scope creep*, is invariably viewed as negative. Change renders your carefully crafted requirements obsolete, and that is frustrating. But businesses and government agencies are judged on their ability to constantly change with their chaotic markets, so their software must be able to change with them, even while it is being created. Given that you have no totalitarian solution to abolish changes, you must accept change during requirements analysis as well as during the rest of application development. You must develop strategies that allow you to cope with such changes.

When change occurs, you must evaluate its consequences objectively and implement them sensibly. Change may increase or decrease scope. Dealing with a scope decrease—a change that reduces the level of automation in a system—might seem easier. However, it is important that you apply the same mechanisms to analyze both types of changes. Your goal is to identify how a change may alter the system. Dependencies between use cases are relevant to the task of understanding change.

6.6 Strategies for Change

Your objective is to handle scope and requirement changes flexibly and accurately. The key is to understand how the overall system must adapt to accommodate the change.

Introducing a new use case typically causes less change than does altering existing use cases. Discovering how the change influences existing functionality accounts for the majority of the effort. The steps undertaken in the Filled iteration are suitable for adding sufficient detail so that you can then use the context matrix (see Section 6.10.1) to complete your picture of how the system will change.

The user community must be involved in defining the additional functionality. We have found it beneficial to walk through the full requirements lifecycle with the additional functionality. Start by defining the Facade iteration of the additional use case. If you are in the position of suggesting change control, you should use the Facade version of the additional use case as the vehicle with which to propose the change. The format is suitable because all the stakeholders are familiar with it. It is also quick to put together, and it is reasonable for inclusion into the matrix. During this process, you should be receptive to the possibility that a new use case may not be required. If possible, it's best to generalize existing functionality to meet the additional requirements.

6.7 Risks and Assumptions

While working on this iteration, you'll discover facets of the system that may not be appropriate content for a use case. Even though these observations are irrelevant to requirements gathering, it is important to record and communicate them to team members and users.

Carefully document the assumptions that underlie your requirements. The system and its scope may change significantly if these assumptions fail. For this reason, you should present the assumptions to the users with your use cases.

The following are risks to the Focused iteration.

- Neglect of a major requirement
- Overengineering of use cases
- A user group that is not comfortable with the use cases

You can control these risks by being aware of them during this iteration. Make sure that your reviewers are aware of the risks so that they can screen the requirements for these problems. If the users are not comfortable with their understanding of use cases, it is worth the effort to educate a representative user and involve him or her actively in the requirements-gathering process.

We recommend an active approach to risk management. For example, to mitigate and manage project risk we use the strategy proposed in *Rapid Development* (McConnell 1996).

6.8 Review

It is essential that somebody review your work for this iteration. Ideal candidates for reviewers are the SMEs because they have the best understanding of the business and the emerging application.

Reviewers look at use cases individually and as a part of the completed system. Each use case must be reviewed for accuracy and completeness. The reviewer must ascertain that the collection of use cases describes an adequate system.

If you are reviewing the Focused iteration, what do you look for?

6.8.1 Opportunities Not Taken

In reviewing the work done in the Focused iteration, you may be able to identify areas where further possibilities remain. Ask yourself the following questions.

- Is there duplicate functionality in the system?
- Do the use cases include unnecessary functionality?
- Are any of the processes overly complex?
- Can the team make improvements?
- Is the level of detail and refinement consistent across use cases developed by different teams and team members? (It is important to consider some of the challenges imposed by teamwork on this process. Chapter 9 discusses these issues in greater depth.)

6.8.2 System Damage

Watch for the following types of faults. You may be reviewing your own or the team's use cases, or you may be a client reviewing the work of an outsourcer.

- Have we inadvertently removed essential parts of the system?
- Will shared functionality work correctly for both processes?
- Does the set of use cases describe a system that meets the business criteria that have prompted this project?
- Does the set of use cases describe a system that meets known technical requirements?

Reacting to the Review

If you're the requirements analyst and some of your changes do not make it through the review, how will it affect you? If the review returns previously rejected functionality to the system, have the reviewer prioritize its importance. During project planning, it is helpful to know which requirements are essential to the system and which are cosmetic.

- Have any references to technology crept in?
- Has there been any attempt to design the system at this point?

In addition to looking for mistakes and omissions in the use cases, you should examine the risk and assumptions documentation and be alert for unidentified risks. You should make detailed comments on all flaws to the requirements analyst. The analyst needs to incorporate the observations and correct any defects found.

6.9 Client Sign-Off

The client's sign-off indicates that the output of this iteration is acceptable, that the assumptions are valid, and that the direction chosen is suitable.

The review and sign-off processes are sequential because we believe that a thorough review is an essential precursor for sign-off. Ideally, the reviewer should have the authority to sign off on the work.

Bold strokes are required of you during this iteration. It is important that the customer understand and accept the changes. We suggest presenting a *before and after* picture of the system to provide an explicit description of facilities that have been removed. The candidate use case list contains this information and is a useful synopsis of your work. The client should review the complete set of use cases.

6.10 Tools

A number of tools are available for your use in the Focused iteration. Let's look at each of them in turn.

6.10.1 Context Matrix

The context matrix (Figure 6.1) contains a summary of the use cases you have written. It is a version of the candidate use case list you developed in the Filled iteration and includes information that relates use cases to one another to determine priority and importance.

Make a copy of your candidate use case list. At the top, add the system description. Add columns for dependency and core.

	Use Case Title	Summary	Core	Dependency
1	The standard title	Short description of the use case	Yes	2,5,6
2			Yes	—
3			No	

Figure 6.1 *Sample Context Matrix*

Fill in each use case title and its description. You can copy and paste this information from the use cases or use the candidate list.

Determine whether the use case is a *core* part of the system. The system description describes the core; compare each use case to it. This is an assignment of importance, or priority, and not a measure of how well the use case description matches the system description.

Be flexible with this determination, and be prepared to change it often. What happens when there is a gray area? Either the use case is not part of the core, or you need to split it into more than one use case.

The intent of the context matrix is to provide context information. It is a working tool and not a deliverable. When you are considering altering a use case, the matrix will show you how the use case relates to the system.

Next, you add information that shows dependencies between high-level use cases. This is important information for making scope decisions. For example, if the use cases are not dependent on a noncore use case, it is a good candidate for scope reduction. To make this decision you must understand the dependency between use cases. The context matrix provides a tight summary of the system that you are proposing. Keep this document accessible, and alter it as your perception of the system evolves.

6.10.2 Dependency Filter

Suppose that a banking system has two types of products: investment accounts and checking accounts. The use cases that represent interactions with these products may depend on each other to some extent. The two use cases could share a use case named *Calculate Foreign Currency Exchange*. This is an example of an *include* relationship. Although a *Deposit into Checking Account* use case contains this functionality, it is also used by the *Deposit into Investment Account* use case. Both use cases must calculate the value of foreign holdings on an effective date. Therefore, there is a dependency between these two use cases, as shown in Figure 6.2.

	Use Case Title	Summary	Core	Dependency
1	*Calculate Foreign Currency Exchange*	. . .	Yes	2
2	*Deposit into Investment Account*	. . .	Yes	—
3	*Deposit into Checking Account*	. . .	Yes	2

Figure 6.2 *Dependencies Reflected in Use Cases*

This dependency is not an indication that you should combine this functionality. This could be a consistent set of use cases. At this point in the development of your use cases, it is sufficient that you make note of the dependencies.

Consider dependency when you are

- Including a use case in the system
- Adding functionality to the system
- Removing functionality from a use case

Now let's continue the example. The use cases relate to a financial services provider that allows customers to access their account information from the Web. During a meeting, the chief information officer decides not to implement the full scope of the system. She reduces scope by deciding not to implement checking account functionality until a later release. Her reasoning is strong. Market research shows that customers are more likely to switch their investment accounts than their checking accounts. Further research shows that availability of Web access is a more dominant factor in choosing an investment account. Therefore, the client will postpone the implementation of checking account access until it reaches the goal of tripling the number of investment accounts.

All that remains is to remove the *Deposit into Checking Account* use case from the candidate list. Figure 6.3 shows the matrix for this system.

What side effects will this action have on the system? Look at both sets of use cases. Where are the dependencies between them? Ask the following questions.

- Is the investment account providing any services to checking that are not used by the investment account? If it is, you have an opportunity to reduce scope without sacrificing functionality.
- Is the investment account using any checking services? If you remove checking, you must keep these functions for continued use by the investment account use cases.
- If the cuts are negotiable or debatable, this type of dependency information is appropriate to the discussion. If dependency is high between use cases, it may not be economical to cut that functionality. You must build most of it anyway.

Throughout this iteration, you examine the system for redundant information and unnecessary functionality. When you locate it, you must make a case for its removal.

Remember that the matrix is a communication tool. Each time you alter a use case, you should update the matrix.

	Use Case Title	Summary	Core	Dependency
1	*Calculate Foreign Currency Exchange*		Yes	2,4
2	*Deposit into Investment Account*		Yes	—

Figure 6.3   *Removing a Use Case from the Context Matrix*

6.10.3 Surplus Functionality Filter

*The Focused iteration is about pruning requirements
detail, duplication, and functionality (scope).*

Reduce scope in this iteration by examining each use case in relation to the system objective. Remove use cases that are tangential to these objectives. Examine each use case in isolation and remove details or features that are not required. Use the dependency information added to the matrix earlier in this chapter.

6.10.4 Narrow the Focus of the System

Now it's time to examine the set of use cases for an odd one out. Look for a use case or set of use cases that does not fit well with the remainder of the system. This use case may represent a subsystem that you can identify as a separate project. Look for noncore use cases that core use cases do not use.

Until your team understands the use cases, avoid the temptation to reduce functionality. Present your findings to the users; it is essential to involve the user community in these decisions.

6.10.5 Identify Surplus Functionality Inside the Use Case

How do you identify surplus functionality? Each use case contains a short description; you should compare the body of the use case to this description to see where additional functionality is being introduced.

This technique is analogous to the comparison you performed between each use case and the system description.

When you suspect that functionality in the use case is excessive, the next step is to decide whether the users can do without it. If they can, it is safe to remove the functionality

> **Midway Check**
>
> The context matrix provides a tight summary of the system that you are proposing. Regular team reviews ensure that everyone shares a similar perspective of the application to be built.

If the users need it and if the functionality really is a bad fit for the use case, it is reasonable to move it elsewhere, either to a new use case or into an existing use case. In either case, it has an effect on the dependency relationships to the system. After altering the system, update the matrix. This update is especially important when people are working in teams. The matrix is a communication mechanism that prevents other team members from repeating your work.

6.10.6 Vocabulary Filter

Another important technique in the Focused iteration is to examine your use of proprietary names. For example, a list of requirements that we saw a few years ago stated that the application must provide a Soundex search capability. Soundex was invented in the late 1800s as a means if identifying lost characters in telegram transmissions. Since then, it has been made obsolete (as you might guess) by a number of cheaper, better technology solutions. Did the requirements analyst really want to specify such outdated technology? Perhaps the analyst meant a *sound-alike feature* or some other nonproprietary feature.

6.11 Deliverables

The deliverables of the Focused iteration include the following.

Problem statement	Complete
Statement of work	Complete
Use cases	Focused level
Use case diagrams	Focused level
Business rule catalog	Almost complete
Risk analysis	Ongoing
Prototype	Not started

6.12 Roles

Table 6.1 shows the roles involved in the Focused iteration.

Table 6.1 Roles in the Focused Iteration

Role	Duties
Requirements analyst	Consolidates use cases and business rules, reinterviewing stakeholders to validate earlier assumptions; documents Focused use cases
Stakeholder	Participates in interviews
Executive sponsor	Requires an occasional status update
Technical architect	Refines nonfunctional requirements; participates in reviews
Project manager	Refines problem statement and statement of work

6.13 Context

During the Focused iteration you reduce the volume of specifications somewhat by making the documentation more efficient. You also bring focus to the dependencies between use cases to help identify what is happening when scope changes.

During the next iteration, you will put final touches on the documentation and refine it until it is suitable for the designers and developers, who will use it in later activities.

6.14 Summary

To meet the challenges of the Focused iteration, you must carefully analyze use cases individually and as a whole. Your goal is to ensure that each of the use cases you will carry into the Finished iteration is efficiently written and describes a necessary task in solving the business problem. You also identify all the dependencies between use cases and consolidate them wherever possible.

7

The Finished Iteration

7.1 Objectives

The Focused iteration, discussed in Chapter 6, completed the refinement of the requirements for your project. You identified the common elements between use cases and exploited them to produce a tight model of the system. Now, in the Finished iteration, you integrate the nonfunctional requirements with the use cases, add the user interface requirements, and package the documentation for the design effort.

Use cases are the primary input to the design phase. They influence the system design by communicating scope and functional descriptions of what the system must do. For example, the nouns and actors in the use cases influence the identification of objects in an object-oriented application development.

The objective of this iteration is to make reasonable decisions to craft nonfunctional requirements into concise sets that support the design of the system architecture. It may not be obvious, but nonfunctional requirements contribute to the success of an application as much as functional requirements do. At the conclusion of this iteration you should be able to visualize the completed system and should have sufficient information to plan iterative development.

7.2 Steps

To complete the Finished iteration, perform the following steps.

1. Add user interface requirements to the use case model.
2. Abstract and combine the nonfunctional requirements and associate them with use cases.
3. Make final scope decisions and get sign-off.
4. Baseline the requirements.

7.2.1 Add User Interface Requirements

Many systems have user interface requirements (batch-driven processing is the main exception). User interface requirements are best modeled outside the use case model, and that is why we discuss them in the final methodology chapter.

Because of the incongruity of user interface requirements with use cases, we have deliberately avoided capturing these requirements until now. Building the user interface is an important part of system development. Customers judge systems by the quality of the interface, and it is the "face" that people use to visualize a system. Why then do use cases put so little emphasis on this important system component? The reason is that the user interface changes more rapidly than the core business components of a system. It is essential to first capture the essence of the system and then decide how to represent this functionality to the users.

Should use cases include the user interface requirements? They can, but if a use case refers to a specific interface component, such as a list box, you will need to update this use case every time you make changes to the user interface, multiplying the effort of designing it. Moreover, details such as the alignment of controls are not easily described in words. In addition, user interface requirements clutter use cases, making them difficult to read, time-consuming to update, and generally distracting.

We choose the combination of standards documents and prototyping to capture user interface requirements. It is outside the scope of this book to investigate the prototyping process. Instead, we discuss how it fits into the use case lifecycle.

7.2.1.1 User Interface Prototypes

A user interface prototype is one tool in our toolset that helps communication between analysts and users. It focuses on the visual layout of the interactions and assists the definition of user interface requirements.

The first task in creating a prototype is to define a *visual metaphor*. This step is both critical and dangerous. Many user interface designers use metaphors that seem highly intuitive and are based in the real world. Yet, in practice, such metaphors can break down and become a barrier between the user and the application.

The metaphor should be something that harkens to real life for the users. For example, a common interface for workflow applications is the desktop, which may include components such as an in-box to hold the incoming work, an out-box to hold the completed work, and a work pool where people can go to get the next piece of work. Other examples of metaphors: a neighborhood (Geocities, Yahoo), a retail store (Amazon.com, Cyberian Outpost), an auction house (uBid, eBay), a conference room or stadium (KOZ.com Community Publishing System, eShare Expressions), and so on. These metaphors work extremely well.

However, the pitfalls of poorly crafted metaphors are numerous. Here's how Alan Cooper, a user interface guru, describes the failed General Magic MagiCap user interface in his book *About Face: The Essentials of User Interface Design*:

> I'm sure it was a lot of fun to design. I'll bet it is a real pain to use. Once you have learned that the substantial-looking building with the big AT&T on its façade is the phone company, you must forever live with going in and out of that building to call people. This most-modern, information-age software drags all of the limitations of the mechanical age into the future and forces us to live with them yet again. Is this progress? (Cooper 1995, p. 62)

After a metaphor has been crafted, the rest of the user interface is created by trial and error. Prototypes are, by definition, iterative deliverables. Create a few windows, show the users, fix and create more, show the users, and on and on.

This book isn't about quality user interface design. After discussing how use cases contribute to the development of user interfaces, we'll refer you to Cooper's fine book or the others listed in the References.

Interface specifics *plus* interface metaphors are essential ingredients for interface prototyping. Which interface specifics have been captured in the use cases?

- Processing flow
- Descriptions of the system's actors and the functionality they require
- Information displayed to each actor
- Information supplied by each actor
- Information processing performed by the system
- Nonfunctional requirements that relate to the interface

The system's processing flow describes how the various components relate to each other. The use case diagram is a good source for this information because it shows packages of related functionality. Use case preconditions describe the order in which users access system functionality.

Use cases relate roles (actors) to functionality, and the interface metaphor may depend on who is expected to use it. For example, system maintenance use cases for the system administrator actor could indicate that a simple, flexible interface would be sufficient, whereas interfaces used by a business analyst role would need to be more friendly.

Detailed use cases often contain data specifics, such as "Enter customer name," or they may contain more general information such as "Enter details to describe the property and its location." Both kinds of data provide valuable interface requirements and can include information displayed to the user or manipulated by or acquired from the user. All this is relevant to user interface design.

The exploration of nonfunctional requirements that progressed from the Filled iteration through this iteration has captured any specific must-have requirements that relate to the interface; such as voice interface, GUI, and so on. These technical constraints influence the higher-level interface design decisions.

Overall, use cases contain information that is essential to user interface design. They state what the user interface must be capable of providing, and they categorize this information by business objective and role. Each use case is concerned with the interactions that take place to achieve a particular objective.

The interface-specific information collected by use cases describes *what* the system must provide and not *how* to provide it. This is a quality criterion for requirements gathering. You are now free to implement the system's constraints and requirements in an interface that delights the users.

We recognize that the user interface prototypes are not necessarily built during the Finished iteration. We present this material here because it is at this point that the use cases provide the optimum amount of information for user interface prototyping. You can enhance the prototype as necessary as use case refinement yields results. You may also find that the prototype identifies weaknesses in the use cases and hence improves them.

7.2.1.2 Standards Guides

Standards are a convenient way to decrease the effort of documenting interface requirements and to increase the accuracy and comprehensiveness of your requirements. A user interface standards document is a useful tool for your requirements-gathering arsenal. This document is specific to an operating system and provides a set of guidelines for the look, feel, and functionality of an interface. Typically, these documents span multiple applications, and that keeps disparate systems closer to each other than they would be otherwise and reduces training and maintenance costs.

You can elect to follow standards that have been published for a platform, or you can choose to build your own so that they are most appropriate for your organization. The standards document records various interface components, their customization, and their interactions.

For example, in a GUI the standards document defines the tabbing order for fields in a window and specifies keyboard and other standard shortcuts.

Enhance your prototype by referring to a standards document, thereby reducing the effort needed to document the user interface layout. The prototype will be presented in conjunction with the standards document, with the understanding that unless otherwise noted, the standards override any omissions in the prototype. The designer and developers design and build the system from a combination of the use cases, the prototype, the window layout, and the standards document.

When the standards change, it is the standards document that is updated and not the use cases. Organizations that are building multiple concurrent projects appreciate being able to update their standards in only one place.

The introduction of the interface prototype has been included as part of the Finished iteration because typically the business is defined before the interface is. But this is not a strict rule. You should begin prototyping the user interface whenever it is useful to your requirements-gathering effort.

7.2.2 Abstract and Combine Nonfunctional Requirements

We discuss nonfunctional requirements in Chapter 6, where we describe the Filled iteration. You have documented nonfunctional requirements as you discovered them. In this iteration, we describe these nonfunctional requirements as use case stereotypes and employ this UML mechanism to tie them to use cases.

Your objective is to find similarity in the nonfunctional requirements so that you can bundle them together and associate them with use cases.

The following steps are involved in abstracting and combining nonfunctional requirements across use cases.

1. Group your use cases by similarity of nonfunctional requirements.
2. Identify stereotypes that can be associated with the functional use cases.
3. Apply the stereotypes to your use case model.

Table 7.1 shows some common stereotype definitions that may apply to your application. (See Appendix C for use case examples.)

Examine the list of nonfunctional requirements that you have been collecting since the Filled iteration. You captured each of them during requirements gathering, and you noted the use cases that they affected. Look for sets of nonfunctional requirements that are repeated in similar use cases. Some of the matches will be close, so consider altering the nonfunctional requirements so that you can apply the same set to many use cases. This will be a trade-off. For example, if some use cases specify a three-second response time and others a four-second requirement, try to choose either three or four seconds as your response time requirement. Discuss these trade-offs with the stakeholders. Explain that your goal is to simplify like nonfunctional requirements and find an acceptable middle ground.

Table 7.1   Stereotype Definitions

Stereotype	Explanation
Secure	Must use secure transactions, to protect the information traveling between the actor and the system. Note that all transactions should be protected from prying eyes, but the use cases of this stereotype are even more critical because they carry identification information about the customers or employees.
Multicustomer interaction	Must provide fail-safe synchronization between what multiple customers see coming from the system.

Create a tiered set of nonfunctional requirements. For example, in a data-intensive business application you find that you have three "types" of use case: simple transaction, complex transaction, and information-only. Simple and complex transactions require history maintenance and support for atomic transactions. In this example, simple transactions must have a subsecond response time and complex transactions must have a three-second response time. Information-only use cases are required to respond to user interaction within ten seconds. Thus, we identify three stereotypes to apply to the use case model: simple, complex, and information-only.

Not all use cases will have nonfunctional stereotypes applied to them. Update your use case documentation and diagrams to show the stereotypes.

7.2.3 Make Final Scope Decisions and Get Sign-Off

Now you present the results of your efforts to the stakeholders for their approval. Provide the completed use cases ahead of time, together with your standards documents, to allow for a proper review. Conduct a walk-through with your stakeholders and describe the purpose of each use case. Discuss any exceptional points and take comments from the stakeholders. The objective is to ascertain that your requirements are accurate and complete and that they describe the system that should be built.

Start with the abstract use cases that you built during the Focused iteration, and progress toward the concrete use cases in the various functional areas, showing how the services are used.

In addition to the stakeholders, an experienced designer should be present during this session to review the use cases. Everyone present should evaluate the use cases against the following criteria. The use cases should

- Specify system requirements to the customer
- Provide input to the designers
- Provide information for testing, training, and documentation
- Describe a system overview suitable for the project sponsor

In addition, each use case should be accurate, comprehensive, and clear.

The reviewed, completed use cases allow the system sponsors to decide what they want built and when. With a small system, this decision is often a simple one: The complete system will be built. Larger systems require a little more care. The stakeholders must decide what should be built and when. This incremental approach to developing large systems is effective in reducing risk and managing change.

Aid the sponsor in making this decision. The use cases contain sufficient details to estimate the development effort, and the context matrix indicates which use cases should be developed in groups. Use the summary to describe use cases to the sponsor.

Before meeting with the sponsor, consider which groups of use cases can sensibly be developed together and determine the best order of development. Use this information as a straw man (a target you expect to get knocked down) for the scope discussions. Document the decision and communicate it to the stakeholders. Identify which use cases will be built in each project iteration and set the time lines for development and delivery.

7.2.4 Baseline the Requirements

*Each requirements baseline represents a
line drawn in the sand.*

A *requirements baseline* is a set of documents that pass related information to the next activity in the software development process. A baseline supports the concept of *activity containment*, a best practice that provides closure to the requirements activity and helps you manage scope.

What information should you pass to the design process? Defining the contents of the requirements baseline increases the consistency of the information being supplied. You should communicate the definition of the baseline to the design team early in this process so that you can consider its feedback. This means that designers get an early chance to request additional information to describe what they will design rather than waiting for you to complete requirements gathering and approval before letting you know what the design needs really are.

Suggested contents for the requirements baseline are as follows.

- *Approved use cases*—These are use cases that have completed the Finished iteration.
- *Use case standards document*—This can be considered an explanation of the contents of each use case.

- *Other standards documents*—These are standards documents that have been identified as providing nonfunctional requirements, such as database design standards and user interface design standards. You are not trying to create an exhaustive set of standards documentation for the entire application but only enough to support the use cases.

Create a requirements baseline that contains this documentation for each of the iteration groups chosen by the project sponsor. Add the requirements baseline to what you've already gathered in configuration management.

To allow requirements tracing, define a procedure for making changes (additions, deletions, or modifications) to the requirements baseline. Define the steps for analyzing the changes and incorporating them into the requirements.

7.3 Tools

Perhaps we should say "tool," because for this iteration we describe only one: the use case review.

7.3.1 Use Case Review

Designers, when reviewing the use cases, look for sufficient clarity to develop an unambiguous understanding of the system. They need to understand both the business needs and the technical needs. If the use cases provide inadequate coverage of an area, it's best to discover it during the review.

The main question to be answered with your review is, Can my team design the application from these use cases?

Here's a checklist for designers.

1. Are the interfaces consistent?
2. Are standards followed?

7.4 Deliverables

The deliverable produced during the Finished iteration is the requirements baseline, which includes the following.

Problem statement	Complete
Statement of work	Complete
Use cases	Complete (Finished iteration)
Use case diagrams	Complete
Business rule catalog	Complete
Risk analysis	Complete

User interface guidelines	Complete
User interface requirements	Complete
Prototype	Complete

7.5 Roles

Table 7.2 shows the roles that participate in the Finished iteration.

7.6 Context

The Finished iteration is the final phase in the requirements lifecycle. It follows the Focused iteration and takes as input the use cases that have been subjected to scope decisions after their similarities have been exploited. During this iteration, you take the nonfunctional requirements that you have been collecting throughout the requirements-gathering process and request input from the users for the design of the user interface requirements. The remainder of the input comes from the project sponsor as you use the results of this iteration to finalize the scope of the system.

7.7 Summary

The Finished iteration completes the requirements-gathering portion of the project lifecycle. During this iteration, you solicit input from the users to outline the user interface requirements that will be implemented during design. You refine the project's use cases to reflect feedback from the stakeholders, get approval from the sponsor to build the project as described, and provide baseline documentation to assist in the next phases of the project.

Table 7.2 Roles in the Finished Iteration

Role	Duties
Requirements analyst	Consolidates use cases and business rules, reinterviews stakeholders to validate earlier assumptions, documents Finished use cases
Stakeholder	Participates in sign-off
Executive sponsor	Requires occasional status updates
Technical architect	Refines nonfunctional requirements, participates in reviews
Project manager	Refines problem statement and statement of work

What Skipper would

Incur the risk,

What Buccaneer would ride,

Without a surety from the wind

Or schedule of the tide?

—Emily Dickinson

Managing the Requirements Activity

Figures 8.1 and 8.2 show two drastically different approaches to getting a software project done. In this chapter we compare what is typically referred to as a waterfall approach (classic lifecycle) to a newer approach called iterative and incremental (iterative lifecycle).

In recent years, several elements of systems development have changed, altering the way managers must think about a project. Project management requires a few new tricks to make the transition to new processes that are being introduced. In reality, these new tricks are the things that good managers have been doing all along and now are simply being formalized. Methodologists follow practitioners, as it should be.

One significant change in methodology in the past five years has been the introduction of the iterative and incremental lifecycle. Instead of a steady, linear lifecycle with well-defined milestones, projects are taking a more circular, adaptive approach to the work.

Milestones, however, are still required. In the new processes, milestones are much closer to the reality of what is being created. Instead of a huge design deliverable with thousands of pages of diagrams and computer printouts, the focus is on producing code as early as humanly possible, using an approach that Grady Booch has referred to as "design a little, code a little." The real milestones are the completion of use cases: determinations of when a particular use case has been logically designed, physically designed, coded, tested, and successfully deployed. This approach is more complex and yet simpler at the same time. It makes life simpler for the developers because it reduces risk for them by letting them try

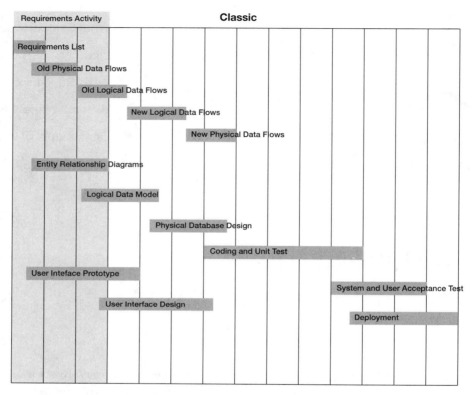

Figure 8.1 *Gantt Chart of a Classic Lifecycle*

things out earlier. It pushes more work onto the operations team, which must have the environment ready sooner, and the project manager, who must juggle these concurrent lifecycles and be fairly sure where each one *should* be and where it actually is.

Another big change has been the increased focus on what have traditionally been the "stepchildren" of the lifecycle: requirements gathering, testing, and transition activities. Quality assurance movements have dictated that we must start paying more attention to these parts of systems development. So many development efforts have failed because of the lack of attention to these activities that the former stepchildren are now full-fledged siblings to analysis, design, and construction. This means that managers need more knowledge about how to manage these formerly peripheral activities as well as those that have been considered more central.

This chapter examines how some of these factors influence the work of the project manager. We certainly can't cover all the recent management changes in one chapter, so we focus on how changes in modern software methodology alter project management.

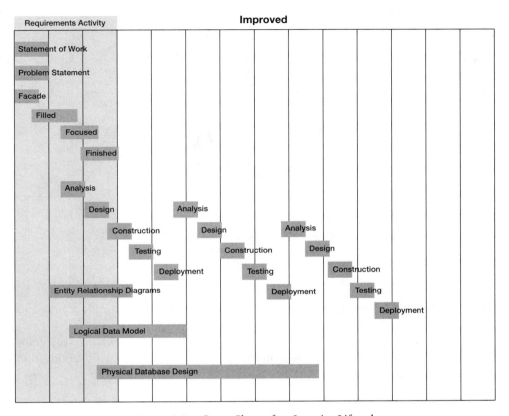

Figure 8.2 *Gantt Chart of an Iterative Lifecycle*

8.1 Managing the Iterative, Incremental Lifecycle

In the world of software development, it is simply not possible to follow a series of steps in which each step is fully completed before the next one begins. Because of the complex nature of the businesses we are modeling and assisting with software, entire systems lifecycles cannot go more than six months without seriously risking the automation of obsolete requirements. And even within that six-month lifecycle, business changes can upset the development effort at any point during requirements gathering, construction, testing—whenever.

Scientists are questioning their own linear pursuits. *Complexity*, one of the celebrated so-called new sciences, describes our world (in terms of physics, biology, economics, computer science, and so on) as so complex that it is pointless to try to predict anything. Essentially, when we write the requirements specification for a system to be built six months hence, we are foolishly predicting that those will be the requirements at that future time. But if you can't predict anything, what's the point?

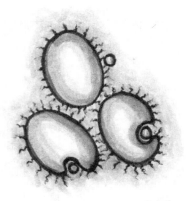

*High-quality use cases should be able
to adapt to their environments.*

The point is that it is more important to *adapt* than to *predict*. The projects that can adapt quickly and efficiently to the inevitable changes are the projects that will succeed. This means that taking a linear approach to development is no longer an option.

David Rubin, a friend of ours in the software business, has a habit of saying, "You know the plan is wrong. Now go with it!" How do you know that the requirements specification you just produced is wrong?

1. It's very difficult to get requirements correct the first time, given imperfect human communication, complex business procedures, and elusive exception conditions.
2. The requirements specification is a prediction for the post-rollout business environment, which is going to be different then from what it is now.

That's why the iterative and incremental lifecycle has replaced the waterfall lifecycle. The new process acknowledges that "it's always wrong" and that you'll have to go back and do it over again.

The best-known iterative and incremental lifecycle at the time of this writing is Rational Software's Rational Unified Process. RUP is a well-thought-out collection of lifecycle phases, activities, roles, and workflows. It embodies the iterative and incremental mentality and provides steps and advice for former "waterfallers" who want to make the switch. We recommend RUP highly.

8.1.1 Why Switch from Waterfall?

The waterfall methodology has been the computer industry's mainstay for several decades. It can be summarized as "Finish one phase before starting the next." Basically, you must

Water falls down, making it difficult to go back up against the rushing stream.

completely finish gathering requirements and documenting them extensively before moving on to analysis, design, and so on.

This approach makes sense in a small context. Why would you code something before being aware of the requirements and attempting a design? Such a method really can't be refuted at any level. However, when this approach shifts to a larger context, things become murkier. If there are 50 use cases and eight people gathering requirements, what are the consequences of completing the requirements specification and wrapping it up in a big bow before continuing on to analysis?

8.1.1.1 Postponing Risk Assessment Doesn't Make It Go Away

Waterfall methodologies push the risk for a project to the back end. When you forgo early testing of the assumptions about what can or can't be done, dangerous risks lurk for weeks or months, only to rear up later and swallow project teams whole. It's not as if the managers do not know that the risks are there; usually, they do. But the methodology says, "Don't even think about writing that code snippet until you've finished the page formatting on the design deliverable." As we've said before, the really good managers don't pay attention to this mandate. They try prototyping the risky areas early anyway, calling it *proof-of-concept* or some other innocent-sounding name. But the waterfall methodology does not condone such behavior, so instead of disciplining these managers, the industry has decided to formalize these approaches and dump the waterfall approach.

We are all familiar with the consequences of waterfall approaches. Everyone puts in extensive overtime toward the end of construction and during testing and transition. The application gets delivered late with fewer features than promised to a less-than-thrilled user community. Ever experience that?

8.1.1.2 The Business Changes Under Your Feet

When the waterfall methodologies were created, it was common for an organization to go an entire year without any fundamental changes in the way it did business. In recent years this has become uncommon. Businesses can't count on going an entire quarter without dramatic changes resulting from competitive pressures, new technology, or market shifts.

In essence, you will never, ever be finished with your requirements document if you take a waterfall approach. No sooner will you be 80 percent of the way through than the company will announce a major reengineering effort that will rock your world.

So what do you do?

8.1.2 The Meaning of "Incremental"

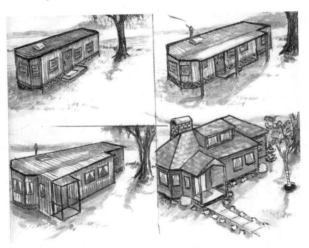

If you build your house incrementally, you can live in it the whole time.

The words *incremental* and *iterative* are often used interchangeably. They are probably almost as maligned as *use case* and *scenario*.

> *Incremental* means creating something one piece at a time and integrating the pieces into the whole a little at a time.

In incremental development, you create something in small parts. If you were building a house incrementally, you'd build one room at a time. First, you'd put up the bathroom. Then you'd add a bedroom. You'd put a little door on this tiny house to keep it warm. At this point you could even start living in it. Next, you'd add a kitchen. Then a living room. Then a dining room and an extra bedroom. The creation of each room is not willy-nilly—it follows a grand design—and the benefit is that you can start living in the house a lot sooner than if you waited for the whole house to be built. What's more, you will need heating, ventilation, plumbing, and electricity for just the bathroom, the first increment. So you get to try working with these elements early in the project, giving yourself an opportunity to evaluate the risks and problems very early.

Alistair Cockburn calls this kind of methodology *build-deliver-learn*. By cutting the application into lots of small chunks of functionality and delivering them separately, you get a chance to learn from your mistakes during the early iterations.

In the context of this book, an incremental approach to requirements specification includes completing batches of use cases and business rules together but not assuming that all artifacts must be completed at the same time.

SEE ALSO: http://members.aol.com/acockburn/

8.1.3 The Meaning of "Iterative"

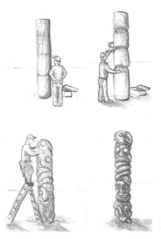

You can build a totem pole by refining the raw log through successive iterations of increasing fidelity.

Iterative means redoing something several times, increasing its richness, comprehensiveness, and consistency each time.

Think of painting a house iteratively. First, you put on a primer coat. This is often a completely different color from the one you are going to use later, but it works well for a primer coat. You just slap it on, not worrying about whether it is perfectly even or whether it looks nice. Then you add the first coat of the finish paint. This coat is the right color, but it is still a little uneven when it is applied. Perhaps another coat is required to smooth out the color and texture because some parts of the wood soak up more paint than others. In the final iteration, you apply the finishing coat of paint. This paint must be evenly applied and nicely textured. It should look exactly right in all places. It should cover every area of the house, even the nooks and crannies.

Look at the illustration of the totem pole being constructed iteratively. Notice how the artisan goes through stages of *doneness*, making each pass a little more detailed and defined. He may have to shave off some carved bits of wood in a later pass. In software development, this is called *recoding*, or, more accurately, *refactoring*.

In the context of this book, an iterative approach to requirements specification includes the refinement of use cases and business rules through a series of brushstrokes, which we categorize as the Facade, Filled, Focused, and Finished iterations.

In *The Unified Software Development Process*, Jacobson, Booch, and Rumbaugh (1999) outline several things that iteration is not:

- Random hacking
- A playpen for developers
- Something that affects only developers
- Redesigning the same thing over and over until the developers finally chance on something that works
- Unpredictable
- An excuse for failing to plan and manage

8.1.4 From Waterfall to Iterative and Incremental

Our friend Steve Frison has mapped a transition from the waterfall methodology to the iterative and incremental methodology. He believes strongly that organizations can't make it in one hop! Following are Frison's steps to get your organization from waterfall to iterative and incremental.

8.1.4.1 Staged Delivery

The first hop is to staged delivery. Most waterfallers can understand and appreciate this. You break a big application into smaller chunks and then proceed in a waterfall lifecycle for each chunk. Each stage has an integration phase during which the new stage is integrated and tested with the older stages.

8.1.4.2 Incremental Construction and Integration

The next big hop is incremental construction and integration. Here, all activities are waterfall activities except construction. Construction proceeds as a series of builds, which are integrated after each short period—perhaps a week or two. This technique dramatically reduces the risks of a big-bang integration but also requires a lot of automation in configuration management and deployment.

8.1.4.3 Incremental Waterfall

During incremental waterfall, each increment is approached from requirements through transition as a separate application. The increment has its own lifecycle, but instead of being delivered to the customer, it simply gets incorporated with the previous increments. Then requirements gathering starts again on the next increment. This approach introduces some important concepts in how to produce increments outside construction.

8.1.4.4 Iterative and Incremental

Finally, the team can begin to experiment with a fully iterative and incremental lifecycle. All activities—requirements gathering, analysis, design, construction, testing, and transition—are performed iteratively and incrementally. True iteration, with increasing fidelity and completeness at each pass, and with some code being scrapped and rewritten, is achieved.

8.1.5 Developers Love It, but Managers Struggle

In our experience, introducing iterative and incremental concepts into the lifecycle is greeted with glee by developers. The usual question is, Why did it take us so long to start this?

Managers, however, glower at the iterative and incremental lifecycle and treat it with disdain. They see the adoption of these new concepts as the destruction of their fondly held document-driven lifecycles of the past. The biggest stumbling block for managers is that the structure of the system is decoupled from the project plan. For years, managers have been building project plans that are tightly coupled to the design of an application that hasn't yet been created. For example, the project plan has estimates for the order entry, sales calculation, and general ledger post subsystems. Even though this arrangement creates a lot more work every time the system's structure morphs throughout the lifecycle, managers cling to their tightly coupled methodology, perhaps because they have invested so much of their expertise in creating it. Now the project plan must be revamped for each major shift in the design. No project planning tools that we know of are linked automatically to the analysis and design tools so that these shifts can be transmitted easily and simply. Instead, the managers wind up changing their hard-won plans to reflect the shifts. Or, worse, the managers resist the changes to the application because it is too much work to change the plan. Significant work is needed from managers to move from the traditional waterfall lifecycle to iterative and incremental. However, the increase in productivity from developers and the dramatic decrease in risk make it worthwhile, even for project managers!

When you plan an iterative and incremental project, take care to get the benefit of overlapping iterations and try not to shorten the lifecycle artificially by starting all iterations at the same time. Later iterations rely on the initial iterations as their input, so if you start them all simultaneously you will starve the later iterations of quality input, and productivity will suffer. Choose a reasonable overlap between successive iterations so that later ones can gain from the earlier ones.

On a project a couple of years ago, we instituted an incremental (but not very iterative) construction cycle that worked well, and the developers liked it. But the manager, who was from a highly structured background, was at her wit's end. She wanted to get rid of the new process but couldn't argue with its success. Finally, she asked the incremental integration team leader, "Could you at least change the name?" He didn't, but the manager learned to live with the new process and actually began to thrive with it after a while.

RUP separates the terminology used by managers and developers. Developers concern themselves with *workflows*, which are the typical activities: *requirements gathering, analysis, design,* and so on. Managers get a new set of terminology to describe the phases, which are not tightly linked to the workflows: *inception, elaboration, construction, transition, evolution.* Managers manage to these phases, and developers happily iterate and increment through their workflows.

Walker Royce describes this topic extensively in his excellent text *Software Project Management: A Unified Framework* (1998).

8.2 The Role of the Scenario in Management

Much of what managers do revolves around collecting, analyzing, and reporting on metrics. If we take away the subsystems of the application for breaking up the work, how can progress be reported and measured? One way is to use scenarios to help manage packages of work.

A scenario—one path through a use case—is an appropriate granularity of functionality for managers. Scenarios move through the phases that RUP defines for managers: inception, elaboration, construction, transition, and evolution. Clusters of scenarios make up each iteration. The end of inception might mean that all the general use cases have been defined. Elaboration might mean that 20 percent of the scenarios have been realized (implemented in code). Construction might mean that all scenarios have been realized in code and are verified to work, and transition implies that all scenarios are in the hands of the users. Evolution is ongoing maintenance, during which scenarios are changed or added to the application.

8.3 Using Scenarios to Plan, Schedule, and Estimate

Scenarios are effective building blocks for creating project plans, especially during design, development, and testing. Geri Schneider and Jason Winters provide details of estimating work with use cases in their book *Applying Use Cases: A Practical Guide* (1998). The methodology was created by Gustav Karner of Objectory AB (later acquired by Rational Software).

We have never used such a detailed methodology for estimating. Frankly, we've also never had much luck with function-point estimating, which is similarly detailed and precise. Perhaps a detailed estimating process based on many interrelated factors is not our style. We tend to create estimates based on a *simple-medium-complex* view of scenarios. Each scenario (or use case variation, if you prefer) becomes a unit of work that must be designed, constructed, and tested. In other words, you use scenarios, instead of modules or programs, as the basis for your estimations. Next, you categorize the scenarios into simple, medium, or complex. Then you assign to those scenarios a number of hours that seems reasonable (be willing to adapt—remember complexity theory) and proceed. As you begin each construction iteration, you must identify into what physical modules the scenario translates. For example, an *Enter Payment by Check* scenario might translate into

- Five Java servlets
- Three database tables
- Changes to five other tables
- An interface to a general ledger system

However, the estimating metric stays at the scenario level. Thus, no work is performed until the whole scenario is finished. But underneath the scenario, you have an effective checklist for developers to follow.

Also, project managers should assign work based on scenarios. Each scenario should be of a granularity (see Chapter 5) that allows it to be assigned to one person or a small group of people. In that way, when construction of the scenario is complete, you have a demonstrable milestone because you can prove that it works. Demonstrable milestones help everyone: the project manager (because they give the project good visibility), developers (because they supply motivation and a sense of pride), and users (because they provide signs of visible progress).

8.4 You Know the Plan Is Wrong

You know the plan is wrong. Now go with it!

—DAVID RUBIN

It sounds counterintuitive, but understanding that your workplan is wrong from the minute you finish it is an important mind-set in project planning. We have worked with project managers who complete their plan and then do everything in their power to protect it and make sure that no changes ever soil it. But projects work better when the project plan is nothing more than an ongoing negotiation. None of us can plan the future perfectly, or even come close to it. But we can make some early attempts with a flexible attitude that the plan is destined to be changed soon after it has been created, and often after that.

The requirements activity is especially spongy in the area of planning. Because you do not have a system definition of any kind, it is even more difficult to plan. Thus, the only thing to do is to create a plan with the tidbits of information you have and proceed somewhat blindly.

8.5 The Atmosphere During Requirements Gathering

Requirements gathering and specification are characterized by hectic activity, fear of the future, and the need for free-flowing adaptability.

8.5.1 Hectic Activity

A completion deadline is usually associated with requirements gathering. But because no one knows much about the new application, it is hard to say how long it will take to gather requirements. This means that you will almost always underestimate it. The other force at work is the various stakeholders, each of whom attempts to have the new computer application accomplish his or her specific goals, perhaps failing to consider the impact on the needs of other stakeholders. The result is scope creep.

So you will have too many requirements to document and too little time to do it. Expect this activity to be hectic no matter how well it is managed. To keep things from getting manic, however, there are two things a manager can do.

- *Exploit preconditions and postconditions to define scope early in use case development.* The preconditions specify the state of the application before the use case, and the postconditions define it afterward. Using this tool allows you to understand and define scope before the use cases are fully developed. Changing preconditions and postconditions are a sign that scope has changed. Use candidate use case lists to manage scope. Adding another use case (or even another scenario) adds to the size of the requirements effort and therefore jeopardizes the deadline.
- *Keep the requirements analysts on track.* Have sessions with each of them often to guide them back to the original objectives of the application.

8.5.2 Fear of the Future

Fear of the future is extremely common during requirements gathering. The team is creating some nontechnical specifications for an application that is to be implemented using all kinds of technology. People ask themselves, Will it work? What risks are we getting ourselves into? These questions are logical. At this moment the only solace for the team is that getting comfortable with uncertainty is a valuable skill to gain. Being able to complete tasks in the present while the future remains uncertain is difficult, especially for people who are methodical and detail-oriented. However, it is an essential skill because it will always be necessary to be able to complete present tasks without falling into "analysis paralysis."

8.5.3 Free-Flowing Adaptability

Requirements gathering must be as free-flowing as possible. There will be times when the entire direction is called into question. Think about these crises this way: Wouldn't you rather face these issues at this time than later in development? Now is the time to wrench from one direction to another. Later it will not be possible without putting the entire project at risk.

8.6 Managing Application and Architecture Requirements

Application designers are interested in functional requirements and business rules. Architects are interested primarily in nonfunctional requirements and technical constraints. In general, you should collect the functional requirements before you collect the nonfunctional requirements. Therefore, it is likely that the architects will need to wait to collect nonfunctional requirements until the application people have at least made a good start on the functional requirements.

Obviously, there will be a lot of overlap. The idea of perfectly consecutive tasks went away when waterfall lifecycles died. However, there is still a waiting period for architects as they allow the first functional requirements to be documented and verified.

8.7 Ensuring Quality in Requirements

In their excellent book *Requirements Engineering: A Good Practice Guide*, Ian Sommerville and Pete Sawyer (1997) outline some important processes to help ensure high-quality requirements and to facilitate changes to the requirements as time goes by. We've updated their list of rules and deleted a few that don't apply to our context.

Physical Management of Artifacts

Physical management of business rules is a tricky proposition. In the past, we simply used the most obvious combination.

- Word processing documents for each use case (Microsoft Word)
- An analysis and design tool for use case diagrams (GDPro, Rational Rose, or Select Enterprise)
- A spreadsheet for business rules storage and candidate use case lists (Microsoft Excel)
- PVCS or MKS Source Integrity to maintain version control of the documents

Frankly, there is probably a better way. In his book *Object-Oriented Project Management with UML*, Murray Cantor (1998) explains that he has used an intranet to store and retrieve use case information. This technique makes a lot of sense. The intranet could also provide a portal to the database of business rules and use case entries, and it could easily be linked to each individual use case Web page. Although we haven't tried this method, we fully intend to do so right after we finish this book! See Figure 8.3 for an example of a document management system for the requirements activity.

8.7.1 Provide Unique Identification for Use Cases and Business Rules

Use cases and business rules, and many of the ideas in this book, are meant to reduce volumes of documentation during requirements gathering. However, large projects will still produce a high volume of documentation. Part of managing such documentation is being able to identify individual items. That's why you should assign numbers to each use case and each business rule.

8.7.2 Use a Database to Store Use Cases and Business Rules

Databases also assist in managing volume. The numbers and names of the use cases should be kept in a multiuser database to facilitate status reporting and scope management. The database should be automatically linked to the analysis and design tool in which the use cases are created. Business rules naturally belong in a database.

8.7.3 Identify Change Cases

This idea of identifying *change cases* comes from Sommerville and Sawyer (1997) and was brought to our attention by our friend and coworker Mat Henshall. It is also an idea that Scott Ambler, the process mentor of Ambysoft, has championed in the last few years. Change cases can be marked in the use case and business rules databases. For each use case and

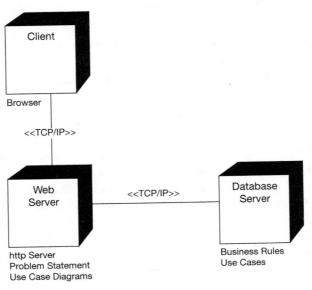

Figure 8.3 *Document Management System*

business rule, there should be a note explaining how likely it is to change, and why. Certain use cases are very susceptible to changes, especially those that are related to legislation or the competitive environment. The effort to isolate such use cases from the rest of the system should be extensive during design and construction.

Anyone who worked on state welfare applications in the late 1980s or early 1990s knows about change cases. By 1995, most states had finished their applications to handle all current federally approved programs—Aid to Families with Dependent Children, food stamps, and so forth. Within two years, the Clinton administration and Congress introduced sweeping new legislation that killed these programs and replaced them with work-for-welfare programs. Most states had to tear out their old applications (some of them only two or three years old) and replace them with something to handle the new legislation. Hopefully, we've learned our lessons, and the next generation of welfare applications is built with extremely adaptable components that can tolerate change, especially in those areas we've identified as change cases.

8.8 A Management Challenge

The requirements activity is a serious management challenge. The most important tool for the manager is willingness to change. Take another look at the time-worn management processes you're using. Dust them off and adapt them to the new techniques of delivering software. You'll be happy you did, and so will your team.

9

Working in Teams

In all but the smallest projects, we approach problems by dividing into teams. The team members share the work and have the same objectives. The concept of adding people to get work completed quickly is an old one. A lot of study has been conducted in the dynamics of teamwork, estimating and managing teams, and what makes a team productive. There are many excellent sources for this information, and this chapter is not concerned with this topic. Rather, this chapter discusses how to develop use cases in teams, including how to split up the system for groups or individuals to work on and how to avoid the quality issues that team development can introduce.

9.1 Organizing by Team

The use case team is an extended team. In addition to the analysts who write the use cases, the team must include reviewers, SMEs, and the sign-off authority. It is essential to identify these resources at the start of requirements analysis to involve them early in the process, to schedule their time, and to ensure that they understand their roles.

Your extended team will include the following.

- *Subject matter experts*—The SMEs are your primary source for requirements and are essential to your team. They understand the business rules and the processes needed in the system. Use case analysts have significant interaction with this role, especially during the Facade and Filled iterations. It is not essential that the SMEs understand use cases unless they also fulfill a reviewing role.
- *Designers*—Use cases are the primary input to the design phase, so you should include a representative from the design team in your extended use case team. The designer's role is to ensure that the use cases contain sufficient input to the design team. Designers should review the use cases as they are being developed and should provide feedback to the use case analysts. To ensure that you are providing a sufficient amount of detail, incorporate their feedback into your use cases.
- *Testers*—If the test team bases its work on use cases, it is appropriate for testers to be involved with use case development. In this way, the testers can understand and plan for the scope of the system and ensure that the use cases are sufficient for testing needs. An informal review role is sufficient to achieve this aim. As with feedback provided by the designers, you should use the testers' input to ensure that there is sufficient detail available for testing.
- *Sign-off authority*—Communicate early and often with your sign-off authority. Keep him or her appraised of the status of your efforts and communicate your project standards. This role should approve the use case template and standards document at the start of this work. This role is also responsible for approving scope decisions.

After identifying each of these roles, communicate them to your team. Give each member of the extended team your project plan, and meet with them to ensure that they understand your expectations for their roles. The SMEs and the sign-off authority may not be full-time resources on the project. Help them understand their time and schedule commitments. If they are not able to commit sufficiently to your project, backup resources must be found.

In addition to paying attention to the composition of the extended team, it is important to balance the experience levels of the team members who will gather the requirements. If you have too few experienced analysts, you risk having mediocre requirements. This will be true regardless of the techniques or methodology used. Experienced analysts are skilled in interviewing users and avoiding the trap of premature design, and they will miss fewer requirements. Each project's requirements-gathering activity also offers an opportunity for team members to better their skills, and they will learn most from experienced mentors.

9.2 Splitting Up the Work

As with all types of project work, one of the preliminary steps is to assign tasks to your staff. How do you split up the work of requirements gathering and documentation among the team members?

Our approach is to involve all use case analysts during the Facade iteration and to use its results to assign work to individuals. Create the Facade iteration during work sessions that include all analysts. This approach provides the work breakdown for individual assignments and communicates the application scope to all analysts. In this way they can grasp the context of the bigger problem within which they create their solutions.

The Facade iteration identifies all the major ways that the user interacts with the application and documents them in the system context use case and the lower-level use cases. The Facade use cases are a convenient unit for assigning work. Each Facade use case is assigned to either an individual or a group depending on the size of the system. If a Facade use case is assigned to a group, its component use cases, the candidate use cases, are assigned to individuals. Be flexible with assignments. The goal is to assign coherent groups of use cases. Be prepared to change the split as your understanding of the system develops.

During the Facade iteration, the system context use case is broken into candidate use cases that are refined and elaborated during the Filled iteration. But it helps team members focus during their requirements gathering.

Assign the system context diagram and the overall use case diagram to an individual who has ownership of these system-level descriptions. As each iteration refines your team's vision of the system, these diagrams should be updated.

9.3 Deploying Configuration Management

We strongly recommend that you employ a well-understood configuration management system for the use cases. Whether you are using a tool that specifically facilitates use case development, such as Rational Rose, or you use a general-purpose word processor, you should be able to find a configuration management product to suit your environment.

The objective is to minimize the amount of work that can be lost due to error (human and computer) and changes. The second objective is to be able to locate and read old versions of your use cases. Whatever your approach, it pays to invest time up-front to ensure that the team (even if it is a team of one) is comfortable with the standards you have set for avoiding loss.

9.4 Avoiding Quality Problems

Team use cases are prone to three specific kinds of faults.

- Missing requirements
- Inconsistent use cases
- Redundant use cases

Let's look at how you can avoid these kinds of problems.

9.4.1 Catch All the Requirements

The first potential problem for team development is that some requirements may be missed. Not all of the requirements fit neatly within a Facade use case; some of them straddle Facade use cases and appear to be requirements of more than one use case. When the team is gathering requirements, each person may assume that another person has responsibility for a requirement. The result is a requirement that does not get documented.

Communication and reviews help to prevent this problem. During reviews, in addition to looking at each use case to ensure that it follows standards and is complete, the reviewers must consider the completeness of the solution. The sum of the use cases must be sufficient to describe the complete system. Check that the inputs and outputs of each use case do not require additional processing.

As we have mentioned in earlier chapters, there are two types of requirements: functional and nonfunctional. Of the two, nonfunctional requirements are the more likely to be neglected. Increase your team's awareness of the importance of capturing these requirements, and have everyone look for them as they find and write functional use cases. Finding and documenting nonfunctional use cases is discussed in Chapter 5.

9.4.2 Create Consistent Use Cases

The biggest snag in team use case development is inconsistency. Your requirements are used to decide what to build, design, and test. All these lifecycle activities depend on the interpretation and understanding of the requirements. Consistency across all the use cases increases the chances of good quality input into later iterations. Creating consistent use cases challenges even a single analyst! Your ideas and methods evolve over the course of a project, so descriptions that were fumbling in one use case may be eloquent in another. In a team setting, this effect is magnified. Not only do people have different ideas, but their elocution also differs.

Use cases can exhibit various kinds of inconsistency.

- *Granularity*—It is necessary to have similar granularity (explained in Chapter 5) across all the use cases that describe a system. To help achieve that, communicate granularity decisions to the entire team. The extended team comes into play here because the people who inherit the use cases as an input to design can add value to your granularity discussions. Ultimately, they will base the design on them. Other stakeholders, such as the executive sponsor, may prefer to see large pieces of the system in a small number of use cases. The system context use case (see Chapter 4) provides this summary view.

- *Level of detail, vocabulary, and the use case template*—You can best address these items by creating a use case standards document, which should provide a concise guide to how you want the team to approach these tasks. To coordinate the vocabulary you use in the use cases, it is a good idea to include some sample use cases. This document should itself be a deliverable.
- *Technique*—Answer the technical questions up-front so that all team members apply the same answers. Many of these technical questions are developed in sidebars throughout this book. An example is, When should I employ the *extend* relationship, and when is a *precondition* more suitable? It is good practice to discuss these questions among your team members early and to agree to their resolution. This technique gives you the jump on this level of consistency.

9.4.3 Avoid Use Case Redundancy

There is little chance for redundancy when you develop the Facade use cases because the resulting set of use cases is small. As you develop the Filled use cases, potentially redundant information is added to the model. The same problems may be being solved, separately, across the set of use cases. It is during the Focused iteration that you abstract some of these solutions so that you can apply one solution to a number of problems.

If the Focused iteration is performed by a group of individuals on their own use cases, you will lose a valuable opportunity to exploit commonality across the system. Instead, the Focused use cases should be written and reviewed by the group. Everyone who is working on the Focused and Finished iterations should have a full view of all the use cases that make up the system; otherwise, similarities, redundancies, and unnecessary scope are identified only across groups of use cases and not across the entire system. Part of the work of focusing the use cases includes reviewing and understanding all the use cases in the application. If each individual does this and focuses his or her use cases, this gives the first cut of the Focused system. After that, the final take on the Focused iteration should be performed as a group.

10

Good judgment comes from experience and experience comes from bad judgment.

—FREDERICK P. BROOKS

Classic Mistakes

10.1 Mistakes, Pitfalls, and Bruised Knees

Making mistakes is the biggest part of learning. To bolster the learning process, great managers encourage their teams to make mistakes early and often. Whether encouraged or not, we've always strived to get on with the mistakes so that we can reach the point at which we're doing things better.

In this chapter, we point out the mistakes we've made or that we've observed others making. Our main reason is not to help you avoid making these mistakes; you'll make them anyway. Instead, our aim is to help you recognize the mistakes when you make them and to help you move quickly to other ways of doing things. The preceding chapters have been "what to do." This chapter is "what to do and then move on."

Antipatterns

Within the patterns movement in the computer industry, a new type of artifact has cropped up called the *antipattern*. Essentially, antipatterns are good solutions to commonly created bad solutions. Perhaps what we've called "classic mistakes" could also be called "antipatterns for requirements."

10.2 Classic Mistakes: Make Them and Move On

Tables 10.1 through 10.7 describe the classic mistakes people make when they're gathering and specifying requirements, particularly those mistakes related to use cases. The tables are organized into general areas: perspective, messiness, thriftiness, overengineering, mismanagement, context, and notation. You can use them as a reference, and perhaps it would be good to bring them out from time to time to remind the team of the usual mistakes that happen. If you and your team tend to err in a particular way—say, overengineering—you can put more focus on that section in your discussions.

Table 10.1 Classic Mistakes of Perspective

Number	Classic Mistake	It Causes	Related Sections
001	Creating inside-out use cases	It is easy for developers to create inside-out use cases, which operate from the perspective of the application and not the user. The problem is that users often don't understand this perspective because it is not natural for them.	2.4.1.2 No Implementation-Specific Language
002	Including user interface details in use cases	Embedding user interface details in use cases is actually quite acceptable—after requirements have been gathered. But during requirements gathering, keep user interface details out. They serve only as a distraction from the interactions that need to occur.	1.5.4 Prototypes 2.4.1.2 No Implementation-Specific Language
003	Expanding the system boundary	It is difficult to keep in mind the scope of the system you're developing. For example, if a security identification system is connected to your application, is it inside the boundary? Or is it an actor? Or should it not be shown on use case diagrams? It depends on whether this project team is responsible for implementing and testing it. If it is an integrated component, it's inside the boundary and not shown in the use case diagram. If it is a separate system done by a separate team, it becomes an actor.	2.4.2.1 Actors and Roles Appendix A
004	Creating use case interactions that don't provide value to an actor	Use cases must generally provide value to an actor. The actor doesn't necessarily have to be the same one who provides the input for the use case.	2.4.1.1 Interactions That Provide Value to Actors

155

Table 10.2 Classic Mistakes of Messiness

Number	Classic Mistake	It Causes	Related Sections
001	Keeping temporary requirements lists	A common mistake is to keep a contraband list of requirements off to the side and then incorporate them into the use cases as they make sense. This means you're doing the work twice; the second time you're just changing the format of the requirements from a list to use cases. This is an acceptable first step into the world of use cases, but it should not become a practice, simply because it is extra work.	Chapter 1, The Trouble with Requirements Chapter 3, A Use Case–Driven Approach to Requirements Gathering
002	Grouping use cases or business rules poorly	It helps a lot to group the use cases, but this is difficult to do. Group use cases and business rules in ways that make sense to the stakeholders. Group use cases using UML packages. Group business rules using category columns in the business rules catalog.	Chapter 9, Working in Teams
003	Having use cases without an owner	Each use case should have an owner. Use cases that are not assigned ownership are often not modified consistently throughout the iterations.	Chapter 8, Managing the Requirements Activity Chapter 9, Working in Teams
004	Having use cases with too many owners	A use case that has too many owners will die a death no less painful than those without any owner. No one really owns it, and people make contradictory changes to the use case, wasting precious time.	Chapter 9, Working in Teams

Number	Classic Mistake	It Causes	Related Sections
005	Including too many cross-references in use case text	Some use case textbooks list various ancillary sections in their use case templates that duplicate information from the use case diagram or other places. Don't include these sections. This is duplicate work that you will have to spend time modifying when things change later in the lifecycle or during maintenance. Here is a subset of these sections: actor lists, included use cases, activity diagrams, user interface, sequence diagrams, subordinate use cases, participating classes. Two exceptions: a primary actor (just one) and extension points.	2.4.3 The Use Case Template
006	Not keeping use cases and business rules in a database	The need to cross-reference, sort, and list the use case titles and business rules means that a database or spreadsheet is the most appropriate place for use cases, especially for a large system.	8.7.2 Use a Database to Store Use Cases and Business Rules
007	Trying to build extensive exception logic into the basic course of events	The purpose of the Exception Paths section in the template is to document paths that occur when something goes wrong. Don't try to put all this in the Basic Course of Events section.	2.4.1.2 No Implementation-Specific Language 2.4.1.3 User-Appropriate Level of Detail 2.4.3 The Use Case Template

Table 10.3 Classic Mistakes of Thriftiness

Number	Classic Mistake	It Causes	Related Sections
001	Skipping iterations	There is a tendency to skip iterations in requirements, especially for those coming from a big-bang waterfall mind-set. For very small projects, it may sometimes make sense, but usually it is wise to go through the four iterations or at least to address all the individual steps detailed in the iteration chapters if fewer iterations are required.	Chapter 4, The Facade Iteration Chapter 5, The Filled Iteration Chapter 6, The Focused Iteration Chapter 7, The Finished Iteration
002	Skipping interview notes that don't fit	If some requirements from the interviews don't fit into the current iteration, people tend to skip them, thinking that they'll come back in the iteration they're supposed to. They might not! Keep free-form notes that don't fit the use cases or business rules of the current iteration and review these notes during each subsequent iteration.	Chapter 4, The Facade Iteration Chapter 5, The Filled Iteration Chapter 6, The Focused Iteration Chapter 7, The Finished Iteration
003	Holding on to use cases that don't belong	Thrifty people hate to throw things away. However, extraneous use cases or business rules that don't belong should be tossed. Version control is helpful here. Throw things away. If you need them later, you can go back a version or two and retrieve them.	Chapter 9, Working in Teams

Table 10.4 Classic Mistakes of Overengineering

Number	Classic Mistake	It Causes	Related Sections
001	Neglecting useful tools within use cases	A use case does not have to be text only. Within a use case, it is perfectly acceptable, even encouraged, to have diagrams, tables, flowcharts, or any other graphic representation that best tells what is happening in the use case. Decision tables for complex logic are a great example.	2.4.3 The Use Case Template
002	Creating CRUD use cases first	CRUD table maintenance is often an acceptable use case, but these use cases should not be the first ones you work on. The first use cases to be created should be those that provide the most value to the actors. CRUD value is almost always subordinate to the major business processes.	5.2.1.1 Identify and Summarize Each Use Case
003	Using computer terminology in use cases	During the requirements activity, all use cases should be in language that the users understand. No computer terminology (LANs, WANs, GUI elements, servers, workstations, screens, windows, and so on) should be used.	2.4.1.2 No Implementation-Specific Language
004	Writing pseudocode for use case text	Use cases are descriptions of interactions between actors and an application. They are not pseudocode or code. They should be written in English (or Spanish or French) and not in OCL, OQL, or anything else remotely machine-readable.	2.4.1.2 No Implementation-Specific Language 2.4.3 The Use Case Template
005	Assuming that the *extend* relationships between use cases dictate class inheritance in design	This is more a mistake of analysis or design. It is natural to assume that the *extend* relationships shown in the use cases will translate into inheritance relationships in a class diagram. There is no correlation between *extend* and class inheritance in design.	Appendix A

continues

Table 10.4 *continued*

Number	Classic Mistake	It Causes	Related Sections
006	Assuming that the *include* relationships between use cases dictate class responsibilities in design	This is a mistake of analysis or design (or both). It is natural to assume that the *include* relationships shown in the use cases will translate to specific classes that should be extracted and assigned specific responsibilities. There is no correlation between *include* and class creation or responsibility assignment in design.	Appendix A
007	Confusing actors with specific people or organizational positions	Actors are roles. One person might play several roles, and one role might be played by several people. To avoid redesigns when organizational or staffing changes occur, you should not couple actor definitions to specific people or organizational positions.	2.4.2.1 Actors and Roles
008	Making business process assumptions that are not verified	There's the way things should work, and then there's the way they do work. While you're creating use cases and business rules, verify, verify, verify. Common sense has nothing to do with it.	Chapter 4, The Facade Iteration Chapter 5, The Filled Iteration Chapter 6, The Focused Iteration Chapter 7, The Finished Iteration
009	Putting everything into one use case diagram	This is extremely common. Why not show every possible use case in one diagram and depict the relationships between all? This is a classic mistake because it is too much for users to take in all at once. Instead, break the system into use case packages, show all packages on one diagram, and then break down the packages into use cases.	5.2.1.3 Review Use Case Granularity

Number	Classic Mistake	It Causes	Related Sections
010	Putting everything into one use case	There should be one use case that describes the entire application: the system context use case. However, it should be at such an abstract level that it is useful only as a general scope statement. Some system context use cases contain a basic course of events that is pages and pages long. This is an abstraction mismatch and should not be done. No use cases should have more than two pages of text for the basic course of events.	5.2.1.3 Review Use Case Granularity
011	Abstracting too much	What? We've been telling you to abstract all along! Can you have too much of a good thing? Of course. How do you tell? Ask your users. If you've abstracted the functionality to such a degree that your users don't understand it any more, it's too much.	5.3.4 Abstraction Filter
012	Using IF-THEN-ELSEs in the use cases	Pseudocode in use cases can make users uncomfortable.	5.2.2.7 Document Exceptions

Table 10.5 Classic Mistakes of Mismanagement

Number	Classic Mistake	It Causes	Related Sections
001	Trying to force simultaneous iterations	Iterations can certainly overlap. However, we've known several managers who think that everything should happen at the same time because it makes their project plans end by the date promised to management. This is the wrong reason. Let iterations overlap naturally, but don't force the issue or a lot will fall through the cracks.	8.1.5 Developers Love It, but Managers Struggle
002	Allowing an imbalance between experience and inexperience	In requirements gathering, a few inexperienced analysts often get paired with too few experienced analysts. Worse yet, no one has business knowledge. Requirements are the most pivotal artifact of the lifecycle. Reduce your investment in them at your peril.	9.1 Organizing by Team
003	Packaging use cases too late	Use case packages are your tool for reducing complexity on diagrams. Use them early and often. If there is a set of functionality that you don't need to deal with right now, lump it into a package and let it sit until the time is right.	5.2.1.3 Review Use Case Granularity
004	Using packages to hide complexity that you're trying to avoid	The purpose of packages is to hide complexity. However, if you use packages of use cases to hide a part of the system that you don't yet understand, you're only putting off the inevitable task of learning that part of the application. If you put it off until later in the requirements activity, you risk running past your deadline when the package turns out to be a lot more complex than you originally thought.	4.3.7 Packages As Place-holders for Functionality

Table 10.6 Classic Mistakes of Context

Number	Classic Mistake	It Causes	Related Sections
001	Confusing *include*, *precondition*, and *assumption*	As long as you use consistent definitions of these three terms, your use cases will be meaningful. We've provided some definitions that make sense to us, but you can use your own, as long as they're applied consistently.	5.3.2 IPA Filter
002	Using two columns in Course of Events section in use case template	This is quite common, and it is even advocated in some textbooks. Here's the question to answer. Usually use cases are interactions between one actor and the application. What happens when multiple actors get involved? Do you then create three columns? Or put both actors in the left column? This seems like a good idea until you try it in complex situations.	2.4.3 The Use Case Template
003	Confusing *include* and *extend*	Confusing the use case adornments is very common. Remember, *includes* (formerly *uses*) is like a function call; *extends* is like inheritance.	2.4.2.2 Associations
004	Underusing use cases during the lifecycle	We believe that use cases are extremely useful after requirements gathering is complete.	2.5 Use Cases Apply Here 8.2 The Role of the Scenario in Management Appendix A

Table 10.7 Classic Mistakes of Notation

Number	Classic Mistake	It Causes	Related Sections
001	Using use cases as scenarios	It's easy to confuse use cases with scenarios. Use cases represent a fairly abstract actor interaction that provides value to the actor. Scenarios are instantiated from use cases and provide specific interactions with specific value.	2.4.4 Paths and Scenarios
002	Using weak verbs in use case names	Use case names are extremely important because they identify the interaction. Poor names are usually too vague or misleading.	4.3.5 Verb Filter
003	Using weak nouns in use cases	Nouns that are computer-specific or just plain bland not only do not help interpretation of the use case text but also point to vague areas of understanding by the requirements analyst.	4.3.6 Noun Filter
004	Portraying application parts as actors	It is common for analysts familiar with only part of the application to take another section of the application and put it outside the boundary of the use case as an actor. This is right only when the outside application part is not the responsibility of this team.	2.4.2.1 Actors and Roles
005	Underusing preconditions and postconditions	Preconditions and postconditions provide an excellent scope management feature for use case creation. If the analyst, the user, and the project manager agree on the preconditions and postconditions for a use case, the analyst is free to find the steps that take the use case from the before to the after. Preconditions and postconditions provide the analyst with a liberating structure.	2.4.3 The Use Case Template 8.5.1 Hectic Activity
006	Using secondary actors inappropriately	Secondary actors should be shown on use case diagrams when the application is likely to require information about them—that is, when the secondary actors are likely to become classes in the class diagram during analysis and design.	2.4.2.1 Actors and Roles

Number	Classic Mistake	It Causes	Related Sections
007	Forgetting that actors can become classes	During analysis and design, the classes that provide the values in use cases are designed and assigned responsibilities. However, actors also become classes when it is important to store information about those actors.	2.4.2.1 Actors and Roles
008	Skipping the system context level use case	The system context use case provides one important thing: scope management. If something changes that affects the system context use case, it is a big change and should get a lot of visibility. This is easier to do if a system context use case exists. If you find yourself resisting this high-level document, create a problem statement instead. It can provide a similar executive-level view of the application.	Appendix A 4.2.7 Create the Facade Use Cases
009	Overusing adornments	The inherent mistake here is thinking of a use case diagram as a system design or data design. It's not. If the adornments (*extend*, *include*, and so on) are starting to clutter the use case diagram, it probably means that the mind-set of the team needs to be pointed toward requirements instead of design.	2.4.2.2 Associations
010	Confusing who extends whom	It is easy to confuse the extender with the extendee. The specialization use case should be at the blunt end of the arrow, and the general use case should be at the sharp end of the arrow.	2.4.2.2 Associations

11

The Case for Use Cases

To be sure, what we've presented in *Use Cases: Requirements in Context* is an incomplete methodology because it focuses entirely on requirements gathering. This was our intent. Having worked in information technology a total of more than twenty years between the two of us, we're weary of methodology wars. There are lifecycle methodologies that address analysis, design, and implementation nicely. Our favorite lifecycle methodology is the Rational Unified Process, although we'd like to see RUP go even deeper on testing and deployment. We're confident that Rational's "Three Amigos" will push into those areas soon.

We're happy to see the emergence of mini-methodologies, often called *process patterns*. People are breaking up their methodological ideas into bits of advice. These tidbits can be fairly coarse-grain, such as the process we describe for requirements, or very fine-grain, such as those described on Scott Ambler's excellent Web site. Think of our advice on requirements gathering as a set of process patterns to help increase quality and decrease effort in the requirements activity. It seems that Extreme Programming, the latest methodology to emerge, is indeed merely a set of process patterns bound together to form a "lite" methodology that is workable for small teams.

SEE ALSO: http://www.ambysoft.com

It doesn't matter which methodology you use for the requirements-gathering activity. We strongly advocate the iterative and incremental model, but waterfall analysis, design, construction, and testing will also work with our processes. If you decide to use the iterative and incremental approach, the four iterations of use cases will map nicely to your process. Typically, you can begin some analysis and design after the Filled iteration, as we show in Chapter 8.

The way you use *Use Cases: Requirements in Context* is up to you, of course. You can take the bits of advice in our process chapters (Chapters 4 through 7) and use the tools wherever they apply to your project. Or you can take the idea of iterating through requirements and try it with fewer or more iterations. Or you can even take the step-by-step approach and use it verbatim. As much as possible, we've tried not to couple the steps tightly to any specific project. We know that these steps work for business systems. For real-time or shrinkwrap systems, we're not as sure. We welcome your feedback through Addison Wesley Longman or through e-mail as to how these steps could be improved given what you've found. And we hope that you can extract useful tools and tips from our book that lighten your daily load a little. Thanks for reading *Use Cases: Requirements in Context,* and good luck in all your efforts.

A

Use Cases Beyond Requirements

Use cases can drive the entire application development lifecycle. This appendix shows how use cases are related to each activity in the lifecycle.

If a use case is your hammer, every requirement is a nail. (This is almost true!)

A.1 Business Modeling

Use cases are being used increasingly for documentation of business process reengineering (BPR) efforts. They can document interaction between actors and processes even if the processes are not automated. In BPR, the system is the system of the organization and not necessarily a computer system. There are several good books on this topic. Our favorite is Ivar Jacobson's *The Objective Advantage* (1995).

A.2 Requirements Gathering

Use Cases: Requirements in Context shows how use cases apply simply and elegantly to the tasks of requirements gathering, documentation, and specification. Use cases provide a structure to weed out duplication and conflicts, and they also give users and analysts flexibility in specifying the system in the best way for the individual situation.

A.3 Analysis

Recall that analysis focuses on building a logical solution that satisfies the users' requirements but does not take physical constraints into account. Use cases are the primary input to analysis. In an object-oriented development effort, analysis tasks often consist, at a minimum, of creating class diagrams and sequence diagrams. Sequence diagrams correlate directly to scenarios within use cases. Each scenario becomes the script for a set of interactions between objects in a sequence diagram. Similarly, the objects that are interacting in the sequence diagram influence the classes that are created in the class diagrams.

A.4 Design

Design takes the logical solution and changes it to work effectively within the physical environment. Constraints such as network latency and database performance are taken into account, and the design is modified to create a system that works the way the users need it to work. Requirements such as a 24-hour, seven-days-per-week uptime influence how the design is changed in this activity.

Design tasks are similar to analysis tasks except that the intent has changed. To allow development of the system, sequence diagrams, class diagrams, and probably some statechart diagrams are refined and added. During the design activity, use cases may become more physical, or implementation-specific, because they may be part of how the system works.

TIP: *Extend* and *include* relationships in your use cases don't translate one-to-one into inheritance and "has responsibility for" relationships in an object-oriented design. The relationships that provide the most value in describing and communicating requirements do not necessarily correlate with a good object-oriented design. Remember that use cases and requirements present the *romantic* view, whereas design documents present the *classical* view (see Chapter 2).

A.4.1 Use Case Hierarchies for User Interface Design

We describe use cases in hierarchies throughout this book. One system context use case is broken into several abstract use cases, which are broken into less-abstract use cases as you traverse down the hierarchy. As shown in the example in Figure A.1, these use cases and their inherent hierarchy can be very useful for user interface design because they show how the users logically break their systems into abstractions. Often, the menu-driven systems that IT groups have produced in the past have been confounding to users because menu choices are not intuitive. Use case hierarchies can help drive the navigation mechanism for a system, whether it is a series of menus, push buttons, Web pages, or whatever.

A.4.2 Using Scenarios As Units of Work for Transaction Processing

When you're building transaction-processing systems, as most line-of-business systems are, it is important to pick the right series of interactions that form transactions, or units of work. Scenarios can help this effort because they express the essence of a unit of work from the user's perspective. When a scenario completes, the user receives his or her value, and this means that the entire unit of work should be committed or rolled back at the end of the scenario. There certainly are times when this approach will not work, but our experience has shown that it makes sense most of the time.

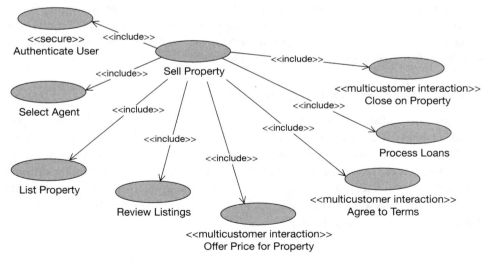

Figure A.1   *Sell Property—Use Case Hierarchy—Finished Use Case Diagram*

A.4.3 Architectural Use Cases

Because the actor in a use case can be a person or another system, it is possible to create use cases for *internal subsystems*. *Architecture* for a system refers to the underlying structure and services that are reusable within the application and probably between applications. It makes sense to create use cases for architectural subsystems as well as for entire applications because it is the interactions that are important. In the same way that an application works for a user, the subsystem must provide certain interfaces and must provide certain results. The black-box approach is important for architectural subsystems in the same way it is for applications.

One popular type of architecture is the three-tier architecture. The application is broken into subsystems that have strong cohesion because they perform similar operations. The three tiers are commonly called *presentation*, *business rules*, and *storage*.

A.4.4 Using Actors As Security Profiles

When you start designing the classes and database tables, you can use actors as the templates for user security profiles. This seems obvious, but unfortunately the linkage is often missed in systems we've seen being developed. Actors represent a class of users. The things that an actor can access in a system are part of the definition of that actor. It makes sense that actors and security profiles in the system implementation be closely coupled.

A.4.5 Using Scenarios to Manage Security

Just as actors can become security profiles, scenarios can be used as the context for assigning access by actors to the system. Most of the time we design security profiles for users to access certain windows or business functions. But it makes sense to set up security for users to access certain scenarios instead. This technique couples the security function to the actual business interactions that occur, something that decreases administration for the security staff and creates yet another use for use cases.

A.4.6 Using Scenarios to Manage Prefetch

Because actors will always move through specific interactions, which are described as scenarios, it makes sense to manage things such as prefetch along the lines of scenarios. *Prefetch* is a term we use that means buffering objects or other memory-resident components somewhere close to the user. In this way, when the user proceeds to the next window or function, all the needed pieces have already been loaded within easy reach. Because you are aware of the path the users will take through the system, you can create prefetch groups based on those scenarios for best performance.

A.5 Construction

During an iterative and incremental lifecycle, the construction activity takes place through several iterations. Each iteration builds a piece of the system's functionality. Each piece is called an *increment*. When you are planning the construction activity, it is difficult to decide how much functionality to place in each construction increment. A good approach is to use scenarios as the building blocks. For example, a construction increment plan might look like the one presented in Table A.1.

A construction increment plan becomes nothing more than a description of the increments that will create specific functionality by a certain date.

A.6 Testing

Testing is where things get really interesting. Scenarios are descriptions of detailed interactions between actors and the system to be built. Test cases are descriptions of detailed interactions between users and the system you have just finished building. When you create test plans, it is extremely useful to go back to the use cases and scenarios and map them one-to-one to test scenarios and test cases. This method provides excellent traceability from the original requirements to the tested system. If the test cases are mapped to use case scenarios and if the tests pass, the system has met its requirements. Period.

A.7 Deployment

In the same way that you can employ use cases and scenarios to help plan construction increments, you can also use them as the measuring stick for the functionality placed in each production release. Deciding the functionality to deliver in a release is an important planning activity because the users see the delivery of each stage of functionality that gets put into production. The way that the stages of delivery build on each other must make sense from the users' perspectives so that they can actually use the stages independent of the upcoming functionality releases.

Table A.1   Construction Increment Plan Example

Increment Number	Completion Date	Scenarios Implemented
B-001	09/06/1999	Enter Credit Card Payment Enter Purchase Order Payment
B-002	09/20/1999	Enter Cash Payment Back Out Payment Transaction

A.8 Project Management

The only constant in systems development is change. We have all seen that every development effort witnesses a transformation of its own requirements, a transformation that occurs at its foundation.

Use cases and scenarios provide a good mechanism for handling one type of change to the scope of a development effort: requirements shift. When the requirements are changed by the users or by management, it is a useful exercise to quantify the resulting effort by showing the increase in the number of scenarios or by showing the number of scenarios that are altered. The ripple effect of requirements change is deceptively large, especially as things progress later in the lifecycle. Scenario-based documentation of requirements shift can help bring the extent of the changes into public scrutiny better than any other method we've seen.

B

Case Study: Sell Property

This appendix shows artifacts produced from a complete lifecycle of four iterations of requirements gathering. Without creating a 500-page appendix, we wanted to give you an impression of how everything comes together. To save space, we provide only short explanations for some of the artifacts (for example, a workplan) that are common knowledge among IT professionals.

This first of two case studies produces the requirements for a real estate agency application. The agency, Acreage-to-City, requires an application that acts as a mediator between the buyer and the seller. The agency provides expertise through its agents and also links the customers with other institutions, such as lenders, as required.

The Acreage-to-City agency is an up-and-comer in the industry. It is looking for a way to leverage technology to gain a strategic advantage in the marketplace. The Internet seems to provide a good way to unite buyers and sellers of real estate, providing both parties with as much information as possible. The executives at the agency are very aware that they need to put something in place quickly to avoid being eclipsed by one of the larger real estate companies. Therefore, they have limited the scope of this first effort to residential sales only.

NOTE: To save space, we've omitted some of the more detailed specifications. For example, use cases covering CRUD functionality have been omitted even though they would be required in a total application requirements document.

B.1 The Facade Iteration

During the Facade iteration, we created the following artifacts.

Problem statement	Complete, but will be revised slightly in future iterations
Statement of work	Complete, but will be revised slightly in future iterations
Risk analysis	Complete, but risks will be added and deleted throughout all iterations
Facade use cases	"Shell" use cases as placeholders for functionality to be filled in later

The project manager for this case study decided not to address business rules during the Facade iteration because interviews with the business rules expert would not be possible until the Filled iteration.

B.1.1 Problem Statement

The Acreage-to-City agency needs to differentiate itself from its competition by providing buyers and sellers of residential real estate with a quantum leap in efficiency and effectiveness. We need to get the right buyer together with the right seller in a way that's unobtrusive and efficient.

B.1.2 Statement of Work

Scope

The following elements are in scope:

- Listing properties
- Searching for properties
- Selecting agents
- Making and responding to offers
- Negotiating terms
- Processing loans for the buyer
- Closing on the deal
- Providing information about the property, such as photos, square footage, price, location, age, and so on
- Residential property

The following elements are out of scope:

- Virtual reality walk-throughs of properties
- Commercial property

Objectives

The objectives of this application are to provide the Acreage-to-City real estate agency with an increased market share by providing a state-of-the-art meeting place for buyers and sellers of real estate. The application should provide all the services necessary to conduct a real estate sale.

Application Overview

This application essentially provides a communication conduit and meeting place for buyers and sellers of residential real estate. It automates and logs the transactions that occur between buyer and seller to speed up the process and match the right property to the right buyer effectively.

User Demography

The main users of this application will be buyers and sellers of real estate. These users may be anywhere in the United States or Canada. The users of this system include the following types of employees of the Acreage-to-City agency: agents, system administrators, and executives.

In addition, there are users from contracted vendors of services: bank loan administrators, legal analysts, and financial analysts.

Constraints

The Internet should be leveraged to link buyers, sellers, and the agency. In many cases, the buyer, seller, and agents will not meet face-to-face.

Assumptions

Sufficient security can be provided using the Internet.

Staffing and Cost

(Staffing and cost plan here.)

Deliverable Outlines

(Outline the deliverables here. Use your methodology to identify deliverables and tables of contents.)

Expected Duration

(Using a GANTT chart, produce a timeline showing when the phases will conclude and the products that will be available at each phase conclusion.)

B.1.3 Risk Analysis

Table B.1   Risk Analysis Example

Number	Category	Risk	Resolution Needed By	Status	Days Lost If It Occurs	Likelihood It Will Happen	Risk Rating
001	Interfaces	The new application needs to interface with SAP, which has not been put into production yet. There could be schedule delays if this project has to wait two months for SAP project.	Jul 1, 2000	Unresolved	50	50%	25
002	User time	The majority of the user group is heavily involved in a reengineering effort. If the project team members cannot get their time, the project will be delayed.	May 15, 2000	Being investigated	70	80%	56

B.1.4 Facade Use Cases

Seller   Sell Property   Buyer

Figure B.1 *System Level Context Use Case—Sell Property Diagram*

Use Case Name:	**Sell Property**
Iteration:	**Facade**
Summary:	System Context Use Case. The seller lists the property, a buyer purchases the property, and the agent guides them through the process and offers advice, caution, and recommendations.
Basic Course of Events:	
Alternative Paths:	
Extension Points:	
Assumptions:	
Preconditions:	
Postconditions:	
Author:	Angela Baltimore
Date:	March 20, 2000

Use Case B.1 *System Level Context Use Case—Sell Property*

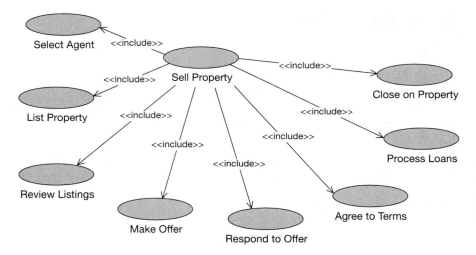

Figure B.2   *Use Case Hierarchy Diagram*

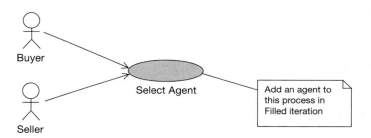

Figure B.3   *Select Agent Diagram*

Use Case Name:	**Select Agent**
Iteration:	**Facade**
Summary:	The customer selects an agent, probably based on the agent's location and expertise and whether the customer has worked with the agent previously.
Basic Course of Events:	
Alternative Paths:	
Exception Paths:	
Extension Points:	

Use Case B.2   *Select Agent—Facade (continues)*

Trigger:	
Assumptions:	
Preconditions:	
Postconditions:	
Related Business Rules:	
Author:	Angela Baltimore
Date:	March 25, 2000—Facade

Use Case B.2 *continued*

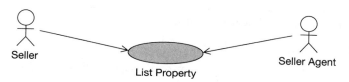

Seller   List Property   Seller Agent

Figure B.4 *List Property*

Use Case Name:	**List Property**
Iteration:	**Facade**
Summary:	The seller lists the property, providing information on location, price, floor layout, and so on. The seller's agent checks the listing and solicits the seller for any additional items required before it can be listed publicly.
Alternative Paths:	
Exception Paths:	
Extension Points:	
Trigger:	
Assumptions:	
Preconditions:	
Postconditions:	
Related Business Rules:	

Use Case B.3 *List Property—Facade*

Author:	Ed Towson
Date:	March 20, 2000—Facade

Use Case B.3 *continued*

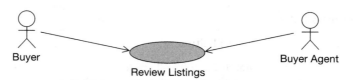

Buyer

Review Listings

Buyer Agent

Figure B.5 *Review Listings*

Use Case Name:	**Review Listings**
Iteration:	**Facade**
Summary:	The buyer browses through the listings of properties using keyword searches or just by listing everything and visually spotting certain criteria (price, location, photo, size, floor plan, age, and so on). The buyer's agent assists by pointing out how to use the listing or by selecting certain properties based on criteria given to the agent by the buyer. The buyer's agent also uses his or her experience in the market to provide cautions or recommendations to the buyer.
Basic Course of Events:	
Alternative Paths:	
Exception Paths:	
Extension Points:	
Trigger:	
Assumptions:	
Preconditions:	
Postconditions:	
Related Business Rules:	
Author:	Ed Towson
Date:	March 23, 2000—Facade

Use Case B.4 *Review Listings—Facade*

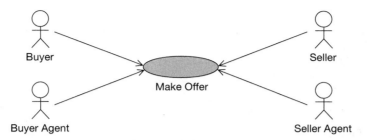

Figure B.6 *Make Offer*

Use Case Name:	**Make Offer**
Iteration:	**Facade**
Summary:	The buyer makes an offer to the seller. The seller's agent and the buyer's agent offer their respective customers advice based on their experience in real estate transactions and their knowledge of the marketplace.
Basic Course of Events:	
Alternative Paths:	
Exception Paths:	
Extension Points:	
Trigger:	
Assumptions:	
Preconditions:	
Postconditions:	
Related Business Rules:	
Author:	Angela Baltimore
Date:	March 22, 2000—Facade

Use Case B.5 *Make Offer—Facade*

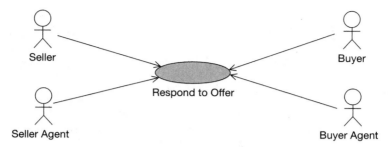

Figure B.7 *Respond to Offer*

Use Case Name:	**Respond to Offer**
Iteration:	**Facade**
Summary:	The seller responds to the buyer's offer either by accepting it, declining it, or presenting a counteroffer. The basic course of events is acceptance. The agents help their customers by offering advice, caution, or recommendations.
Basic Course of Events:	
Alternative Paths:	
Exception Paths:	
Extension Points:	
Trigger:	
Assumptions:	
Preconditions:	
Postconditions:	
Related Business Rules:	
Author:	Ed Towson
Date:	March 27, 2000—Facade

Use Case B.6 *Respond to Offer—Facade*

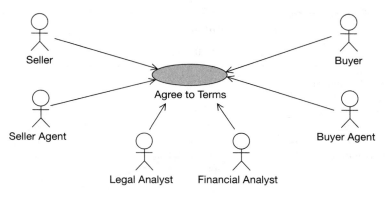

Figure B.8 *Agree to Terms*

Use Case Name:	**Agree to Terms**
Iteration:	**Facade**
Summary:	The buyer and the seller agree to the terms of the sale, including any required changes to the existing property, the items included with the property, the date of possession, the financing, and any other conditions of sale. The agents help their respective customers by offering advice, caution, or recommendations. The financial analyst helps the buyer understand the extent to which the buyer's finances will stretch. The legal analyst provides advice on legal issues and approves the contract.
Basic Course of Events:	
Alternative Paths:	
Exception Paths:	
Extension Points:	
Trigger:	
Assumptions:	
Preconditions:	
Postconditions:	
Related Business Rules:	

Use Case B.7 *Agree to Terms—Facade (continues)*

Author:	Angela Baltimore
Date:	March 20, 2000—Facade

Use Case B.7 *continued*

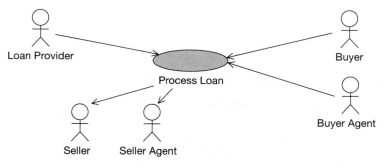

Figure B.9 *Process Loan*

Use Case Name:	**Process Loan**
Iteration:	**Facade**
Summary:	The loan provider and the buyer work out the terms of the loan if the buyer requires one. Terms include the interest rate, points, term, escrow, insurance, and so on.
Basic Course of Events:	
Alternative Paths:	
Exception Paths:	
Extension Points:	
Trigger:	
Assumptions:	
Preconditions:	
Postconditions:	
Related Business Rules:	
Author:	Felix Westerville
Date:	March 27, 2000—Facade

Use Case B.8 *Process Loan—Facade*

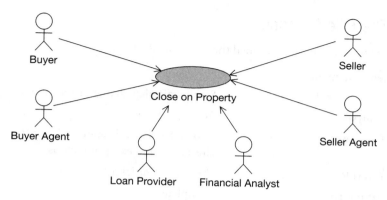

Figure B.10 *Close on Property*

Use Case Name:	**Close on Property**
Iteration:	**Facade**
Summary:	The buyer and the seller close the transaction on the property. Advice and recommendations come from the other actors.
Basic Course of Events:	
Alternative Paths:	
Exception Paths:	
Extension Points:	
Trigger:	
Assumptions:	
Preconditions:	
Postconditions:	
Related Business Rules:	
Author:	Felix Westerville
Date:	March 20, 2000—Facade

Use Case B.9 *Close on Property—Facade*

B.2   The Filled Iteration

During the Filled iteration, we refined the following artifacts.

Problem statement	No changes
Statement of work	Small workplan changes (not shown)
Risk analysis	Added two risks
Filled use cases	Added details: basic course of events and alternative and exception paths
Business rules	Created an initial list
Context matrix	Complete
Nonfunctional requirements	Started
Scenario test	Important scenarios completed

A new use case for security, *Authenticate User*, was added.

B.2.1   Risk Analysis

Table B.2 Risk Analysis: Filled Iteration

Number	Category	Risk	Resolution Needed By	Status	Days Lost If It Occurs	Likelihood It Will Happen	Risk Rating
001	Interfaces	The new application needs to interface with SAP, which has not been put into production yet. There could be schedule delays if this project has to wait two months for the SAP project.	Jul 1, 2000	Unresolved	50	50%	25
002	User time	The majority of the user group is heavily involved in a reengineering effort. If the project team members cannot get their time, the project will be delayed.	May 15, 2000	Being investigated	70	80%	56
003	Qualified project manager	The project manager originally slated to take this project through deployment has quit the company. A new, equally qualified person must be found before the analysis activity starts.	May 20, 2000	Interviews under way	200	20%	40
004	Commercial versus residential	The executive sponsor has said that the agency may decide to prioritize commercial real estate sales above residential. If this is done now or in the future, it will cause rework.	May 1, 2000	Decision request provided to executive sponsor	30	50%	15

B.2.2 Filled Use Cases

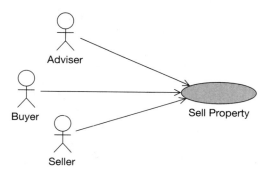

Figure B.11 *System Level Context Use Case: Sell Property*

Use Case Name:	**Sell Property**
Iteration:	**Filled**
Summary:	System Context Use Case. The seller lists the property, a buyer purchases the property, and the agent guides them through the process and offers advice, caution, and recommendations.
Basic Course of Events:	1. The seller selects an agent. 2. The system responds by assigning an agent and notifying the seller's agent. 3. The seller lists the property to sell. 4. The system responds by displaying this property in the property listing and linking it for searches. 5. The buyer selects an agent. 6. The buyer reviews the property listings by entering search criteria. 7. The system responds by displaying properties that match the buyer's search criteria. 8. The buyer finds a property and makes an offer on it. 9. The system responds by notifying the seller and the seller's agent. 10. The seller responds to the offer with a counteroffer. 11. The system responds by notifying the buyer and the buyer's agent.

Use Case B.10 *Sell Property—Filled (continues)*

	12. The buyer and the seller agree to terms. 13. The system responds by recording the agreement. 14. The buyer indicates that a loan is required. 15. The system responds by locating an appropriate loan provider. 16. The buyer and the loan provider agree to loan terms. 17. The system responds by recording the terms of the loan. 18. The buyer and the seller close on the property. 19. The system responds by recording the details of the close.
Alternative Paths:	N/A
Extension Points:	N/A
Trigger:	N/A
Assumptions:	N/A
Preconditions:	N/A
Postconditions:	N/A
Related Business Rules:	N/A
Author:	Angela Baltimore
Date:	March 20, 2000—Facade; March 26, 2000—Filled

Use Case B.10   *continued*

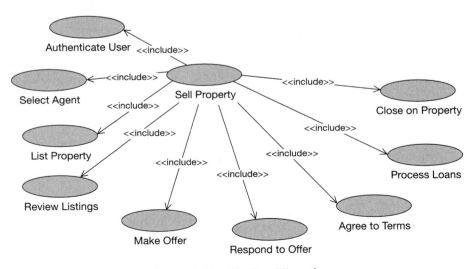

Figure B.12   *Use Case Hierarchy*

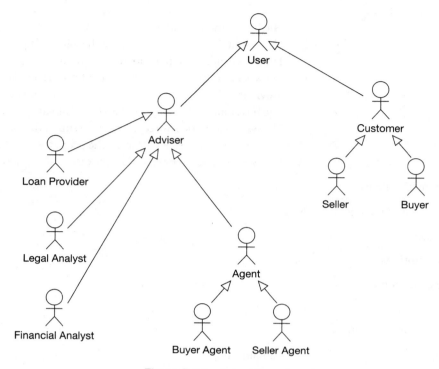

Figure B.13 *Actor Hierarchy*

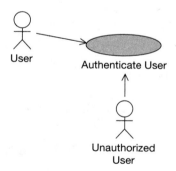

Figure B.14 *Authenticate User*

Use Case Name:	**Authenticate User**
Iteration:	**Filled**
Summary:	All users who request entry to the system must prove they are who they say they are (authentication). This applies to users inside the company as well as outside. Who the user is determines what he or she has access to (authorization).
Basic Course of Events:	1. This use case begins when the user enters a user identification and password. 2. The system responds by checking the combination of user identification and password against the recorded list of valid users. 3. The system responds by notifying the user that the user identification and password are valid and allowing the user access to the application.
Alternative Paths:	None
Exception Paths:	In step 2, if the user identification and password combination is not valid, the system responds by notifying the user that the combination was invalid and asks the user to try again. If the user tries three times unsuccessfully, the system responds by disallowing the user and marking as suspended the user record of any and all user identifications tried. In step 2, if the user identification that is tried is in suspended mode, the system responds by notifying the user that this identification has been suspended and the user must contact a system administrator.
Extension Points:	None
Trigger:	The user requires access to the system.
Assumptions:	None
Preconditions:	The system is operational.
Postconditions:	The validated user is allowed access to the system.
Related Business Rules:	None
Author:	Shelley Foerster
Date:	June 5, 2000—Facade; June 5, 2000—Filled

Use Case B.11   *Authenticate User—Filled*

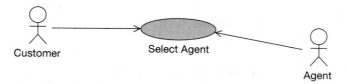

Figure B.15   *Select Agent*

Use Case Name:	**Select Agent**
Iteration:	**Filled**
Summary:	The customer selects an agent, probably based on the agent's location and expertise and whether the customer has worked with the agent previously.
Basic Course of Events:	1. This use case begins when the customer requests a list of agents. 2. The system responds with a list of agents, with information on their location and expertise. 3. The customer responds by choosing an agent.
Alternative Paths	None
Exception Paths:	In step 1, if the customer suddenly decides not to choose an agent, the customer indicates this. The system responds by warning the customer of the dangers of not having an agent and then records that the customer has not chosen an agent.
Extension Points:	None
Trigger:	The customer indicates the desire to choose an agent.
Assumptions:	None
Preconditions:	The customer has decided to choose an agent.
Postconditions:	The customer has chosen a specific agent.
Related Business Rules:	None
Author:	Angela Baltimore
Date:	March 25, 2000—Facade; March 27, 2000—Filled

Use Case B.12   *Select Agent—Filled*

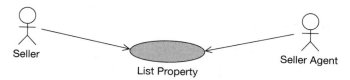

Figure B.16 *List Property*

Use Case Name:	**List Property**
Iteration:	**Filled**
Summary:	The seller puts a property up for sale, including a set of information that classifies it uniquely for prospective buyers.
Basic Course of Events:	1. This use case begins when the seller enters the information required to list a property. 2. The system responds by saving the listing and notifying the seller's agent that the listing has been entered. 3. The seller's agent checks the listing and solicits the seller for additional information or clarifications. Then the seller's agent completes the listing and confirms it. 4. The system records the confirmation and lists the property publicly.
Alternative Paths:	In step 3, if there are no clarifications or additions required, as judged by the seller's agent, the seller's agent simply confirms the listing.
Exception Paths:	None
Extension Points:	None
Trigger:	The seller has decided to sell a property.
Assumptions:	None
Preconditions:	The seller has chosen an agent or has chosen not to have an agent.
Postconditions:	The property is available for viewing on the system by prospective buyers.

Use Case B.13 *List Property—Filled (continues)*

Related Business Rules:	None
Author:	Ed Towson
Date:	March 20, 2000—Facade; April 2, 2000—Filled

Use Case B.13 *continued*

Figure B.17   *Review Listings*

Use Case Name:	**Review Listings**
Iteration:	**Filled**
Summary:	The buyer browses through the listings of properties with the help of the buyer's agent.
Basic Course of Events:	1. This use case begins when the buyer requests to view properties. 2. The system responds by providing the buyer with methods for searching: keyword or specific criteria such as price, location, photo, size, floor plan, age, and so on. 3. The buyer's agent enters advice for the buyer into the system and points out certain properties that the buyer may have overlooked.
Alternative Paths:	In step 3, if the buyer did not choose an agent, this step does not exist.
Exception Paths:	None
Extension Points:	None
Trigger:	The buyer wishes to purchase a property but does not know of a suitable property yet.
Assumptions:	None

Use Case B.14   *Review Listings—Filled (continues)*

Preconditions:	At least one property has been listed.
Postconditions:	None
Related Business Rules:	None
Author:	Ed Towson
Date:	March 23, 2000—Facade; March 26, 2000—Filled

Use Case B.14   *continued*

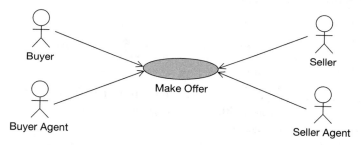

Figure B.18   *Make Offer*

Use Case Name:	**Make Offer**
Iteration:	**Filled**
Summary:	The buyer makes an offer to the seller. The seller's agent and the buyer's agent offer their respective customers advice based on their experience in real estate transactions and their knowledge of the marketplace.
Basic Course of Events:	1. This use case begins when a buyer registers a bid against a property on the system. 2. The system responds by saving the bid and presenting agent criteria to the buyer. 3. The buyer chooses specific criteria and chooses a buyer's agent. 4. The system responds by registering the agent choice and notifying the seller and the seller's agent that an offer has been made. 5. The seller receives the offer.

Use Case B.15   *Make Offer—Filled (continues)*

	6. The system responds by notifying the buyer that the seller has seen the offer (there is no implication of acceptance or rejection).
Alternative Paths:	In step 3, if the buyer chooses not to use an agent, the system warns the buyer of the hazards of proceeding without an agent. If the buyer insists, the system allows the buyer to proceed to the next step (and through all future steps) without an agent.
Exception Paths:	None
Extension Points:	None
Trigger:	The buyer decides to make an offer on a specific property.
Assumptions:	None
Preconditions:	The seller has listed the property. The buyer and the seller have either chosen agents or have decided not to choose agents.
Postconditions:	The offer is made and received by the seller.
Related Business Rules:	None
Author:	Angela Baltimore
Date:	March 22, 2000—Facade; March 27, 2000—Filled

Use Case B.15 *continued*

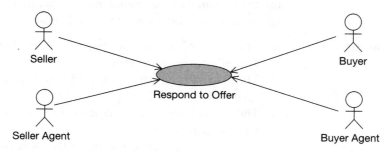

Figure B.19 *Respond to Offer*

Use Case Name:	**Respond to Offer**
Iteration:	**Filled**
Summary:	The seller responds to the buyer's offer either by accepting it, declining it, or presenting a counteroffer. The basic course of events is acceptance. The agents help their cusomers by offering advice, caution, or recommendations.
Basic Course of Events:	1. This use case begins when the seller prepares a counteroffer and submits it. 2. The system responds by presenting the counteroffer to the buyer and the buyer's agent. 3. The buyer responds by accepting the counteroffer. 4. The system responds by notifying the seller that the counteroffer was accepted.
Alternative Paths:	In step 1, if the seller accepts the buyer's offer, the seller simply registers acceptance of the offer and the system responds by notifying the buyer and the buyer's agent. In step 4, if the buyer does not accept the seller's offer, the buyer submits another counteroffer, which is presented to the seller, and then processing returns to step 1.
Exception Paths:	None
Extension Points:	None
Trigger:	An offer has been made by a prospective buyer.
Assumptions:	None
Preconditions:	An offer has been made.
Postconditions:	The buyer has received the offer and the seller has received a counteroffer.
Related Business Rules:	None
Author:	Ed Towson
Date:	March 27, 2000—Facade; March 28, 2000—Filled

Use Case B.16 *Respond to Offer—Filled*

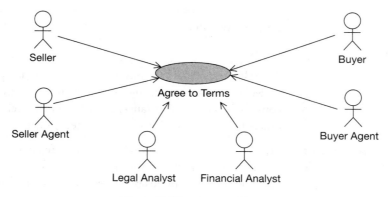

Figure B.20   *Agree to Terms*

Use Case Name:	**Agree to Terms**
Iteration:	**Filled**
Summary:	The buyer and the seller agree to the terms of the sale, including any required changes to the existing property, the items included with the property, the date of possession, the financing, and any other conditions of sale. The agents help their respective customers by offering advice, caution, or recommendations.
Basic Course of Events:	1. This use case begins when the buyer and the seller both indicate that an agreement is possible. 2. The system responds by notifying the buyer, the buyer's agent, the seller, the seller's agent, the legal analyst, and the financial analyst that the agreement process is ready to begin. 3. The buyer submits a proposal of terms. 4. The system responds by allowing all actors to view the proposal of terms and make their changes. 5. The actors make their changes. 6. The system responds by making the actors' changes public to all. 7. The actors discuss the changes and come to an agreement on each proposed change, item by item. 8. The system responds by consolidating the agreed-to changes and making the proposal of terms public again.

Use Case B.17   *Agree to Terms—Filled (continues)*

	9. The actors indicate their agreement. 10. This use case ends when the system indicates that the proposal of terms is final.
Alternative Paths:	In step 3, the buyer's agent may submit a proposal of terms to the buyer, who may then submit it as his or her own. In step 3, the seller may also be the one to submit a proposal of terms. In step 3, the seller's agent may submit a proposal of terms to the seller, who may then submit it as his or her own.
Exception Paths:	In step 9, if the buyer or seller does not agree to the proposal of terms as it stands, the objecting party enters the issue. Then the objecting party modifies the proposal, and processing returns to step 4.
Extension Points:	None
Trigger:	Buyer and seller indicate that agreement to terms can begin.
Assumptions:	None
Preconditions:	An offer has been made and accepted.
Postconditions:	Terms are agreed to by the buyer and the seller.
Related Business Rules:	None
Author:	Angela Baltimore
Date:	March 20, 2000—Facade; March 28, 2000—Filled

Use Case B.17 *continued*

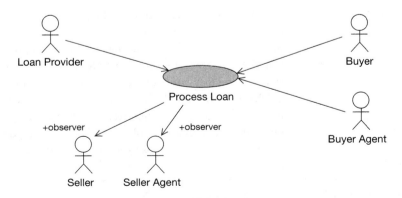

Figure B.21 *Process Loan*

Use Case Name:	**Process Loan**
Iteration:	**Filled**
Summary:	The loan provider and the buyer work out the terms of the loan if the buyer requires one. Terms include the interest rate, points, term, escrow, insurance, and so on.
Basic Course of Events:	1. This use case begins when the buyer and the seller have agreed to terms. 2. The buyer indicates that a loan is required. 3. The system responds by contacting the loan provider with the details of the buyer's loan requirement. 4. The loan provider uses the buyer's loan requirement as input to create a loan proposal. 5. The system responds by sending the loan proposal to the buyer and the buyer's agent. 6. The buyer makes a counteroffer to the loan provider. 7. The system responds by sending the counteroffer to the loan provider. 8. The loan provider accepts the counteroffer. 9. The system responds by sending notification of the loan provider's acceptance to the buyer and the buyer's agent. 10. The buyer indicates acceptance of the loan. 11. The system responds by recording the buyer's acceptance of the loan and files the approved loan application with the loan provider.
Alternative Paths:	In step 6, if the buyer approves the initial loan proposal, jump to step 8.
Exception Paths:	In step 6, if the buyer decides that this loan provider cannot provide an appropriate loan for this purchase, the buyer indicates to the system that another loan provider is needed. The system responds by returning to step 3. In step 4, if the loan provider decides that the buyer is not eligible for any loan, the loan provider makes note of this in the system and the system responds by notifying the buyer that no loan is possible from this loan provider. The buyer may then choose another loan provider or may cancel the offer.

Use Case B.18   *Process Loan—Filled (continues)*

Extension Points:	None
Trigger:	The buyer requires financing and initiates a loan search.
Assumptions:	None
Preconditions:	Buyer requires financing.
Postconditions:	The loan is approved and recorded.
Related Business Rules:	None
Author:	Felix Westerville
Date:	March 27, 2000—Facade; March 31, 2000—Filled

Use Case B.18 *continued*

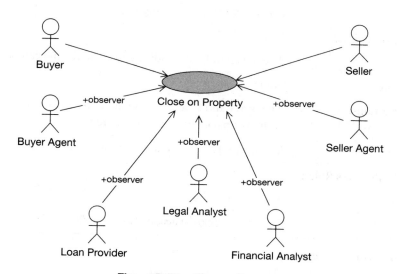

Figure B.22 *Close on Property*

Use Case Name:	**Close on Property**
Iteration:	**Filled**
Summary:	The buyer and the seller close the transaction on the property. Advice and recommendations come from the other actors.

Use Case B.19 *Close on Property—Filled (continues)*

Basic Course of Events:	1. This use case begins when the buyer and seller request to view the contract. 2. The system responds by presenting the contract and by requesting confirmation by the buyer and the seller. 3. The buyer and the seller confirm the sale. 4. This use case ends when the system records the sale as confirmed and registers the property in the buyer's name.
Alternative Paths:	None
Exception Paths:	In step 3, if the buyer or the seller does not confirm the sale, both parties are notified that the transaction did not occur, and the system records that the transaction was aborted during the closing stage.
Extension Points:	None
Trigger:	The buyer and seller indicate that the closing can occur.
Assumptions:	None
Preconditions:	The buyer and seller have agreed to terms. The buyer's source of payment has been secured.
Postconditions:	The property is closed and the transaction is complete.
Related Business Rules:	None
Author:	Felix Westerville
Date:	March 20, 2000—Facade; April 1, 2000—Filled

Use Case B.19 *continued*

B.2.3 Business Rules

Table B.3 Business Rules Example

Rule ID	Name	Description	Category	Static/Dynamic	Source
001	Customer can change agents	Customers can change the agent they are using at any time during the transaction with no penalty.	Structural fact	Dynamic	Interview with executive sponsor 03/20/2000
002	Customer can transact without an agent	Customers can transact business as buyers or sellers without having an agent. However, each time a customer chooses to transact business without an agent, he or she must be warned of the downside of not having an agent.	Structural fact	Dynamic	Interview with executive sponsor 03/22/2000
003	Customers not using agents are charged less	When customers decide not to use an agent to transact business, they will be charged less than customers who use agents.	Structural fact	Dynamic	JRP session 03/21/2000
004	Agent fees depend on number of interactions	The fees the customer is charged are based on the number of interactions with an agent. Each interaction requiring an agent will be charged to the customer as a one-hour minimum. If the agent spends more than one hour, the customer will be charged in quarter-hour segments.	Computation	Dynamic	JRP session 03/21/2000
005	Seller may pull property almost any time	The seller may retract the offer to sell the property at any time except after the seller has made a counteroffer to a prospective buyer. After this has occurred, if the seller and buyer are still in active negotiation, the seller must first notify all involved agents and the active buyer.	Action restricting	Dynamic	JRP session 03/21/2000

B.2.4   Context Matrix

Table B.4   Context Matrix

Number	Use Case	Summary	Core	This Use Case Depends On
CM001	Authenticate User	All users who request entry to the system must prove they are who they say they are (authentication). This applies to users inside the company as well as outside. Who the users are determines what they have access to (authorization).	No	None
CM002	Agree to Terms	The buyer and the seller agree to the terms of the sale, including any required changes to the existing property, the items included with the property, the date of possession, the financing, and any other conditions of sale. The agents help their respective customers by offering advice, caution, or recommendations.	Yes	Respond to offer
CM003	Close on Property	The buyer and the seller close the transaction on the property. Advice and recommendations come from the other actors.	Yes	Agree to Terms
CM004	List Property	The seller puts a property up for sale, including information that classifies it uniquely for prospective buyers.	Yes	None
CM005	Make Offer	The buyer makes an offer to the seller. The seller's agent and the buyer's agent offer their respective customers advice based on their experience in real estate transactions and their knowledge of the marketplace.	Yes	List Property Review Listings

continues

Table B.4 *continued*

Number	Use Case	Summary	Core	This Use Case Depends On
CM006	Process Loan	The loan provider and the buyer work out the terms of the loan if the buyer requires one. Terms include the interest rate, points, term, escrow, insurance, and so on.	No	None
CM007	Respond to Offer	The seller responds to the buyer's offer either by accepting it, declining it, or presenting a counteroffer. The basic course of events is acceptance. The agents help their customers by offering advice, caution, or recommendations.	Yes	Make Offer
CM008	Review Listings	The buyer browses through the listings of properties with the help of the buyer's agent.	Yes	List Property
CM009	Select Agent	The customer selects an agent, probably based on the agent's location and expertise and whether the customer has worked with the agent previously.	No	None

B.2.5 Nonfunctional Requirements

Table B.5 **Nonfunctional Requirements**

Number	Category	Requirement	Applies to Use Cases	Exceptions
SP-NF001	Availability	The system must be available to internal and external users 24 hours a day, 7 days a week, 99.9 percent of the time.	All	None
SP-NF002	Cost of ownership	None	To be determined	To be determined

Applies to Number	Category	Requirement	Use Cases	Exceptions
SP-NF003	Maintainability	The system must be maintainable by the IT staff, who currently have skills in Visual Basic, ActiveX, MS Internet Information Server, MS SQL Server, and MS Transaction Server.	All	None
SP-NF004	Data integrity	Information on property closures must be unalterable by anyone after the closing occurs.	All	None
SP-NF005	Development cost	Cost of development must not exceed $2,500,000, including hardware, packages, and custom development.	All	None
SP-NF006	Delivery date	The system must have at least core functionality in place by January 31, 2001.	All	To be determined
SP-NF007	Extensibility	The system should be built in a way that Acreage-to-City can involve other agencies on a pay-per-use basis.	All	None
SP-NF008	Flexibility	The system should be able to handle interfaces with the following financial institutions: NationsBank, CitiBank, and National City Bank.	Process Loan	N/A
SP-NF009	Installability	None	All	None
SP-NF010	Leveragability, reuse	None	All	None

continues

Table B.5 *continued*

Number	Category	Requirement	Applies to Use Cases	Exceptions
SP-NF011	Operability	System operations must be easily handled by the current IT staff.	All	None
SP-NF012	Performance	Online response for agents should be within 10 seconds 90 percent of the time. Online response for customers should be within 7 seconds 95 percent of the time.	All	None
SP-NF013	Portability	The system should be usable by customers or agents with any of the following Internet browsers: Netscape Navigator 3.x or later, MS Internet Explorer 3.x or later.	All	None
SP-NF014	Quality	None	N/A	N/A
SP-NF015	Fault tolerance, robustness	None	N/A	N/A
SP-NF-16	Scalability	This system should provide the specified response times with a load of 500 concurrent users.	All	None

B.2.6 Testing Using Scenarios

Use Case Name:	**Agree to Terms**
Iteration:	**Filled**
Scenario:	1. The buyer (John Forrest) and the seller (Tina Hart) both indicate that an agreement is possible. 2. The system responds by notifying John Forrest, Tina Hart, the buyer's agent (Harold Beanton), and the seller's agent (Claretta Watersmith) that the agreement process is ready to begin. 3. Tina Hart submits a proposal of terms. 4. The system responds by allowing all actors to view the proposal of terms and make their changes. 5. John Forrest changes the possession date from February 15 to February 10 and requests that Tina Hart include the set of shelves in the garage with the property; the others do not make any changes. 6. The system makes John Forrest's changes public to all other actors. 7. The actors discuss John Forrest's possession date change, and Tina Hart asks that it be moved to February 11. Everyone agrees to that possession date. The set of shelves is also added. 8. The system responds by consolidating the agreed-to changes and making the proposal of terms public again to all actors. 9. The actors indicate their agreement. 10. The system responds by indicating that the proposal of terms is final.
Author:	Angela Baltimore with Claretta Watersmith
Date:	March 27, 2000

Use Case B.20 *Testing Using Scenarios*

B.3 The Focused Iteration

During the Focused iteration, we refined the following artifacts.

Problem Statement	No changes
Statement of Work	Small workplan changes (not shown)
Risk Analysis	Added one risk
Focused Use Cases	Refined use cases, merged *Make Offer* and *Respond to Offer* to create *Offer Price for Property*
Business Rules	Added one business rule to clarify a term

The *Make Offer* and *Respond to Offer* use cases were merged into the *Offer Price for Property* use case. The users, jointly with the requirements analysts, decided that there was not much inherent value in the two smaller use cases and that they should be combined.

B.3.1 Risk Analysis

Table B.6   Risk Analysis: Focused Iteration

Number	Category	Risk	Resolution Needed By	Status	Days Lost If It Occurs	Likelihood It Will Happen	Risk Rating
001	Interfaces	The new application needs to interface with SAP, which has not been put into production yet. There could be schedule delays if this project has to wait two months for the SAP project.	Jul 1, 2000	Unresolved	50	50%	25
002	User time	The majority of the user group is heavily involved in a reengineering effort. If the project team members cannot get their time, the project will be delayed.	May 15, 2000	Being investigated	70	80%	56
003	Qualified project manager	The project manager originally slated to take this project through deployment has quit the company. A new, equally qualified person must be found before the analysis activity starts.	May 20, 2000	Interviews under way	200	20%	40
004	Commercial versus residential	The executive sponsor has said that the agency may decide to prioritize commercial real estate sales above residential. If this is done now or in the future, it will cause rework.	May 1, 2000	Decision request provided to executive sponsor	30	50%	15

continues

Table B.6 *continued*

Number	Category	Risk	Resolution Needed By	Status	Days Lost If It Occurs	Likelihood It Will Happen	Risk Rating
005	Undo property closings	If the agency allows customers to "undo" property closures, this will cause a tremendous amount of additional work for this project and for the agents involved in each sale that gets undone.	May 1, 2000	Decision request provided to executive sponsor	300	5%	15

B.3.2 Focused Use Cases

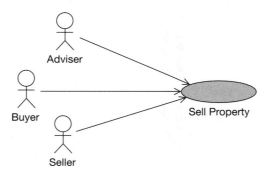

Figure B.23   *System Level Context Use Case Diagram: Sell Property*

Use Case Name:	**Sell Property**
Iteration:	**Focused**
Summary:	System Context Use Case. The seller lists the property, a buyer purchases the property, and the agent guides them through the process and offers advice, caution, and recommendations.
Basic Course of Events:	1. The seller selects an agent. 2. The system responds by assigning an agent and notifying the seller's agent. 3. The seller lists the property. 4. The system responds by displaying this property in the property listing and linking it for searches. 5. The buyer selects an agent. 6. The buyer reviews the property listings by entering search criteria. 7. The system responds by displaying properties that match the buyer's search criteria. 8. The buyer finds a property and makes an offer on it. 9. The system responds by notifying the seller and the seller's agent. 10. The seller responds to the offer with a counteroffer. 11. The system responds by notifying the buyer and the buyer's agent.

Use Case B.21   *System Level Context Sell Property—Focused (continues)*

	12. The buyer and the seller agree to terms. 13. The system responds by recording the agreement. 14. The buyer indicates that a loan is required. 15. The system responds by locating an appropriate loan provider. 16. The buyer and the loan provider agree to loan terms. 17. The system responds by recording the terms of the loan. 18. The buyer and the seller close on the property. 19. The system responds by recording the details of the closing.
Alternative Paths:	N/A
Extension Points:	N/A
Trigger:	N/A
Assumptions:	N/A
Preconditions:	N/A
Postconditions:	N/A
Related Business Rules:	N/A
Author:	Angela Baltimore
Date:	March 20, 2000—Facade; March 26, 2000—Filled; April 2, 2000—Focused

Use Case B.21 *continued*

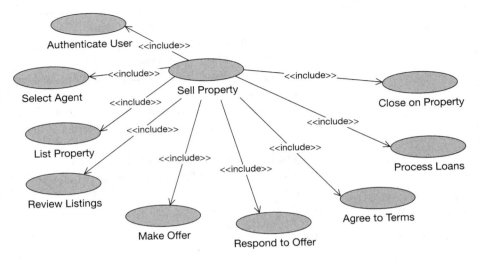

Figure B.24 *Use Case Hierarchy*

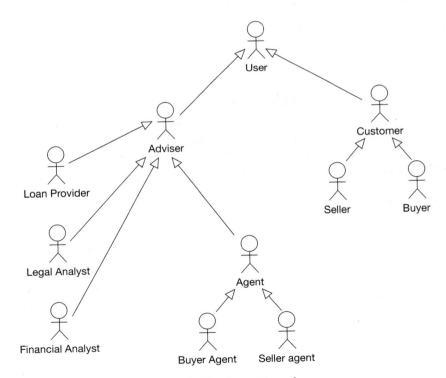

Figure B.25 *Actor Hierarchy*

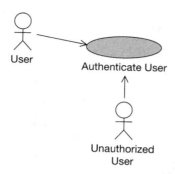

Figure B.26 *Authenticate User*

Use Case Name:	**Authenticate User**
Iteration:	**Focused**
Summary:	All users who request entry to the system must prove they are who they say they are (authentication). This applies to users inside the company as well as outside. Who the user is determines what he or she has access to (authorization).
Basic Course of Events:	1. This use case begins when the user enters a user identification and password. 2. The system responds by checking the combination of user identification and password against the recorded list of valid users. 3. The system responds by notifying the user that the user identification and password are valid and allows the user access to the application.
Alternative Paths:	None
Exception Paths:	In step 2, if the user identification and password combination is not valid, the system responds by notifying the user that the combination was invalid and asks the user to try again. If the user tries three times unsuccessfully, the system responds by disallowing the user and marking as suspended the user record of any and all user identifications tried. In step 2, if the user identification that is tried is in suspended mode, the system responds by notifying the user that this identification has been suspended and the user must contact a system administrator.

Use Case B.22 *Authenticate User—Focused (continues)*

Extension Points:	None
Trigger:	The user requires access to the system.
Assumptions:	None
Preconditions:	The system is operational.
Postconditions:	The validated user is allowed access to the system.
Related Business Rules:	None
Author:	Shelley Foerster
Date:	June 5, 2000—Facade; June 5, 2000—Filled; June 11, 2000—Focused

Use Case B.22 *continued*

Figure B.27 *Select Agent*

Use Case Name:	**Select Agent**
Iteration:	**Focused**
Summary:	The customers select their agents, probably based on the agents' location and expertise and whether the customers have worked with the agent previously.
Basic Course of Events:	1. This use case begins when the customer requests a list of agents.
	2. The system responds with a list of agents with information on their location and expertise.
	3. The customer makes a short list of agents.
	4. The system responds by notifying the agents on the short list.
	5. The agents respond by contacting the customer and answering questions the customer has about their experience or qualifications.
	6. The customer responds by choosing an agent.

Use Case B.23 *Select Agent—Focused (continues)*

Alternative Paths:	None
Exception Paths:	In step 1, if the customer suddenly decides not to choose an agent, the customer indicates this, and the system responds by warning the customer of the dangers of not having an agent and records that the customer has not chosen an agent.
Extension Points:	None
Trigger:	The customer indicates that he or she would like to choose an agent.
Assumptions:	None
Preconditions:	The customer has decided to choose an agent.
Postconditions:	The customer has chosen a specific agent.
Related Business Rules:	None
Author:	Angela Baltimore
Date:	March 25, 2000—Facade; March 27, 2000—Filled; April 1, 2000—Focused

Use Case B.23 *continued*

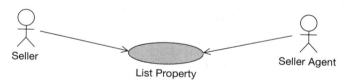

Seller

List Property

Seller Agent

Figure B.28 *List Property*

Use Case Name:	**List Property**
Iteration:	**Focused**
Summary:	The seller puts a property up for sale, including a set of information that classifies the property uniquely for prospective buyers.

Use Case B.24 *List Property—Focused (continues)*

Basic Course of Events:	1. This use case begins when the seller enters the information required to list a property. 2. The system responds by saving the listing and notifying the seller's agent that the listing has been entered. 3. The seller's agent checks the listing and solicits the seller for additional information or clarifications. Then the seller's agent completes the listing and confirms it. 4. The system records the confirmation and lists the property publicly.
Alternative Paths:	In step 3, if there are no clarifications or additions required, as judged by the seller's agent, the seller's agent simply confirms the listing.
Exception Paths:	None
Extension Points:	None
Trigger:	The seller has decided to sell a property.
Assumptions:	None
Preconditions:	The seller has chosen an agent or has chosen not to have an agent.
Postconditions:	The property is available for viewing on the system by prospective buyers.
Related Business Rules:	None
Author:	Ed Towson
Date:	March 20, 2000—Facade; April 2, 2000—Filled; April 3, 2000—Focused

Use Case B.24 *continued*

Figure B.28 *Review Listings*

Use Case Name:	**Review Listings**
Iteration:	**Focused**
Summary:	The buyer browses through the listings of properties with the help of the buyer's agent.
Basic Course of Events:	1. This use case begins when the buyer requests to view properties. 2. The system responds by providing the buyer with methods for searching: keyword or specific criteria (price, location, photo, size, floor plan, age, and so on). 3. The buyer's agent enters advice for the buyer into the system and points out certain properties that the buyer may have overlooked.
Alternative Paths:	In step 3, if the buyer did not choose an agent, this step does not exist.
Exception Paths:	None
Extension Points:	None
Trigger:	The buyer wishes to purchase a property but does not know of a suitable property yet.
Assumptions:	None
Preconditions:	At least one property has been listed.
Postconditions:	None
Related Business Rules:	None
Author:	Ed Towson
Date:	March 23, 2000—Facade; March 26, 2000—Filled; April 1, 2000—Focused

Use Case B.25 *Review Listings—Focused*

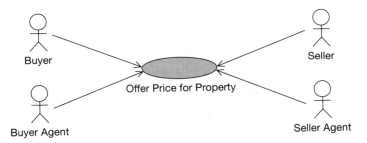

Figure B.30   *Offer Price for Property*

Use Case Name:	**Offer Price for Property**
Iteration:	**Focused**
Summary:	The buyer makes an offer to the seller. The seller's agent and the buyer's agent offer their respective customers advice based on their experience in real estate transactions and their knowledge of the marketplace.
Basic Course of Events:	1. This use case begins when a buyer registers a bid against a property on the system. 2. The system responds by saving the bid. The system then presents agent criteria to the buyer. 3. The buyer chooses specific criteria and chooses an agent. 4. The system responds by registering the agent choice and by notifying the seller and the seller's agent that an offer has been made. 5. The seller receives the offer. 6. The system responds by notifying the buyer that the seller has seen the offer (there is no implication of acceptance or rejection). 7. The seller prepares a counteroffer and submits it. 8. The system responds by presenting the counteroffer to the buyer and the buyer's agent. 9. The buyer responds by accepting the counteroffer. 10. The system responds by notifying the seller that the counteroffer was accepted.

Use Case B.26   *Offer Price for Property—Focused (continues)*

Alternative Paths:	In step 3, if the buyer chooses not to use an agent, the system warns the buyer of the hazards of proceeding without an agent. If the buyer insists, the system allows the buyer to proceed to the next step (and through all future steps) without an agent. In step 7, if the seller accepts the buyer's offer, the seller simply registers acceptance of the offer. The system responds by notifying the buyer and the buyer's agent. In step 4, if the buyer does not accept the seller's offer, the buyer submits another counteroffer, which is presented to the seller, and then processing returns to step 5.
Exception Paths:	None
Extension Points:	None
Trigger:	The buyer has decided to make an offer on a specific property.
Assumptions:	None
Preconditions:	The property has been listed. The buyer and seller have either chosen agents or decided not to choose agents.
Postconditions:	The buyer and seller have reached agreement on a price.
Related Business Rules:	None
Author:	Angela Baltimore
Date:	April 6, 2000—Focused

Use Case B.26 *continued*

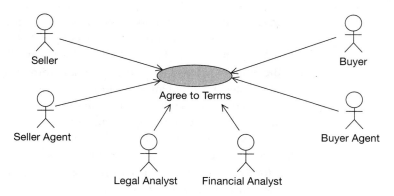

Figure B.31 *Agree to Terms*

Use Case Name:	**Agree to Terms**
Iteration:	**Focused**
Summary:	The buyer and the seller agree to the terms of the sale, including any required changes to the existing property, the items included with the property, the date of possession, the financing, and any other conditions of sale. The agents help their respective customers by offering advice, caution, or recommendations.
Basic Course of Events:	1. This use case begins when the buyer and the seller indicate that an agreement is possible. 2. The system responds by notifying the buyer, the buyer's agent, the seller, the seller's agent, the legal analyst, and the financial analyst that the agreement process is ready to begin. 3. The buyer or the seller submits a proposal of terms. 4. The system responds by allowing all actors to view the proposal of terms and make their changes. 5. The actors make their changes. 6. The system responds by making the actors' changes public to all. 7. The actors discuss the changes and come to an agreement on each proposed change, item by item.

Use Case B.27 *Agree to Terms—Focused (continues)*

	8. The system responds by consolidating the agreed-upon changes and making the proposal of terms public again. 9. The actors indicate their agreement. 10. This use case ends when the system indicates that the proposal of terms is final.
Alternative Paths:	In step 3, the buyer's agent may submit a proposal of terms to the buyer, who may then submit it as his or her own. In step 3, the seller may also be the one to submit a proposal of terms. In step 3, the seller's agent may submit a proposal of terms to the seller, who may then submit it as his or her own.
Exception Paths:	In step 9, if the buyer or the seller does not agree to the proposal of terms as it stands, the objecting party enters the issue. Then the objecting party modifies the proposal, and processing returns to step 4.
Extension Points:	None
Trigger:	Buyer and seller indicate that agreement to terms can begin.
Assumptions:	None
Preconditions:	An offer has been made and accepted.
Postconditions:	Terms are agreed to by buyer and seller.
Related Business Rules:	None
Author:	Angela Baltimore
Date:	March 20, 2000—Facade; March 28, 2000—Filled; April 2, 2000—Focused

Use Case B.27 *continued*

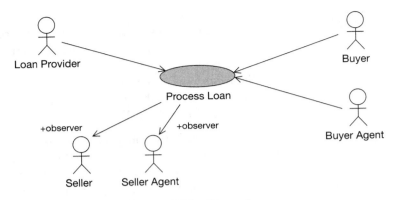

Figure B.32 *Process Loan*

Use Case Name:	**Process Loan**
Iteration:	**Focused**
Summary:	The loan provider and the buyer work out the terms of the loan if the buyer requires one. Terms include the interest rate, points, term, escrow, insurance, and so on.
Basic Course of Events:	1. This use case begins when the buyer and the seller have agreed to terms. 2. The buyer indicates that a loan is required. 3. The system responds by contacting the loan provider with the details of the buyer's loan requirements. 4. The loan provider uses the buyer's loan requirement as input to create a loan proposal. 5. The system responds by sending the loan proposal to the buyer and the buyer's agent. 6. The buyer makes a counteroffer to the loan provider. 7. The system responds by sending the counteroffer to the loan provider. 8. The loan provider accepts the counteroffer. 9. The system responds by sending notification of the loan provider's acceptance to the buyer and the buyer's agent. 10. The buyer indicates acceptance of the loan. 11. The system responds by recording the buyer's acceptance of the loan and files the approved loan application with the loan provider.

Use Case B.28 *Process Loan—Focused (continues)*

Alternative Paths:	In step 6, if the buyer approves the initial loan proposal, jump to step 8.
Exception Paths:	In step 6, if the buyer decides that this loan provider cannot provide an appropriate loan for this purchase, the buyer indicates to the system that another loan provider is needed. The system responds by returning to step 3. In step 4, if the loan provider decides that the buyer is not eligible for a loan, the loan provider makes note of this in the system and the system responds by notifying the buyer that no loan is possible from this loan provider. The buyer may then choose another loan provider or may cancel the offer.
Extension Points:	None
Trigger:	The buyer requires financing and initiates a loan search.
Assumptions:	None
Preconditions:	The buyer requires financing.
Postconditions:	The loan is approved and recorded.
Related Business Rules:	None
Author:	Felix Westerville
Date:	March 27, 2000—Facade; March 31, 2000—Filled; April 1, 2000—Focused

Use Case B.28 *continued*

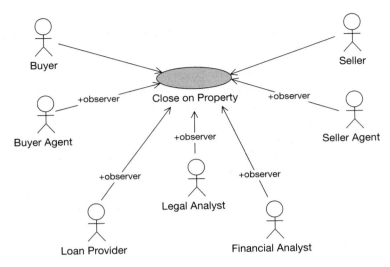

Figure B.33   *Close on Property*

Use Case Name:	**Close on Property**
Iteration:	**Focused**
Summary:	The buyer and seller close the transaction on the property. Advice and recommendations come from the other actors.
Basic Course of Events:	1. This use case begins when the buyer and the seller request to view the contract. 2. The system responds by presenting the contract and by requesting confirmation by buyer and seller. 3. The buyer and the seller confirm the sale. 4. This use case ends when the system records the sale as confirmed and registers the property in the buyer's name.
Alternative Paths:	None
Exception Paths:	In step 3, if the buyer or the seller does not confirm the sale, both parties are notified that the transaction did not occur, and the system records that the transaction was aborted during the closing stage.
Extension Points:	None

Use Case B.29   *Close on Property—Focused (continues)*

Trigger:	The buyer and the seller indicate that the closing can occur.
Assumptions:	None
Preconditions:	The buyer and the seller have agreed to terms. The buyer's source of payment has been secured.
Postconditions:	The property is closed and the transaction is complete.
Related Business Rules:	None
Author:	Felix Westerville
Date:	March 20, 2000—Facade; April 1, 2000—Filled; April 1, 2000—Focused

Use Case B.29 *continued*

B.3.3 Business Rules

Table B.7 Business Rules Example

Rule ID	Name	Description	Category	Static/ Dynamic	Source
001	Customer can change agents	Customers can change the agent they are using at any time during the transaction with no penalty.	Structural fact	Dynamic	Interview with executive sponsor 03/20/2000
002	Customer can transact without an agent	Customers can transact business as buyers or sellers without having an agent. However, each time a customer chooses to transact business without an agent, he or she must be warned of the downside of not having an agent.	Structural fact	Dynamic	Interview with executive sponsor 03/22/2000
003	Customers not using agents are charged less	When customers decide not to use an agent to transact business, they will be charged less than customers who use agents.	Structural fact	Dynamic	JRP session 03/21/2000
004	Agent fees depend on number of interactions	The fees the customer is charged are based on the number of interactions with an agent. Each inter-action requiring an agent will be charged to the customer as a one-hour minimum. If the agent spends more than one hour, the customer will be charged in quarter-hour segments.	Computation	Dynamic	JRP session 03/21/2000
005	Seller may pull property almost any time	The seller may retract the offer to sell the property at any time except after the seller has made a counteroffer to a prospective buyer. After this has occurred, if the seller and buyer are still in active negotiation, the seller must first notify all involved agents and the active buyer.	Action restricting	Dynamic	JRP session 03/21/2000

continued

Table B.7 *continued*

Rule ID	Name	Description	Category	Static/Dynamic	Source
006	Number of counteroffers limited	The number of counteroffers between buyer and seller is limited to ten for the buyer and ten for the seller. After this maximum has been reached, one or both agents or an agency designee will step in and conduct a review of the transaction with the customers.	Action triggering	Dynamic	Interview with agent 04/02/2000
007	Definition of "active negotiation"	An active negotiation is a transaction that has occurred within the past five business days.	Structural fact	Dynamic	Interview with executive sponsor 04/02/2000

B.4 The Finished Iteration

During the Finished iteration, we refined the following artifacts.

Problem statement	No changes
Statement of work	Small workplan changes (not shown)
Risk analysis	Deleted a risk that was addressed by adding a business rule
Finished use cases	Added nonfunctional requirements as stereotypes, made other small adjustments
Business rules	Added one business rule
User interface guidelines	Started and completed (not shown)
Prototype	Started (not shown)

B.4.1 Risk Analysis

Table B.8 Risk Analysis: Finished Iteration

Number	Category	Risk	Resolution Needed By	Status	Days Lost If It Occurs	Likelihood It Will Happen	Risk Rating
001	Interfaces	The new application needs to interface with SAP, which has not been put into production yet. There could be schedule delays if this project has to wait two months for the SAP project.	Jul 1, 2000	Unresolved	50	50%	25
002	User time	The majority of the user group is heavily involved in a reengineering effort. If the project team members cannot get their time, the project will be delayed.	May 15, 2000	Being investigated	70	80%	56
003	Qualified project manager	The project manager originally slated to take this project through deployment has quit the company. A new, equally qualified person must be found before the analysis activity starts.	May 20, 2000	Interviews under way	200	20%	40
004	Commercial versus residential	The executive sponsor has said that the agency may decide to prioritize commercial real estate sales above residential. If this is done now or in the future, it will cause rework.	May 1, 2000	Decision request provided to executive sponsor	30	50%	15

B.4.2 Finished Use Cases

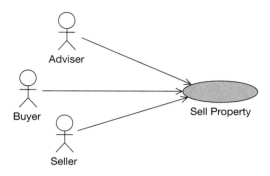

Figure B.34 *System Level Context Use Case: Sell Property*

Use Case Name:	**Sell Property**
Iteration:	**Finished**
Summary:	System Context Use Case. The seller lists the property, a buyer purchases the property, and the agent guides them through the process and offers advice, caution, and recommendations.
Basic Course of Events:	1. The seller selects an agent. 2. The system responds by assigning an agent and notifying the seller's agent. 3. The seller lists the property to sell. 4. The system responds by displaying this property in the property listing and linking it for searches. 5. The buyer selects an agent. 6. The buyer reviews the property listings by entering search criteria. 7. The system responds by displaying properties that match the buyer's search criteria. 8. The buyer finds a property and makes an offer on it. 9. The system responds by notifying the seller and the seller's agent. 10. The seller responds to the offer with a counteroffer. 11. The system responds by notifying the buyer and the buyer's agent. 12. The buyer and the seller agree to terms.

Use Case B.30 *System Level Context Sell Property—Finished (continues)*

	13. The system responds by recording the agreement. 14. The buyer indicates that a loan is required. 15. The system responds by locating an appropriate loan provider. 16. The buyer and the loan provider agree to loan terms. 17. The system responds by recording the terms of the loan. 18. The buyer and the seller close on the property. 19. The system responds by recording the details of the close.
Alternative Paths:	N/A
Extension Points:	N/A
Trigger:	N/A
Assumptions:	N/A
Preconditions:	N/A
Postconditions:	N/A
Related Business Rules:	N/A
Author:	Angela Baltimore
Date:	March 20, 2000—Facade; March 26, 2000—Filled; April 2, 2000—Focused; April 10, 2000—Finished

Use Case B.30 *continued*

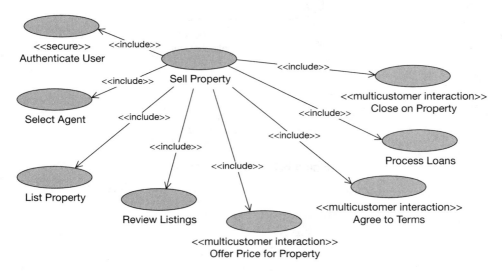

Figure B.35 *Use Case Hierarchy*

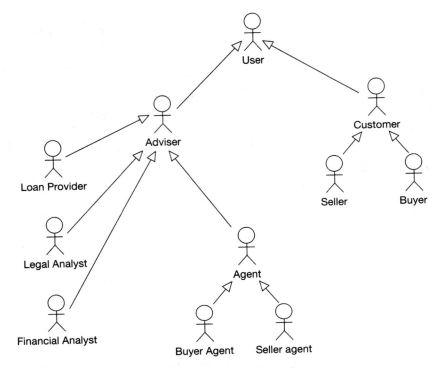

Figure B.36   *Actor Hierarchy*

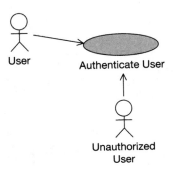

Figure B.37   *Authenticate User*

Use Case Name:	**Authenticate User**
Iteration:	**Finished**
Summary:	All users who request entry to the system must prove they are who they say they are (authentication). This applies to users inside the company as well as outside. Who the user is determines what he or she has access to (authorization).
Basic Course of Events:	1. This use case begins when the user enters a user identification and password. 2. The system responds by checking the combination of user identification and password against the recorded list of valid users. 3. The system responds by notifying the user that the user identification and password are valid and allows the user access to the application.
Alternative Paths:	None
Exception Paths:	In step 2, if the user identification and password combination is not valid, the system responds by notifying the user that the combination was invalid and asks the user to try again. If the user tries three times unsuccessfully, the system responds by disallowing the user and marking as suspended the user record of any and all user identifications tried. In step 2, if the user identification that is tried is in suspended mode, the system responds by notifying the user that this identification has been suspended and the user must contact a system administrator.
Extension Points:	None
Trigger:	The user requires access to the system.
Assumptions:	None
Preconditions:	The system is operational.
Postconditions:	The validated user is allowed access to the system.
Related Business Rules:	None
Author:	Shelley Foerster
Date:	June 5, 2000—Facade; June 5, 2000—Filled; June 11, 2000—Focused; June 14, 2000—Finished

Use Case B.31 *Authenticate User—Finished*

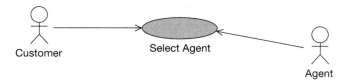

Figure B.38 *Select Agent*

Use Case Name:	**Select Agent**
Iteration:	**Finished**
Summary:	The customers select their agents, probably based on the agents' location and expertise and whether the customers have worked with the agents previously.
Basic Course of Events:	1. This use case begins when the customer requests a list of agents. 2. The system responds with a list of agents, with information on their location and expertise. 3. The customer responds by choosing an agent.
Alternative Paths	None
Exception Paths:	In step 1, if the customer decides not to choose an agent, the customer indicates this. The system responds by warning the customer of the dangers of not having an agent and records that the customer has not chosen an agent.
Extension Points:	None
Trigger:	The customers indicate that they would like to choose an agent.
Assumptions:	None
Preconditions:	The customer has decided to choose an agent.
Postconditions:	The customer has chosen a specific agent.
Related Business Rules:	None
Author:	Angela Baltimore
Date:	March 25, 2000—Facade; March 27, 2000—Filled; April 3, 2000—Focused; April 6, 2000—Finished

Use Case B.32 *Select Agent—Finished*

Figure B.39   *List Property*

Use Case Name:	**List Property**
Iteration:	**Finished**
Summary:	The seller puts a property up for sale, including a set of information that classifies the property uniquely for prospective buyers.
Basic Course of Events:	1. This use case begins when the seller enters the information required to list a property. 2. The system responds by saving the listing and notifying the seller's agent that the listing has been entered. 3. The seller's agent checks the listing and solicits the seller for additional information or clarifications. Then the seller's agent completes the listing and confirms it. 4. The system records the confirmation and lists the property publicly.
Alternative Paths:	In step 3, if there are no clarifications or additions required, as judged by the seller's agent, the seller's agent simply confirms the listing.
Exception Paths:	None
Extension Points:	None
Trigger:	The seller has decided to sell a property.
Assumptions:	None
Preconditions:	The seller has chosen an agent or chosen not to have an agent.
Postconditions:	The property is available for viewing on the system by prospective buyers.

Use Case B.33   *List Property—Finished (continues)*

Related Business Rules:	None
Author:	Ed Towson
Date:	March 20, 2000—Facade; April 2, 2000—Filled; April 3, 2000—Focused; April 6, 2000—Finished

Use Case B.33 *continued*

Buyer   Review Listings   Buyer Agent

Figure B.40 *Review Listings*

Use Case Name:	**Review Listings**
Iteration:	**Finished**
Summary:	The buyer browses through the listings of properties with the help of the buyer's agent.
Basic Course of Events:	1. This use case begins when the buyer requests to view properties. 2. The system responds by providing the buyer with methods for searching: keyword or specific criteria (price, location, photo, size, floor plan, age, and so on). 3. The buyer's agent enters advice for the buyer into the system and points out certain properties that the buyer may have overlooked.
Alternative Paths:	In step 3, if an agent was not chosen by the buyer, this step does not exist.
Exception Paths:	None
Extension Points:	None
Trigger:	The buyer wishes to purchase a property but does not know of a suitable property yet.

Use Case B.34 *Review Listings—Filled (continues)*

Assumptions:	None
Preconditions:	At least one property has been listed.
Postconditions:	None
Related Business Rules:	None
Author:	Ed Towson
Date:	March 23, 2000—Facade; March 26, 2000—Filled; April 1, 2000—Focused; April 7, 2000—Finished

Use Case B.34 *continued*

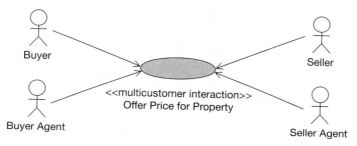

Figure B.41 *Offer Price for Property*

Use Case Name:	**Offer Price for Property**
Iteration:	**Finished**
Summary:	The buyer makes an offer to the seller. The seller's agent and the buyer's agent offer their respective customers advice based on their experience in real estate transactions and their knowledge of the marketplace.
Basic Course of Events:	1. This use case begins when a buyer registers a bid against a property on the system. 2. The system responds by saving the bid. The system then presents agent criteria to the buyer. 3. The buyer chooses specific criteria and chooses an agent. 4. The system responds by registering the agent choice and notifying the seller and the seller's agent that an offer has been made.

Use Case B.35 *Offer Price for Property—Finished (continues)*

	5. The seller receives the offer. 6. The system responds by notifying the buyer that the seller has seen the offer (there is no implication of acceptance or rejection). 7. The seller prepares a counteroffer and submits it. 8. The system responds by presenting the counteroffer to the buyer and the buyer's agent. 9. The buyer responds by accepting the counteroffer. 10. The system responds by notifying the seller that the counteroffer was accepted.
Alternative Paths:	In step 3, if the buyer chooses not to use an agent, the system warns the buyer of the hazards of proceeding without an agent. If the buyer insists, the system allows the buyer to proceed to the next step (and through all future steps) without an agent. In step 7, if the seller accepts the buyer's offer, the seller simply registers acceptance of the offer and the system responds by notifying the buyer and the buyer's agent. In step 4, if the buyer does not accept the seller's offer, the buyer submits another counteroffer, which is presented to the seller and then processing returns to step 5.
Exception Paths:	None
Extension Points:	None
Trigger:	The buyer has decided to make an offer on a specific property.
Assumptions:	None
Preconditions:	The property has been listed. The buyer and the seller have either chosen agents or decided not to choose agents.
Postconditions:	The buyer and the seller have reached agreement on a price.
Related Business Rules:	None
Author:	Angela Baltimore
Date:	April 6, 2000—Focused; April 10, 2000—Finished

Use Case B.35 *continued*

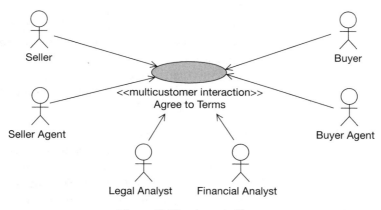

Figure B.42 *Agree to Terms*

Use Case Name:	**Agree to Terms**
Iteration:	**Finished**
Summary:	The buyer and the seller agree to the terms of the sale, including any required changes to the existing property, the items included with the property, the date of possession, the financing, and any other conditions of sale. The agents help their respective customers by offering advice, caution, or recommendations.
Basic Course of Events:	1. This use case begins when the buyer and the seller indicate that an agreement is possible. 2. The system responds by notifying the buyer, the buyer's agent, the seller, the seller's agent, the legal analyst, and the financial analyst that the agreement process is ready to begin. 3. The buyer submits a proposal of terms. 4. The system responds by allowing all actors to view the proposal of terms and make their changes. 5. The actors make their changes. 6. The system responds by making the actors' changes public to all. 7. The actors discuss the changes and come to an agreement on each proposed change, item by item.

Use Case B.36 *Agree to Terms—Finished (continues)*

	8. The system responds by consolidating the agreed-upon changes and making the proposal of terms public again. 9. The actors indicate their agreement. 10. This use case ends when the system indicates that the proposal of terms is final.
Alternative Paths:	In step 3, the buyer's agent may submit a proposal of terms to the buyer, who may then submit it as his or her own. In step 3, the seller may also be the one to submit a proposal of terms. In step 3, the seller's agent may submit a proposal of terms to the seller, who may then submit it as his or her own.
Exception Paths:	In step 9, if the buyer or seller does not agree to the proposal of terms as it stands, the objecting party enters the issue. Then the objecting party modifies the proposal, and processing returns to step 4.
Extension Points:	None
Trigger:	Buyer and seller indicate that agreement to terms can begin.
Assumptions:	None
Preconditions:	An offer has been made and accepted.
Postconditions:	Terms are agreed to by the buyer and the seller.
Related Business Rules:	None
Author:	Angela Baltimore
Date:	March 20, 2000—Facade; March 28, 2000—Filled; April 3, 2000—Focused; April 3, 2000—Finished

Use Case B.36 *continued*

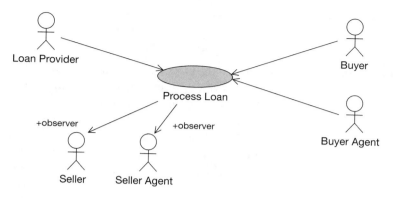

Figure B.43 *Process Loan*

Use Case Name:	**Process Loan**
Iteration:	**Finished**
Summary:	The loan provider and the buyer work out the terms of the loan if the buyer requires one. Terms include the interest rate, points, term, escrow, insurance, and so on.
Basic Course of Events:	1. This use case begins when the buyer and the seller have agreed to terms. 2. The buyer indicates that a loan is required. 3. The system responds by contacting the loan provider with the details of the buyer's loan requirement. 4. The loan provider uses the buyer's loan requirement as input to create a loan proposal. 5. The system responds by sending the loan proposal to the buyer and the buyer's agent. 6. The buyer makes a counteroffer to the loan provider. 7. The system responds by sending the counteroffer to the loan provider. 8. The loan provider accepts the counteroffer. 9. The system responds by sending notification of the loan provider's acceptance to the buyer and the buyer's agent. 10. The buyer indicates acceptance of the loan. 11. The system responds by recording the buyer's acceptance of the loan and files the approved loan application with the loan provider.

Use Case B.37 *Process Loan—Finished (continues)*

Alternative Paths:	In step 6, if the buyer approves of the initial loan proposal, jump to step 8.
Exception Paths:	In step 6, if the buyer decides that this loan provider cannot provide an appropriate loan for this purchase, the buyer indicates to the system that another loan provider is needed. The system responds by returning to step 3. In step 4, If the loan provider decides that the buyer is not eligible for any loan, the loan provider makes note of this in the system and the system responds by notifying the buyer that no loan is possible from this loan provider. The buyer may then choose another loan provider or may cancel the offer.
Extension Points:	None
Trigger:	The buyer requires financing and initiates the loan search.
Assumptions:	None
Preconditions:	The buyer requires financing.
Postconditions:	The loan is approved and recorded.
Related Business Rules:	None
Author:	Felix Westerville
Date:	March 27, 2000—Facade; March 31, 2000—Filled; April 1, 2000—Focused; April 10, 2000—Finished

Use Case B.37   *continued*

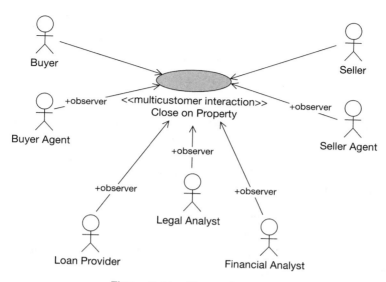

Figure B.44 *Close on Property*

Use Case Name:	**Close on Property**
Iteration:	**Finished**
Summary:	The buyer and the seller close the transaction on the property. Advice and recommendations come from the other actors.
Basic Course of Events:	1. This use case begins when the buyer and the seller request to view the contract. 2. The system responds by presenting the contract and requesting confirmation by the buyer and the seller. 3. The buyer and the seller confirm the sale. 4. This use case ends when the system records the sale as confirmed and registers the property in the buyer's name.
Alternative Paths:	None
Exception Paths:	In step 3, if the buyer or the seller does not confirm the sale, both parties are notified that the transaction did not occur, and the system records that the transaction was aborted during the closing stage.

Use Case B.38 *Close on Property—Finished (continues)*

Extension Points:	None
Trigger:	The buyer and the seller indicate that the closing can occur.
Assumptions:	None
Preconditions:	The buyer and the seller have agreed to terms. The buyer's source of payment has been secured.
Postconditions:	The property is closed and the transaction is complete.
Related Business Rules:	None
Author:	Felix Westerville
Date:	March 20, 2000—Facade; April 1, 2000—Filled; April 1, 2000—Focused; April 6, 2000—Finished

Use Case B.38   *continued*

B.4.3 Business Rules

Table B.9 Business Rules Example

Rule ID	Name	Description	Category	Static/ Dynamic	Source
001	Customer can change agents	Customers can change the agent they are using at any time during the transaction with no penalty.	Structural fact	Dynamic	Interview with executive sponsor 03/20/2000
002	Customer can transact without an agent	Customers can transact business as buyers or sellers without having an agent. However, each time a customer chooses to transact business without an agent, he or she must be warned of the downside of not having agent.	Structural fact	Dynamic	Interview with executive sponsor 03/22/2000
003	Customers not using agents are charged less	When customers decide not to use an agent to transact business, they will be charged less than customers who use agents.	Structural fact	Dynamic	JRP session 03/21/2000
004	Agent fees depend on number of interactions	The fees the customer is charged are based on the number of interactions with an agent. Each interaction requiring an agent will be charged to the customer as a one-hour minimum. If the agent spends more than one hour, the customer will be charged in quarter-hour segments.	Computation	Dynamic	JRP session 03/21/2000
005	Seller may pull property almost any time	The seller may retract the offer to sell the property at any time except after the seller has made a counteroffer to a prospective buyer. After this has occurred, if the seller and buyer are still in active negotiation, the seller must first notify all involved agents and the active buyer.	Action restricting	Dynamic	JRP session 03/21/2000

Rule ID	Name	Description	Category	Static/Dynamic	Source
006	Number of counteroffers limited	The number of counteroffers between buyer and seller is limited to ten for the buyer and ten for the seller. After this maximum has been reached, one or both agents or an agency designee will step in and conduct a review of the transaction with the customers.	Action triggering	Dynamic	Interview with agent 04/02/2000
007	Definition of "active negotiation"	An active negotiation is a transaction that has occurred within the past five business days.	Structural fact	Dynamic	Interview with executive sponsor 04/02/2000
008	No "undo" after property closure	After a property has closed, any protests from buyer or seller will go to an arbitration board, set up at the mutual agreement of our agency, the buyer, and the seller. No protests after closure will be handled any other way.	Structural fact	Static	Interview with agent 05/08/2000

C

Case Study: Track Costume Sales

This appendix shows artifacts produced from a complete lifecycle of four iterations of requirements gathering. Without creating a 500-page appendix, we wanted to give you an impression of how everything comes together. To save space, we provide only short explanations for some of the artifacts (for example, a workplan) that are common knowledge among IT professionals.

This second of two case studies produces the requirements for an application for a costume design shop. The company requires an application that can provide historical sales information to show trends in costume fashion. Currently, no sales information is being tracked electronically, so this system must provide inputs for everything related to selling costumes.

The T. J. Eye Catchers costume design company is a small shop that caters to individual customers, including fitness instructors, bodybuilders, ice skaters, child performers, and other performers. The new system will help the designers forecast and respond to future surges in demand for designs, which are now causing problems during peak-and-valley demand cycles.

NOTE: We have deleted some details to avoid cluttering this appendix. For example, we have omitted use cases for CRUD functionality as well as use cases to address "cancel order," both of which would need to be included in an actual system. These appendixes are quite large as it is, so we've taken steps to shorten them by eliminating some of the more grueling details.

C.1 The Facade Iteration

During the Facade iteration, we created the following artifacts.

Problem statement	Complete but will be revised slightly in future iterations
Statement of work	Complete but will be revised slightly in future iterations
Risk analysis	Complete, but risks will be added and deleted throughout all iterations
Facade use cases	"Shell" use cases as placeholders for functionality to be filled in later
Business rules	Created an initial list

C.1.1 Problem Statement

The T. J. Eye Catchers costume design company needs to forecast and respond to the rapid cycles of fashion that are currently hindering our ability to produce the best display costumes for the front window and for our catalog. Currently, we do not track any sales information electronically.

C.1.2 Statement of Work

Scope

The following elements are in scope:

- Handling customer appointments
- Costume tracking
- Customer tracking
- Sales tracking
- Trend identification
- All show-biz costumes
- Halloween costumes

The following element is out of scope:

- Commercial customers (mass uniform orders)

Objectives

The objectives of this application are to provide the T. J. Eye Catchers costume design company with an application that allows the designers to forecast styles and trends of costumes. The forecasting capability must have extensive graphic capability to allow the designers to spot trends visually.

Application Overview

This application is a line-of-business financial application. It will store the information that is critical to T. J. Eye Catchers for revenue, profit, tax, and strategy.

User Demography

The only users of this system will be employees of the company.

- Designers
- Office administrator
- System administrator

Constraints

There are no constraints at the current time.

Assumptions

Designers will have sufficient computer literacy skills by the time the first deployment of the application occurs.

Staffing and Cost

(Staffing and cost plan here.)

Deliverable Outlines

(Outline the deliverables here. Use your methodology to identify deliverables and tables of contents.)

Expected Duration

(Using a GANTT chart, produce a timeline showing when the phases (as identified in the methodology) will conclude and the products that will be available at the conclusion of each phase.)

C.1.3 Risk Analysis

Table C.1 Risk Analysis: Facade Iteration

Number	Category	Risk	Resolution Needed By	Status	Days Lost If It Occurs	Likelihood It Will Happen	Risk Rating
001	Interfaces	Currently, the system is defined as requiring a design component for creating costumes online. This will require a very complex computer-aided design (CAD) tool, which we have not located in the industry. If we cannot find one, we will have to develop it, and that will have a tremendous impact on scope.	Jul 1, 2000	Continuing search for package	500	10%	50
002	Designers' computer literacy	Currently, the costume designers have no computer skills. If they are to use a computer for their line-of-business transactions, they must begin learning how to use a mouse and so on immediately so that they can use this application when it is ready. (The office administrator is computer-literate.)	Jul 1, 2000	Sent memo to executive sponsor	30	50%	15

C.1.4 Facade Use Cases

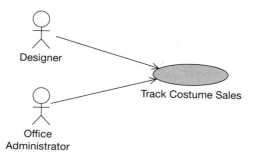

Designer

Track Costume Sales

Office
Administrator

Figure C.1 *System Level Context Use Case: Track Costume Sales Diagram*

Use Case Name:	**Track Costume Sales**
Iteration:	**Facade**
Summary:	System Context Use Case. This system needs to track the information related to customers, appointments, designs, orders, and sales. The purpose of the system is to provide historical sales data that allows the owner to visualize trends.
Basic Course of Events:	
Alternative Paths:	
Exception Paths:	
Extension Points:	
Trigger:	
Assumptions:	
Preconditions:	
Postconditions:	
Related Business Rules:	
Author:	Tammie Thurber
Date:	June 2, 2000—Facade

Use Case C.1 *System Level Context Use Case—Track Costume Sales*

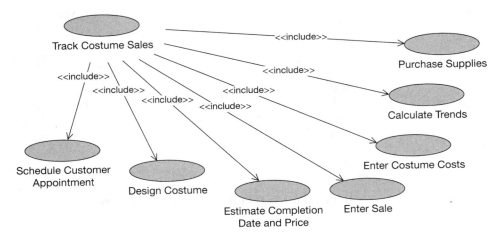

Figure C.2   *Use Case Hierarchy Diagram*

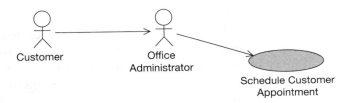

Figure C.3   *Schedule Customer Appointment*

Use Case Name:	**Schedule Customer Appointment**
Iteration:	**Facade**
Summary:	The office administrator works with the customer to determine an appointment with a designer that suits each person's schedule. As the appointment approaches, the system reminds the office administrator to confirm the appointment with both parties.
Basic Course of Events:	
Alternative Paths:	
Exception Paths:	
Extension Points:	

Use Case C.2   *Schedule Customer Appointment—Facade (continues)*

Trigger:	
Assumptions:	
Preconditions:	
Postconditions:	
Related Business Rules:	
Author:	Tammie Thurber
Date:	June 3, 2000—Facade

Use Case C.2 *continued*

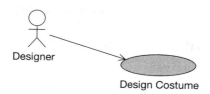

Designer

Design Costume

Figure C.4 *Design Costume*

Use Case Name:	**Design Costume**
Iteration:	**Facade**
Summary:	The designer creates a new costume design, which consists of a pattern, style, and size. The designer uses the application to create a design that will waste the least fabric and conforms to the customer's measurements.
Basic Course of Events:	
Alternative Paths:	
Exception Paths:	
Extension Points:	
Trigger:	
Assumptions:	
Preconditions:	

Use Case C.3 *Design Costume—Facade (continues)*

Postconditions:	
Related Business Rules:	
Author:	Todd Kurstak
Date:	June 3, 2000—Facade

Use Case C.3   *continued*

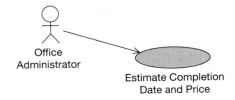

Office
Administrator

Estimate Completion
Date and Price

Figure C.5   *Estimate Completion Date and Price*

Use Case Name:	**Estimate Completion Date and Price**
Iteration:	**Facade**
Summary:	The office administrator enters the estimated completion date and price into the system after the designer has decided what is needed. The system provides a list of all other ongoing work to help the office administrator with the completion date decision. It also provides a list of similar costumes made previously at that price.
Basic Course of Events:	
Alternative Paths:	
Exception Paths:	
Extension Points:	
Trigger:	
Assumptions:	
Preconditions:	
Postconditions:	

Use Case C.4   *Estimate Completion Date and Price—Facade (continues)*

Related Business Rules:	
Author:	Todd Kurstak
Date:	June 3, 2000—Facade

Use Case C.4 *continued*

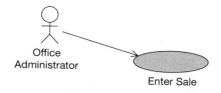

Office
Administrator

Enter Sale

Figure C.6 *Enter Sale*

Use Case Name:	**Enter Sale**
Iteration:	**Facade**
Summary:	The office administrator enters the sale amount, identified by customer, date, order, designer, and design information (fabric, color, and so on).
Basic Course of Events:	
Alternative Paths:	
Exception Paths:	
Extension Points:	
Trigger:	
Assumptions:	
Preconditions:	
Postconditions:	
Related Business Rules:	
Author:	Todd Kurstak
Date:	June 3, 2000—Facade

Use Case C.5 *Enter Sale—Facade*

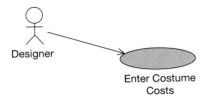

Figure C.7   *Enter Costume Costs*

Use Case Name:	**Enter Costume Costs**
Iteration:	**Facade**
Summary:	Immediately after completing the costume, the designer enters the total of all costs that went into it: labor, fabric, novelties, consultations (if applicable), and so on.
Basic Course of Events:	
Alternative Paths:	
Exception Paths:	
Extension Points:	
Trigger:	
Assumptions:	
Preconditions:	
Postconditions:	
Related Business Rules:	
Author:	Shelley Foerster
Date:	June 5, 2000—Facade

Use Case C.6   *Enter Costume Costs—Facade*

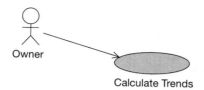

Figure C.8 *Calculate Trends*

Use Case Name:	**Calculate Trends**
Iteration:	**Facade**
Summary:	The owner needs to know the costume sales trends. For example, certain fabrics go in and out of style with customers. The owner needs to know the sales trends for all the variables in costume design: fabric, cut, novelties (sequins, shimmer, rhinestones, and so on), color combinations, and so on. These trends are based on the sales made in the previous weeks or months. The owner also needs to analyze customer activity, such as identifying the best and worst customers by volume, referrals, and so on. (This use case is the whole reason for building this application.)
Basic Course of Events:	
Alternative Paths:	
Exception Paths:	
Extension Points:	
Trigger:	
Assumptions:	
Preconditions:	
Postconditions:	
Related Business Rules:	
Author:	Tammie Thurber
Date:	June 2, 2000—Facade

Use Case C.7 *Calculate Trends—Facade*

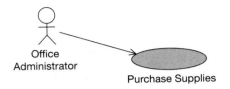

Figure C.9   *Purchase Supplies*

Use Case Name:	**Purchase Supplies**
Iteration:	**Facade**
Summary:	The office administrator records a purchase of supplies when the shipment arrives (fabric, novelties, elastic, and so on).
Basic Course of Events:	
Alternative Paths:	
Exception Paths:	
Extension Points:	
Trigger:	
Assumptions:	
Preconditions:	
Postconditions:	
Related Business Rules:	
Author:	Todd Kurstak
Date:	June 2, 2000—Facade

Use Case C.8   *Purchase Supplies—Facade*

C.1.5 Business Rules

Table C.2   Business Rules: Facade Iteration

Number	Name	Description	Category	Static/Dynamic	Source
001	Provide discounts for referrals	When a current customer provides a referral to the company and the referred party makes a purchase, the customer receives a $20 discount off future costume purchases.	Inference	Dynamic	Interview with owner 5/7/2000
002	Referral discounts must be used quickly	If a referral discount has been granted to a customer, it must be used on a costume within one year unless the customer contacts the company to request an extension.	Structural fact	Dynamic	Interview with owner 5/7/2000
003	Accept alterations only for faithful customers	No alterations will be accepted unless the transaction is approved by the owner for a long-time customer.	Structural fact	Static	Interview with owner 5/7/2000
004	Costume price is labor plus materials	The price of a costume is calculated as the cost of all supplies, materials, and novelties plus the cost of the designer's labor.	Computation	Static	Interview with owner 5/3/2000
005	No checks accepted from first-time customers	If a customer has not purchased anything from the company previously, he or she must pay cash in advance of receiving the costume.	Structural fact	Static	Interview with office administrator 5/6/2000 Confirmed by owner 5/10/2000

continues

Table C.2 *continued*

Number	Name	Description	Category	Static/Dynamic	Source
006	Some consultations are charged for	Consultations cost the customer only in the following circumstances: (1) if the customer has not paid for orders previously, (2) if the total order comes to less than $200, or (3) if the owner approves a paid consultation for this order	Structural fact	Dynamic	Interview with owner 5/10/2000
007	Consultations are charged at the regular designer rate	Consultation charges are calculated at the same hourly rate as design and sewing work.	Computation	Static	Interview with owner 5/10/2000

C.2 The Filled Iteration

During the Filled iteration, we refined the following artifacts.

Problem statement	No changes
Statement of work	Small workplan changes (not shown), added profitability to out-of-scope list
Risk analysis	No changes
Filled use cases	Added detail to basic course of events and alternative and exception paths
Business rules	No changes
Context matrix	Created initial draft
Nonfunctional requirements	Created an initial list
Testing using scenarios	N/A

A new use case, *Enter Order*, was added. Unless orders are entered, there is no way to track the costume while it is being designed. Also, the orders that are not sold provide useful statistics for analyzing trends.

The *Purchase Supplies* use case was deleted because it did not apply to the scope of tracking sales. It only aided profitability calculations, which are now out of scope.

C.2.1 Statement of Work

Scope

The following elements are in scope:

- Handling customer appointments
- Costume tracking
- Customer tracking
- Sales tracking
- Trend identification
- All show-biz costumes
- Halloween costumes

The following elements are out of scope:

- Mass uniform orders
- Profitability
- Costume design (CAD style)

C.2.2 Filled Use Cases

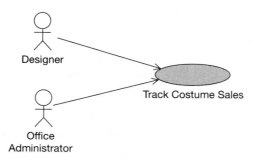

Figure C.10   *System Level Context Use Case: Track Costume Sales*

Use Case Name:	**Track Costume Sales**
Iteration:	**Filled**
Summary:	System Context Use Case. This system needs to track the information related to customers, appointments, designs, orders, and sales. The purpose of the system is to provide historical sales data to allow the owner to visualize trends.
Basic Course of Events:	1. The office administrator schedules a customer appointment. 2. The system responds by saving the appointment and customer information and by notifying the designer when the customer arrives. 3. The designer consults with the customer, estimates a price and date for availability, and enters the data into the system. 4. The system responds by arranging the designer's schedule to produce the item by the date specified to the customer. 5. The office administrator enters the order. 6. The system responds by saving the order information. 7. When the designer meets with the customer, the designer enters the customer's measurements and design preferences.

Use Case C.9   *Track Costume Sales—Filled (continues)*

	8. The system responds by optimizing the pattern for the fabric and the customer's measurements.
	9. The designer designs and sews the costume and, when it is complete, enters the costume costs.
	10. The system responds by calculating the profit or loss on the costume, given the quoted price.
	11. When the customer arrives for the final fitting, the office administrator enters the sale information.
	12. The system responds by saving the sale information.
	13. The owner requests visual trend calculations based on customers' preferences.
	14. The system responds with visual trend calculations.
	15. The owner responds by changing the business to capitalize on the upcoming trends noted.
Alternative Paths:	N/A
Exception Paths:	N/A
Extension Points:	N/A
Trigger:	N/A
Assumptions:	N/A
Preconditions:	N/A
Postconditions:	N/A
Related Business Rules:	N/A
Author:	Tammie Thurber
Date:	June 2, 2000—Facade; June 5, 2000—Filled

Use Case C.9 *continued*

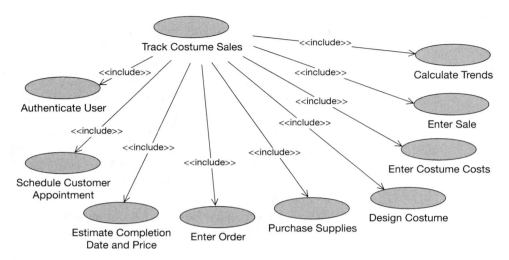

Figure C.11   *Use Case Hierarchy*

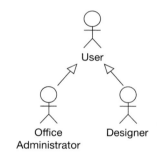

Figure C.12   *Actor Hierarchy*

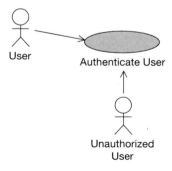

Figure C.13   *Authenticate User*

Use Case Name:	**Authenticate User**
Iteration:	**Filled**
Summary:	All users who request entry to the system must prove they are who they say they are (authentication). This applies to users inside the company as well as outside. Who the users are determines what they have access to (authorization).
Basic Course of Events:	1. This use case begins when the user enters a user identification and password. 2. The system responds by checking the combination of user identification and password against the recorded list of valid users. 3. The system responds by notifying the user that the user identification and password are valid and allows user access to the application.
Alternative Paths:	None
Exception Paths:	In step 2, if the user identification and password combination is not valid, the system responds by notifying the user that the combination was invalid and asks the user to try again. If the user tries three times unsuccessfully, the system responds by disallowing the user and marking as suspended the user record of any and all user identifications tried. In step 2, if the user identification that is tried is in suspended mode, the system responds by notifying the user that this identification has been suspended and the user must contact a system administrator.
Extension Points:	None
Trigger:	The user requires access to the system.
Assumptions:	None
Preconditions:	The system is operational.
Postconditions:	The validated user is allowed access to the system.
Related Business Rules:	None
Author:	Shelley Foerster
Date:	June 5, 2000—Facade; June 5, 2000—Filled

Use Case C.10 *Authenticate User—Filled*

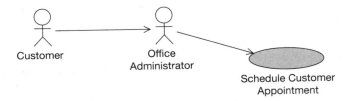

Figure C.14   *Schedule Customer Appointment*

Use Case Name:	**Schedule Customer Appointment**
Iteration:	**Filled**
Summary:	Enter an appointment with the designer and customer to take initial measurements and to determine the best design for the customer.
Basic Course of Events:	1. This use case begins when the office administrator, using date/time parameters supplied by the customer, requests a list of available times when the designer and customer can have a consultation. 2. The system responds with a list of available appointment times. 3. The office administrator picks one of the times or enters a different time based on the customer's preference. 4. The system records the appointment time and, later, notifies the designer of the upcoming appointment.
Alternative Paths:	In step 1, if the office administrator has more than one appointment to record, the system allows multiple appointment entry.
Exception Paths:	In step 3, if the time chosen by the office administrator conflicts with another appointment or with the designer in completing another costume, the system warns the office administrator. The office administrator can respond by overriding the system and entering the appointment, shuffling this and other appointments until the appointment fits, or choosing another appointment date.
Extension Points:	None

Use Case C.11   *Schedule Customer Appointment—Filled (continues)*

Trigger:	The customer requests an appointment.
Assumptions:	None
Preconditions:	Basic information about the customer already exists in the system.
Postconditions:	The appointment is stored, and the system alerts the designer before the appointment comes to pass.
Related Business Rules:	None
Author:	Tammie Thurber
Date:	June 3, 2000—Facade; June 7, 2000—Filled

Use Case C.11 *continued*

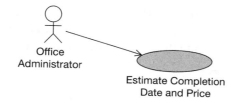

Figure C.15 *Estimate Completion Date and Price*

Use Case Name:	**Estimate Completion Date and Price**
Iteration:	**Filled**
Summary:	The office administrator enters the estimated completion date and price with input from the designer. The system provides a list of all other ongoing work to help the office administrator with the completion date decision. It also provides a list of similar costumes made previously at that price.
Basic Course of Events:	1. This use case begins when the office administrator needs to estimate a completion date and price. The office administrator enters information about the design, the customer's measurements, and the fabric and novelties involved. The office administrator also enters information regarding the urgency of this costume.

Use Case C.12 *Estimate Completion Date and Price—Filled (continues)*

	2. The system responds by calculating an estimated quantity of labor, materials, and profit and a retail price.
	3. The office administrator responds by accepting the price and providing it to the customer.
	4. The system responds by saving this information and scheduling the work into the designer's schedule.
Alternative Paths:	In step 3, if the office administrator does not wish to accept the price, the office administrator may override the price and the system will save both the calculated and the overridden price.
Exception Paths:	In step 4, if the system is not able to fit this work into the designer's schedule by the date/time indicated, the system responds by alerting the office administrator of this problem. The office administrator can respond by overriding the system, by shuffling this and other work until the date/time can be met, or by changing the date/time.
Extension Points:	None
Trigger:	The customer and the designer have identified a costume design, including details regarding the fabric, novelties, and customer's urgency.
Assumptions:	None
Preconditions:	Basic information exists in the system about the customer, order, and design.
Postconditions:	The estimated completion date and price have been attached to the order.
Related Business Rules:	None
Author:	Todd Kurstak
Date:	June 3, 2000—Facade; June 9, 2000—Filled

Use Case C.12 *continued*

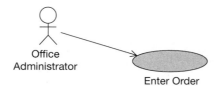

Figure C.16 *Enter Order*

Use Case Name:	**Enter Order**
Iteration:	**Filled**
Summary:	The office administrator enters the customer's order, including quoted price, design preferences, and estimated completion date.
Basic Course of Events:	1. This use case begins when the office administrator enters a customer order, including quoted price design preferences and estimated completion date. 1.1 (Optional) The office administrator enters additional costume orders until the entire order is complete. 2. The system responds by saving the order information.
Alternative Paths:	None
Exception Paths:	None
Extension Points:	None
Trigger:	The customer agrees to order a costume.
Assumptions:	None
Preconditions:	Basic information about the customer exists in the system.
Postconditions:	The order is stored.
Related Business Rules:	None
Author:	Tammie Thurber
Date:	June 5, 2000—Filled

Use Case C.13 *Enter Order—Filled*

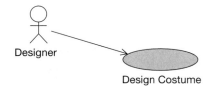

Figure C.17 *Design Costume*

Use Case Name:	**Design Costume**
Iteration:	**Filled**
Summary:	The designer creates a new costume design, which consists of a pattern, style, and size. The designer uses the application to create a design that wastes the least amount of fabric and conforms to the customer's measurements.
Basic Course of Events:	1. This use case begins when the designer indicates that she is ready to begin designing the costume and enters the fabric and novelties that will be used and the amount that is on hand. 2. The system responds by displaying the information stored so far about the customer and a costume. 3. The designer creates the costume design interactively. 4. The system responds by producing a design that the designer can use to begin cutting the fabric.
Alternative Paths:	In step 2, if some information is still missing regarding the customer or the design, the system responds by prompting the designer for the additional information. If the designer chooses not to enter the additional information, the system responds by attempting to create a costume design anyway.
Exception Paths:	In step 4, if there is not enough of a particular supply (fabric, novelty, and so on) on hand, the system responds by notifying the designer, who makes arrangements to purchase the missing supply.
Extension Points:	None
Trigger:	The designer has completed all previously scheduled appointments and work and is ready to design this costume.

Use Case C.14 *Design Costume—Filled (continues)*

Assumptions:	None
Preconditions:	Basic information exists on the customer and the design.
Postconditions:	A costume design is complete and ready to sew.
Related Business Rules:	None
Author:	Todd Kurstak
Date:	June 3, 2000—Facade; June 6, 2000—Filled

Use Case C.14 *continued*

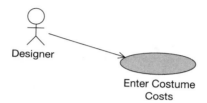

Designer

Enter Costume
Costs

Figure C.18 *Enter Costume Costs*

Use Case Name:	**Enter Costume Costs**
Iteration:	**Filled**
Summary:	Immediately after completing the costume, the designer enters into the system the total of all costs that went into it: labor, fabric, novelties, consultations (if applicable), and so on.
Basic Course of Events:	1. This use case begins when the designer has completed the costume and enters into the system the total costs of material and labor. 2. The system responds by saving this information.
Alternative Paths:	None
Exception Paths:	None
Extension Points:	None
Trigger:	Costume design and sewing are complete.
Assumptions:	None

Use Case C.15 *Enter Costume Costs—Filled (continues)*

Preconditions:	Basic information about the customer, order, and design exists in the system.
Postconditions:	Costume costs have been attached to the order.
Related Business Rules:	None
Author:	Shelley Foerster
Date:	June 5, 2000—Facade; June 5, 2000—Filled

Use Case C.15 *continued*

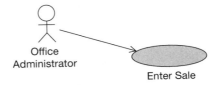

Office
Administrator

Enter Sale

Figure C.19   *Enter Sale*

Use Case Name:	**Enter Sale**
Iteration:	**Filled**
Summary:	The office administrator enters the sale amount, identified by customer, date, order, designer, and design information (fabric, color, and so on).
Basic Course of Events:	1. This use case begins when the office administrator enters the customer, date, costume, and sales amount for the sale. 2. The system responds by saving this information.
Alternative Paths:	None
Exception Paths:	None
Extension Points:	None
Trigger:	The customer has paid for the order.
Assumptions:	None
Preconditions:	Basic information exists in the system about the customer, order, and design.

Use Case C.16   *Enter Sale—Filled (continues)*

Postconditions:	A sale is attached to the order and is recorded for later trend calculation.
Related Business Rules:	None
Author:	Todd Kurstak
Date:	June 3, 2000—Facade; June 9, 2000—Filled

Use Case C.16 *continued*

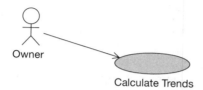

Owner

Calculate Trends

Figure C.20 *Calculate Trends*

Use Case Name:	**Calculate Trends**
Iteration:	**Filled**
Summary:	The owner needs to know the costume sales trends. For example, certain fabrics go in and out of style with customers. The owner needs to know the sales trends for all the variables in costume design: fabric, cut, novelties (sequins, shimmer, rhinestones, and so on), color combinations, and so on. These trends are based on the sales made in the previous weeks or months. The owner also needs to analyze customer activity, such as identifying the best and worst customers by volume, referrals, and so on.
Basic Course of Events:	1. This use case begins when the owner requests trend information. 2. The system responds with visual trend information for the variables specified: fabric, cut, novelties (sequins, shimmer, rhinestones, and so on), color combinations, and so on. 3. The owner responds by using this information to change some aspect of the business.

Use Case C.17 *Calculate Trends—Filled (continues)*

Alternative Paths:	None
Exception Paths:	In step 1, if no data is available from which to produce trends, the system responds by displaying a message stating that no information is available.
Extension Points:	None
Trigger:	The owner begins periodic business planning.
Assumptions:	None
Preconditions:	None
Postconditions:	Trend information is displayed.
Related Business Rules:	None
Author:	Tammie Thurber
Date:	June 2, 2000—Facade; June 12, 2000—Filled

Use Case C.17   *continued*

C.2.3 Business Rules

Table C.3 Business Rules: Filled Iteration

Number	Name	Description	Category	Static/Dynamic	Source
001	Provide discounts for referrals	If a current customer provides a referral to the company and the referred party makes a purchase, the customer receives a $20 discount off a future costume purchase.	Inference	Dynamic	Interview with owner 5/7/2000
002	Referral discounts must be used quickly	If a referral discount has been granted to a customer, it must be used on a costume within one year unless the customer contacts the company to request an extension.	Structural fact	Dynamic	Interview with owner 5/7/2000
003	Accept alterations only for faithful customers	No alterations will be accepted unless the transaction is approved by the owner for a long-time customer.	Structural fact	Static	Interview with owner 5/7/2000
004	Costume price is labor plus materials	The price of a costume is calculated as the cost of all supplies, materials, and novelties plus the cost of the designer's labor.	Computation	Static	Interview with owner 5/3/2000
005	No checks are accepted from first-time customers	If a customer has not purchased anything from the company previously, he or she must pay cash in advance of receiving the costume.	Structural fact	Static	Interview with office administrator 5/6/2000 Confirmed by owner 5/10/2000

continues

279

Table C.3 continued

Number	Name	Description	Category	Static/Dynamic	Source
006	Some consultations are charged for	Consultations cost the customer in only the following circumstances: if the customer has not paid for orders previously, if the total order comes to less than $200, or if the owner approves a paid consultation for this order	Structural fact	Dynamic	Interview with owner 5/10/2000
007	Consultations are charged at the regular designer rate	Consultation charges are calculated at the same hourly rate as design and sewing work.	Computation	Static	Interview with owner 5/10/2000

C.2.4 Context Matrix

Table C.4 Context Matrix: Filled Iteration

Number	Use Case	Summary	Core	This Use Case Depends On
CM001	Authenticate User	All users who request entry to the system must prove they are who they say they are (authentication). This applies to users inside the company as well as outside. Who the users are determines what they have access to (authorization).	No	None
CM002	Calculate Trends	The owner needs to know the costume sales trends. For example, certain fabrics go in and out of style with customers. The owner needs to know the sales trends for all the variables in costume design: fabric, cut, novelties (sequins, shimmer, rhinestones, and so on), color combinations, and so on. These trends are based on the sales made in the previous weeks or months. The owner also needs to analyze customer activity, such as identifying the best and worst customers by volume, referrals, and so on.	Yes	Enter Costume Costs Enter Sale Enter Order
CM003	Design Costume	The designer creates a new costume design, which consists of a pattern, style, and size. The designer uses the application to create a design that wastes the least amount of fabric and conforms to the customer's measurements.	No	Enter Order
CM004	Enter Costume Costs	Immediately after completing the costume, the designer enters the total of all costs that went into it: labor, fabric, novelties, consultations (if applicable), and so on.	Yes	Enter Order

continues

Table C.4 *continued*

Number	Use Case	Summary	Core	This Use Case Depends On
CM005	Enter Sale	The office administrator enters the sale amount, identified by customer, date, order, designer, and design information (fabric, color, and so on).	Yes	Enter Order
CM006	Estimate Completion Date and Price	The designer decides on the estimated completion date and price and tells the customer. The system provides a list of all other ongoing work to help with the completion date decision. It also provides a list of similar costumes made previously at that price.	No	Schedule Customer Appointment
CM007	Purchase Supplies	The office administrator records a purchase of supplies when the shipment arrives (fabric, novelties, elastic, and so on).	No	None
CM008	Schedule Customer Appointment	The office administrator creates an appointment with the designer and customer to take initial measurements and to determine the best design for the customer.	No	None
CM009	Enter Order	The office administrator enters the customer's order, including quoted price, design preferences, and estimated completion date.	No	Schedule Customer Appointment

C.2.5 Nonfunctional Requirements

Table C.5   Nonfunctional Requirements: Filled Iteration

Number	Category	Requirement	Applies to Use Cases	Exceptional Cases
TC-NF001	Availability	The system must be available to internal and external users 24 hours a day, 7 days a week, 99.9 percent of the time.	All	None
TC-NF002	Cost of ownership	None	N/A	N/A
TC-NF003	Maintainability	None	N/A	N/A
TC-NF004	Data integrity	None	N/A	N/A
TC-NF005	Development cost	Cost of development must not exceed $500,000, including hardware, packages, and custom development.	All	None
TC-NF006	Delivery date	The system must have at least core functionality in place by November 15, 2000.	Core	To be determined
TC-NF007	Extensibility	Application should be able to interface with CAD-style design packages in the future.	Design Costume	None
TC-NF008	Flexibility	None	N/A	N/A
TC-NF009	Installability	The application must have an uninstall utility that erases all traces of the application on a machine.	None	None
TC-NF010	Leveragability, reuse	None	N/A	N/A

continues

Table C.5 *continued*

Number	Category	Requirement	Applies to Use Cases	Exceptional Cases
TC-NF011	Operability	Operations must be easy for the office administrator to handle, including backup/recovery, audit, security, nightly batch cycles, and so on.	All	None
TC-NF012	Performance	For use cases in which the customer is waiting, either in person or on the phone, response times must be 5 seconds or less for all interactions 90 percent of the time.	Schedule Customer Appointment Authenticate User Estimate Completion Date and Price Enter Sale Enter Order	None
TC-NF013	Performance	For use cases when there is no customer waiting, response times must be 10 seconds or less for all interactions 90 percent of the time.	Calculate Trends	None
TC-NF014	Portability	None	N/A	N/A
TC-NF015	Quality	The number of problems experienced during user acceptance testing should be no more than four problems multiplied by the number of use cases.	All	None
TC-NF016	Fault tolerance, robustness	None	N/A	N/A
TC-NF017	Scalability	The system should provide the specified response times given a load of three concurrent users.	All	None

C.2.6 Testing Using Scenarios

Use Case Name:	**Schedule Customer Appointment**
Iteration:	**Filled**
Scenario:	1. Jenny Carmela, a fitness instructor, calls for an appointment on July 5, 2000. She needs a posing bikini and fitness outfit for the Nationals on August 22.
	2. Terri, the office administrator, logs on to the system with her user ID and password and requests a list of available times when Karen, the designer, can meet with Jenny for a consultation.
	3. The system responds with the following openings: • July 7 1 PM–8 PM • July 15 1 PM–9 PM • July 16 1 PM–9 PM • etc.
	4. Jenny requests July 7 at 3:30 PM, which Terri chooses in the system.
	5. The system responds by recording this appointment with Karen and Jenny.
	6. When Karen logs on to the system July 6 at 4 PM, the system notifies her of her upcoming appointment the following day.
Author:	Tammie Thurber with Karen Lavton
Date:	June 6, 2000

Use Case C.18 *Schedule Customer Appointment Testing Scenario—Filled*

Use Case Name:	**Enter Costume Costs**
Iteration:	**Filled**
Scenario:	1. Karen, the designer, completes Jenny Carmela's fitness outfit and logs on to the system using her user ID and password.
	2. Karen chooses Jenny's order and the fitness outfit from a listing of all outstanding orders.

Use Case C.19 *Enter Costume Costs Testing Scenario—Filled (continues)*

	3. Karen enters all the supplies that went into the outfit:
	  • 1.5 yards of yellow fireworks hologram fabric at $49 per yard
	  • 12 gross of rhinestones at $30 per gross (thread and elastic are not recorded)
	4. The system responds by saving this information with Jenny's order.

Author:	Tammie Thurber
Date:	June 3, 2000—Facade; June 7, 2000—Filled

Use Case C.19 *continued*

C.3 The Focused Iteration

During the Focused iteration, we refined the following artifacts.

Problem statement	No changes
Statement of work	Small workplan changes (not shown)
Risk analysis	Added one risk
Focused use cases	Refined use cases, deleted two use cases
Business rules	Added one business rule

The *Design Costume* use case was removed because it did not contribute value to calculating trends in customer preferences. After the design information was captured at the time of the order, it was not necessary to have the application involved in the creation of the pattern. In addition, the designers' budding computer literacy skills did not make it a good idea to introduce concepts such as CAD.

C.3.1 Risk Analysis

Table C.6 Risk Analysis: Focused Iteration

Number	Category	Risk	Resolution Needed By	Status	Days Lost If It Occurs	Likelihood It Will Happen	Risk Rating
001	Interfaces	Currently, the system is defined as requiring a design component for creating costumes online. This will require a very complex CAD-style design tool, which we have not located in the industry. If we cannot find one, we will have to develop it, and that will have a tremendous impact on scope.	Jul 1, 2000	Continuing search for package	500	10%	50
002	Designers' computer literacy	Currently, the costume designers have no computer skills. If they are to use a computer for their line-of-business transactions, they must begin learning how to use a mouse and so on immediately to be able to begin using this application when it is ready. (The office administrator is computer-literate.)	Jul 1, 2000	Sent memo to executive sponsor	30	50%	15
003	New store-front schedule impact	Plans to open a new storefront on Sep 1 will likely have an impact on our ability to deliver this application because the attention of the designers will be focused on the opening and they will be unable to assist with this application.	Aug 1, 2000	Booked meeting with executive sponsor	15	75%	10

C.3.2 Focused Use Cases

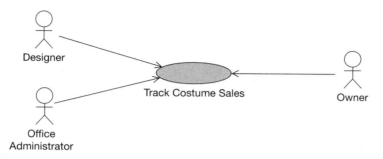

Figure C.21 *System Level Context Use Case: Track Costume Sales*

Use Case Name:	**Track Costume Sales**
Iteration:	**Focused**
Summary:	System Context Use Case. This system needs to track the information related to customers, appointments, designs, orders, and sales. The purpose of the system is to provide historical sales data to allow the owner to visualize trends.
Basic Course of Events:	1. The office administrator schedules a customer appointment. 2. The system responds by saving the appointment and customer information and by notifying the designer when the customer arrives. 3. The designer consults with the customer, estimates a price and date for availability, and enters this information into the system. 4. The system responds by arranging the designer's schedule to produce the item by the date specified to the customer. 5. The office administrator enters the order. 6. The system responds by saving the order information. 7. When the designer meets with the customer, the designer enters the customer's measurements and design preferences. 8. The system responds by optimizing the pattern for the fabric and the customer's measurements.

Use Case C.20 *System Level Context—Focused (continues)*

	9. The designer designs and sews the costume and, when it is complete, enters the costume costs.
	10. The system responds by calculating the profit or loss on this costume, given the quoted price.
	11. When the customer arrives for the final fitting, the office administrator enters the sale information.
	12. The system responds by saving the sale information.
	13. The owner requests visual trend calculations based on customers' preferences.
	14. The system responds with visual trend calculations.
	15. The owner responds by changing the business to capitalize on the upcoming trends noted.
Alternative Paths:	N/A
Exception Paths:	N/A
Extension Points:	N/A
Trigger:	N/A
Assumptions:	N/A
Preconditions:	N/A
Postconditions:	N/A
Related Business Rules:	N/A
Author:	Tammie Thurber
Date:	June 2, 2000—Facade; June 5, 2000—Filled; June 11, 2000—Focused

Use Case C.20   *continued*

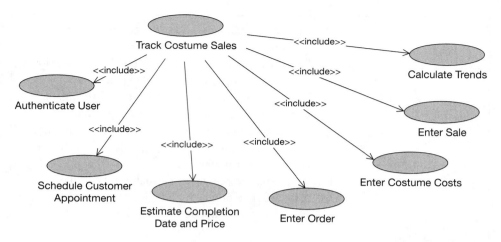

Figure C.22   *Use Case Hierarchy*

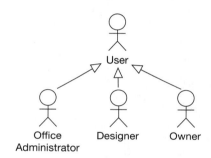

Figure C.23   *Actor Hierarchy*

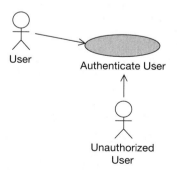

Figure C.24   *Authenticate User*

Use Case Name:	**Authenticate User**
Iteration:	**Focused**
Summary:	All users who request entry to the system must prove they are who they say they are (authentication). This applies to users inside the company as well as outside. Who the users are determines what they have access to (authorization).
Basic Course of Events:	1. This use case begins when the user enters a user identification and password. 2. The system responds by checking the combination of user identification and password against the recorded list of valid users. 3. The system responds by notifying the user that the user identification and password are valid and allows the user access to the application.
Alternative Paths:	None
Exception Paths:	In step 2, if the user identification and password combination is not valid, the system responds by notifying the user that the combination was invalid and asks the user to try again. If the user tries three times unsuccessfully, the system responds by disallowing the user and marking as suspended the user record of any and all user identifications tried. In step 2, if the user identification that is tried is in suspended mode, the system responds by notifying the user that this identification has been suspended and the user must contact a system administrator.
Extension Points:	None
Trigger:	The user requires access to the system.
Assumptions:	None
Preconditions:	The system is operational.
Postconditions:	The validated user is allowed to access the system.
Related Business Rules:	None
Author:	Shelley Foerster
Date:	June 5, 2000—Facade; June 5, 2000—Filled; June 11, 2000—Focused

Use Case C.21 *Authenticate User—Focused*

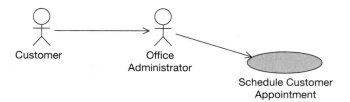

Figure C.25　*Schedule Customer Appointment*

Use Case Name:	**Schedule Customer Appointment**
Iteration:	**Focused**
Summary:	Enter an appointment with the designer and the customer to take initial measurements and to determine the best design for the customer.
Basic Course of Events:	1. This use case begins when the office administrator, using date/time parameters supplied by the customer. requests a list of available times when the designer and customer can have a consultation. 2. The system responds with a list of available appointment times. 3. The office administrator picks one of the times or enters a different time based on the customer's preference. 4. The system records the appointment time and, later, notifies the designer of the upcoming appointment.
Alternative Paths:	In step 1, if the office administrator has more than one appointment to record, the system allows multiple appointment entry.
Exception Paths:	In step 3, if the time chosen by the office administrator conflicts with another appointment or with the designer in completing another costume, the system warns the office administrator. The office administrator can respond by overriding the system and entering the appointment, by shuffling this and other appointments until the appointment fits, or by choosing another appointment date.

Use Case C.22　*Schedule Customer Appointment—Focused (continues)*

Extension Points:	None
Trigger:	The customer requests an appointment.
Assumptions:	None
Preconditions:	Basic information about the customer already exists in the system.
Postconditions:	The appointment is stored, and the system alerts the designer before the appointment comes to pass.
Related Business Rules:	None
Author:	Tammie Thurber
Date:	June 3, 2000—Facade; June 7, 2000—Filled; June 13, 2000—Focused

Use Case C.22 *continued*

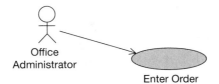

Office Administrator

Enter Order

Figure C.26 *Enter Order*

Use Case Name:	**Enter Order**
Iteration:	**Focused**
Summary:	The office administrator enters the customer's order, including quoted price, design preferences, and estimated completion date.
Basic Course of Events:	1. This use case begins when the office administrator enters a customer order, including quoted price design preferences and estimated completion date. 1.1 (Optional) The office administrator enters additional costume orders until the entire order is complete. 2. The system responds by saving the order information.
Alternative Paths:	None

Use Case C.23 *Enter Order—Focused (continues)*

Exception Paths:	None
Extension Points:	None
Trigger:	The customer agrees to order a costume.
Assumptions:	None
Preconditions:	Basic information about the customer exists in the system
Postconditions:	The order is stored.
Related Business Rules:	None
Author:	Tammie Thurber
Date:	June 5, 2000—Filled; June 11, 2000—Focused

Use Case C.23   *continued*

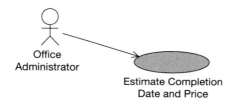

Office
Administrator

Estimate Completion
Date and Price

Figure C.27   *Estimate Completion Date and Price*

Use Case Name:	**Estimate Completion Date and Price**
Iteration:	**Focused**
Summary:	The office administrator enters the estimated completion date and price. The system provides a list of all other ongoing work to help with the completion date decision. It also provides a list of similar costumes made previously at that price.
Basic Course of Events:	1. This use case begins when the office administrator needs to estimate a completion date and price. The office administrator enters information about the design, the customer's measurements, and the fabric and novelties involved. The office administrator also enters information regarding the urgency for this costume.

Use Case C.24   *Estimate Completion Date and Price—Focused (continues)*

	2. The system responds by calculating an estimated quantity of labor, materials, and profit and a retail price. 3. The office administrator responds by accepting the price and providing it to the customer. 4. The system responds by saving this information and scheduling the work into the designer's schedule.
Alternative Paths:	None
Exception Paths:	In step 2, if the system is not able to fit this work into the designer's schedule by the date/time indicated, the system responds by alerting the office administrator of this problem. The office administrator can respond by overriding the system, by shuffling this and other work until the date/time can be met, or by changing the date/time.
Extension Points:	None
Trigger:	The customer and designer have identified a costume design, including details regarding the fabric, novelties, and customer's urgency.
Assumptions:	None
Preconditions:	Basic information exists in the system about the customer, order, and design.
Postconditions:	The estimated completion date and price have been attached to the order.
Related Business Rules:	None
Author:	Todd Kurstak
Date:	June 3, 2000—Facade; June 9, 2000—Filled; June 13, 2000—Focused

Use Case C.24 *continued*

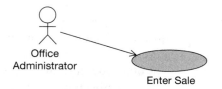

Figure C.28 *Enter Sale*

Use Case Name:	**Enter Sale**
Iteration:	**Focused**
Summary:	The office administrator enters the sale amount, identified by customer, date, order, designer, and design information (fabric, color, and so on).
Basic Course of Events:	1. This use case begins when the office administrator enters the customer, date, costume, and sales amount for the sale. 2. The system responds by saving this information.
Alternative Paths:	None
Exception Paths:	None
Extension Points:	None
Trigger:	The customer has paid for the order.
Assumptions:	None
Preconditions:	Basic information exists in the system about the customer, order, and design.
Postconditions:	A sale is attached to the order and is recorded for later trend calculation.
Related Business Rules:	None
Author:	Todd Kurstak
Date:	June 3, 2000—Facade; June 9, 2000—Filled; June 15, 2000—Focused

Use Case C.25 *Enter Sale—Focused*

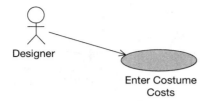

Figure C.29 *Enter Costume Costs*

Use Case Name:	**Enter Costume Costs**
Iteration:	**Focused**
Summary:	Immediately after completing the costume, the designer enters the total of all costs that went into it, such as labor, fabric, novelties, consultations (if applicable), and so on.
Basic Course of Events:	1. This use case begins when the designer has completed the costume and enters the total costs of material and labor. 2. The system responds by saving this information.
Alternative Paths:	None
Exception Paths:	None
Extension Points:	None
Trigger:	The costume design and sewing are complete.
Assumptions:	None
Preconditions:	Basic information about the customer, order, and design exists in the system.
Postconditions:	Costume costs have been attached to the order.
Related Business Rules:	None
Author:	Shelley Foerster
Date:	June 5, 2000—Facade; June 5, 2000—Filled; June 20, 2000—Focused

Use Case C.26 *Enter Costume Costs—Focused*

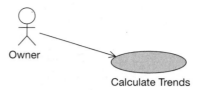

Figure C.30   *Calculate Trends*

Use Case Name:	**Calculate Trends**
Iteration:	**Focused**
Summary:	The owner needs to know the costume sales trends. For example, certain fabrics go in and out of style with customers. The owner needs to know the sales trends for all the variables in costume design: fabric, cut, novelties (sequins, shimmer, rhinestones, and so on), color combinations, and so on. These trends are based on the sales made during the previous weeks or months. The owner also needs to analyze customer activity, such as identifying the best and worst customers by volume, referrals, and so on.
Basic Course of Events:	1. This use case begins when the owner requests trend information. 2. The system responds with visual trend information for the variables specified: fabric, cut, novelties (sequins, shimmer, rhinestones, and so on), color combinations, and so on. 3. The owner responds by using this information to change some aspect of the business.
Alternative Paths:	None
Exception Paths:	In step 1, if no data is available from which to produce trends, the system responds by displaying a message stating that no information is available.
Extension Points:	None
Trigger:	The owner begins periodic business planning.
Assumptions:	None

Use Case C.27   *Calculate Trends—Focused (continues)*

Preconditions:	None
Postconditions:	Trend information is displayed.
Related Business Rules:	None
Author:	Tammie Thurber
Date:	June 2, 2000—Facade; June 12, 2000—Filled; June 13, 2000—Focused

Use Case C.27 *continued*

C.3.3 Business Rules

Table C.7 Business Rules: Focused Iteration

Number	Name	Description	Category	Static/Dynamic	Source
001	Provide discounts for referrals	If a current customer provides a referral to the company and the referred party makes a purchase, the customer receives a $20 discount off a future costume purchase.	Inference	Dynamic	Interview with owner 5/7/2000
002	Referral discounts must be used quickly	If a referral discount has been granted to a customer, it must be used on a costume within one year unless the customer contacts the company to request an extension.	Structural fact	Dynamic	Interview with owner 5/7/2000
003	Accept alterations only for faithful customers	No alterations will be accepted unless the transaction is approved by the owner for a long-time customer.	Structural fact	Static	Interview with owner 5/7/2000
004	Costume price is labor plus materials	The price of a costume is calculated as the cost of all supplies, materials, and novelties plus the cost of the designer's labor.	Computation	Static	Interview with owner 5/3/2000
005	No checks accepted from first-time customers	If a customer has not purchased anything from the company previously, he or she must pay cash in advance of receiving the costume.	Structural fact	Static	Interview with office administrator 5/6/2000 Confirmed by owner 5/10/2000

Number	Name	Description	Category	Static/ Dynamic	Source
006	Some consultations are charged for	Consultations cost the customer only in the following circumstances: if the customer has not paid for the order previously, if the total order comes to less than $200, or if the owner approves a paid consultation for this order	Structural fact	Dynamic	Interview with owner 5/10/2000
007	Consultations are charged at the regular designer rate	Consultation charges are calculated at the same hourly rate as design and sewing work.	Computation	Static	Interview with owner 5/10/2000
008	Payment in cash	Payment must be made using cash, cashier's check, bank, or post office money order or credit card, but not personal checks.	Structural fact	Static	Interview with owner 5/15/2000

C.4 The Finished Iteration

During the Finished iteration, we refined the following artifacts:

Problem statement	No changes
Statement of work	Small workplan changes (not shown)
Risk analysis	No changes
Finished use cases	Added nonfunctional requirements as stereotypes, made other small adjustments
Business rules	No changes
User interface guidelines	Started (not shown)
Prototype	Started (not shown)

The *Enter Costume Costs* use case was deleted because it did not contribute directly to the need for trend analysis. It might be added later after the first phase of deployment.

C.4.1 Finished Use Cases

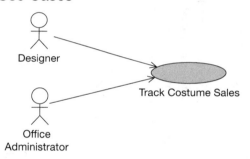

Figure C.31   *System Level Context Use Case: Track Costume Sales Diagram*

Use Case Name:	**Track Costume Sales**
Iteration:	**Finished**
Summary:	System Context Use Case. This system needs to track the information related to customers, appointments, designs, orders, and sales. The purpose of the system is to provide historical sales data to allow the owner to visualize trends.
Basic Course of Events:	1. The office administrator schedules a customer appointment.

Use Case C.28   *System Level Context Use Case—Track Costume Sales (continues)*

2. The system responds by saving the appointment and customer information and by notifying the designer as the appointment nears.

3. The designer consults with the customer, estimates a price and date for availability, and enters this information into the system.

4. The system responds by arranging the designer's schedule to produce the item by the date specified to the customer.

5. The office administrator enters the order.

6. The system responds by saving the order information.

7. When the designer meets with the customer, the designer enters the customer's measurements and design preferences.

8. The system responds by optimizing the pattern for the fabric and the customer's measurements.

9. The designer designs and sews the costume and, when it is complete, enters the costume costs.

10. The system responds by calculating the profit or loss on this costume, given the quoted price.

11. When the customer arrives for the final fitting, the office administrator enters the sale information.

12. The system responds by saving the sale information.

13. The owner requests visual trend calculations based on customers' preferences.

14. The system responds with visual trend calculations.

15. The owner responds by changing the business to capitalize on the upcoming trends noted.

Alternative Paths:	N/A
Exception Paths:	N/A
Extension Points:	N/A
Trigger:	N/A
Assumptions:	N/A
Preconditions:	N/A
Postconditions:	N/A
Related Business Rules:	N/A

Use Case C.28 *continues*

Author:	Tammie Thurber
Date:	June 2, 2000—Facade; June 5, 2000—Filled; June 11, 2000—Focused; June 22, 2000—Finished

Use Case C.28 *continued*

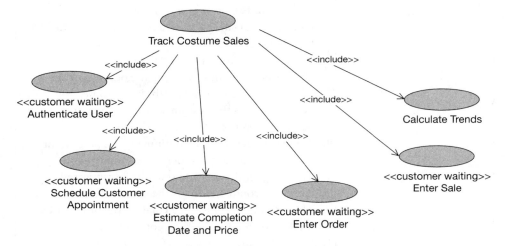

Figure C.32 *Use Case Hierarchy*

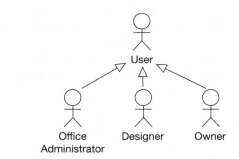

Figure C.33 *Actor Hierarchy*

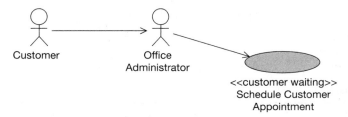

Figure C.34 *Schedule Customer Appointment*

Use Case Name:	**Schedule Customer Appointment**
Iteration:	**Finished**
Summary:	Enter an appointment with the designer and customer to take initial measurements and to determine the best design for the customer.
Basic Course of Events:	1. This use case begins when the office administrator, using date/time parameters supplied by the customer, requests a list of available times when the designer and customer can have a consultation. 2. The system responds with a list of available appointment times. 3. The office administrator picks one of the times or enters a different time based on the customer's preference. 4. The system records the appointment time and later notifies the designer of the upcoming appointment.
Alternative Paths:	In step 1, if the office administrator has more than one appointment to record, the system allows multiple appointment entry.
Exception Paths:	In step 3, if the time the office administrator chooses conflicts with another appointment or with the designer in completing another costume, the system warns the office administrator. The office administrator can respond by overriding the system and entering the appointment, by shuffling this and other appointments until the appointment fits, or by choosing another appointment date.
Extension Points:	None
Trigger:	The customer requests an appointment.
Assumptions:	None
Preconditions:	Basic information about the customer already exists in the system.
Postconditions:	The appointment is stored, and the system alerts the designer before it comes to pass.

Use Case C.29 *Schedule Customer Appointment—Finished (continues)*

Related Business Rules:	None
Author:	Tammie Thurber
Date:	June 3, 2000—Facade; June 7, 2000—Filled; June 13, 2000—Focused; June 22, 2000—Finished

Use Case C.29   *continued*

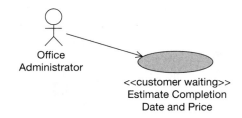

Figure C.35   *Estimate Completion Date and Price*

Use Case Name:	**Estimate Completion Date and Price**
Iteration:	**Finished**
Summary:	The office administrator enters the estimated completion date and price. The system provides a list of all other ongoing work to help with the completion date decision. It also provides a list of similar costumes made previously at that price.
Basic Course of Events:	1. This use case begins when the office administrator needs to estimate a completion date and price. The office administrator enters information about the design, the customer's measurements, and the fabric and novelties involved. The office administrator also enters information regarding the urgency for this costume. 2. The system responds by calculating an estimated quantity of labor, materials, and profit and a retail price. 3. The office administrator responds by accepting the price and providing it to the customer. 4. The system responds by saving this information and scheduling the work into the designer's schedule.

Use Case C.30   *Estimate Completion Date and Price—Finished (continues)*

Alternative Paths:	None
Exception Paths:	In step 2, if the system is cannot fit this work into the designer's schedule by the date/time indicated, the system responds by alerting the designer of this problem. The office administrator can respond by overriding the system, by shuffling this and other work until the date/time can be met, or by changing the date/time.
Extension Points:	None
Trigger:	The customer and the designer have identified a costume design, including details regarding the fabric, novelties, and the customer's urgency.
Assumptions:	None
Preconditions:	Basic information exists in the system about the customer, order, and design.
Postconditions:	The estimated completion date and price have been attached to the order.
Related Business Rules:	None
Author:	Todd Kurstak
Date:	June 3, 2000—Facade; June 9, 2000—Filled; June 13, 2000—Focused; June 19, 2000—Finished

Use Case C.30 *continued*

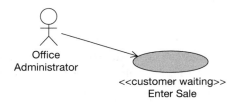

Figure C.36   *Enter Sale*

Use Case Name:	**Enter Sale**
Iteration:	**Finished**
Summary:	The office administrator enters the sale amount, identified by customer, date, order, designer, and design information (fabric, color, and so on).
Basic Course of Events:	1. This use case begins when the office administrator enters the customer name, date, costume, and amount of the sale. 2. The system responds by saving this information.
Alternative Paths:	None
Exception Paths:	None
Extension Points:	None
Trigger:	The customer has paid for the order.
Assumptions:	None
Preconditions:	Basic information exists in the system about the customer, order, and design.
Postconditions:	A sale is attached to the order and is recorded for later trend calculation.
Related Business Rules:	None
Author:	Todd Kurstak
Date:	June 3, 2000—Facade; June 9, 2000—Filled; June 15, 2000—Focused; June 21, 2000—Finished

Use Case C.31   *Enter Sale—Finished*

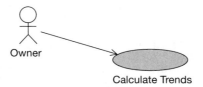

Figure C.37 *Calculate Trends*

Use Case Name:	**Calculate Trends**
Iteration:	**Finished**
Summary:	The owner needs to know the costume sales trends. For example, certain fabrics go in and out of style with customers. The owner needs to know the sales trends for all the variables in costume design: fabric, cut, novelties (sequins, shimmer, rhinestones, and so on), color combinations, and so on. These trends are based on the sales made during the previous weeks or months. The owner also needs to analyze customer activity, such as identifying the best and worst customers by volume, referrals, and so on.
Basic Course of Events:	1. This use case begins when the owner requests trend information. 2. The system responds with visual trend information for the variables specified: fabric, cut, novelties (sequins, shimmer, rhinestones, and so on), color combinations, and so on. 3. The owner responds by using this information to change some aspect of the business.
Alternative Paths:	None
Exception Paths:	In step 1, if no data is available from which to produce trends, the system responds by displaying a message stating that no information is available.
Extension Points:	None
Trigger:	None
Assumptions:	The owner begins periodic business planning.

Use Case C.32 *Calculate Trends—Finished (continues)*

Preconditions:	None
Postconditions:	Trend information is displayed.
Related Business Rules:	None
Author:	Tammie Thurber
Date:	June 2, 2000—Facade; June 12, 2000—Filled; June 13, 2000—Focused; June 22, 2000—Finished

Use Case C.32 *continued*

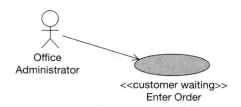

Figure C.38 *Enter Order*

Use Case Name:	**Enter Order**
Iteration:	**Finished**
Summary:	The office administrator enters the customer's order, including quoted price, design preferences, and estimated completion date.
Basic Course of Events:	1. This use case begins when the office administrator enters a customer order, including quoted price, design preferences, and estimated completion date. 1.1 (Optional) The office administrator enters additional costume orders until the entire order is complete. 2. The system responds by saving the order information.
Alternative Paths:	None
Exception Paths:	None
Extension Points:	None

Use Case C.33 *Enter Order—Finished (continues)*

Trigger:	The customer agrees to order a costume.
Assumptions:	None
Preconditions:	Basic information about the customer exists in the system
Postconditions:	The order is stored.
Related Business Rules:	None
Author:	Tammie Thurber
Date:	June 5, 2000—Filled; June 11, 2000—Focused; June 19, 2000—Finished

Use Case C.33 *continued*

C.4.2 Business Rules

Table C.8 Business Rules: Finished Iteration

Number	Name	Description	Category	Static/Dynamic	Source
001	Provide discounts for referrals	If a current customer provides a referral to the company and the referred party makes a purchase, the customer receives a $20 discount off a future costume purchase.	Inference	Dynamic	Interview with owner 5/7/2000
002	Referral discounts must be used x must be used quickly	If a referral discount has been granted to a customer, it must be used within one year unless the customer contacts the company to request an extension.	Structural fact	Dynamic	Interview with owner 5/7/2000
003	Accept alterations only for faithful customers	No alterations will be accepted unless the transaction is approved by the owner for a long-time customer.	Structural fact	Static	Interview with owner 5/7/2000
004	Costume price is labor plus materials	The price of a costume is calculated as the cost of all supplies, materials, and novelties plus the cost of the designer's labor.	Computation	Static	Interview with owner 5/3/2000
005	No checks accepted from first-time customers	If a customer has not purchased anything from the company previously, he or she must pay cash in advance of receiving the costume.	Structural fact	Static	Interview with office administrator 5/6/2000 Confirmed by owner 5/10/2000
006	Some consultations are charged for	Consultations cost the customer only in the following circumstances: if the customer has not paid for orders previously, if the total order comes to less than $200, or if the owner approves a paid consultation for this order	Structural fact	Dynamic	Interview with owner 5/10/2000

Number	Name	Description	Category	Static/Dynamic	Source
007	Consultations are charged at the regular designer rate	Consultation charges are calculated at the same hourly rate as design and sewing work.	Computation	Static	Interview with owner 5/10/2000
008	Payment in cash	Payment must be made using cash, cashier's check, bank or post office money order, or credit card, but not by personal checks.	Structural fact	Static	Interview with owner 5/15/2000

Bibliography

Alexander, C. 1996. Keynote address presented at the 1996 OOPSLA Conference, San Jose, CA.

Bennett, D. 1997. *Designing Hard Software*, Prentice Hall.

Booch, G., J. Rumbaugh, and I. Jacobson. 1998. *The Unified Modeling Language User Guide*, Addison Wesley.

Cantor, M. 1998. *Object-Oriented Project Management with UML*, John Wiley & Sons.

Constantine, L., and L. Lockwood. 1999. *Software for Use: A Practical Guide to Models and Methods of Usage Centered Design*, ACM Press.

Cooper, A. 1995. *About Face: The Essentials of User Interface Design*, IDG Books Worldwide.

de Bono, E. 1982. *de Bono's Thinking Course*, Rev. Edition.

Jacobson, I. 1995. *The Object Advantage: Business Process Reengineering with Object Technology*, Addison Wesley.

Jacobson, I. 1996. Use Cases Tutorial, OOPSLA Conference, San Jose, CA.

Jacobson, I., G. Booch, and J. Rumbaugh. 1999. *The Unified Software Development Process*, Addison Wesley Longman.

Jacobson, I., M. Christerson, P. Jonsson, and G. Overgaard. 1992. *Object-Oriented Software Engineering: A Use Case Driven Approach*, ACM Press.

Jones, C. 1996. *Applied Software Measurement: Assuring Productivity and Quality*, second edition, McGraw Hill.

Larman, C. 1997. *Applying UML and Patterns: An Introduction to Object-Oriented Analysis and Design*, Prentice Hall.

McConnell, S. 1996. *Rapid Development: Taming Wild Software Schedules*, Microsoft Press.

Pirsig, R. 1974. *Zen and the Art of Motorcycle Maintenance: An Inquiry into Values*, William Morrow & Company.

Ross, R. 1997. *The Business Rule Book: Classifying, Defining and Modeling Rules, Version 4.0*, Business Rules Solutions, Inc..

Royce, W. 1998. *Software Project Management: A Unified Framework*, Addison Wesley Longman.

Rumbaugh, J., I. Jacobson, and G. Booch. 1998. *The Unified Modeling Language User Guide*, Addison Wesley.

Rumbaugh, J., I. Jacobson, and G. Booch. 1999. *The Unified Modeling Language Reference Guide*, Addison Wesley.

Schneider, G., and J. Winters. 1998. *Applying Use Cases: A Practical Guide*, Addison Wesley Longman.

Sommerville, I., and P. Sawyer. 1997. *Requirements Engineering: A Good Practice Guide*, John Wiley & Sons.

Index

Note: Italicized page numbers indicate locations of figures/tables

Object-Oriented Software Engineering
A Use Case Driven Approach
Ivar Jacobson, Magnus Christerson, Patrik Jonsson, and
Gunnar Overgaard

How can software developers, programmers, and managers meet the challenges of their jobs and begin to resolve the software crisis? This book, the classic treatment of use cases, is based on Objectory, the first commercially available comprehensive object-oriented process for developing large-scale industrial systems. Ivar Jacobson developed Objectory as a result of 20 years of experience building real software-based products. The approach takes a global view of system development and focuses on minimizing the system's life cycle cost.

0-201-54435-0 • Hardcover • 552 pages • ©1992

Use Case Driven Object Modeling with UML
A Practical Approach
Doug Rosenberg with Kendall Scott
Addison-Wesley Object Technology Series

This book presents a streamlined approach to UML modeling that includes a minimal but sufficient set of diagrams and techniques you can use to get from use cases to code quickly and efficiently. *Use Case Driven Object Modeling with UML* provides practical guidance that will allow software developers to produce UML models quickly and efficiently, while maintaining traceability from user requirements through detailed design and coding. The authors draw upon their extensive industry experience to present proven methods for driving the object modeling process forward from use cases in a simple and straightforward manner.

0-201-43289-7 • Paperback • 192 pages • ©1999

Applying Use Cases
A Practical Guide
Geri Schneider and Jason P. Winters
Addison-Wesley Object Technology Series

Applying Use Cases provides a practical and clear introduction to developing use cases, demonstrating their use via a continuing case study. Using the Unified Software Development Process as a framework and the Unified Modeling Language as a notation, the authors lead the reader through the application of use cases in different phases of the process, focusing on where and how use cases are best applied. This book also offers insight into the common mistakes and pitfalls that can plague an object-oriented project.

0-201-30981-5 • Paperback • 208 pages • ©1998